FAR FROM HOME

Southern Literary Studies

FRED HOBSON, SERIES EDITOR

FAR FROM HOME

SELECTED LETTERS *of* WILLIAM HUMPHREY

[*Edited by* ASHBY BLAND CROWDER]

Louisiana State University Press
Baton Rouge

Published by Louisiana State University Press

Manufactured in the United States of America
First printing

DESIGNER: Michelle A. Neustrom
TYPEFACE: Chaparral Pro
PRINTER AND BINDER: Thomson-Shore, Inc.

LIBRARY OF CONGRESS CATALOGING-IN-PUBLICATION DATA

Humphrey, William.
Far from home : selected letters of William Humphrey / edited by Ashby Bland Crowder.
p. cm. — (Southern literary studies)
Includes index.
ISBN 978-0-8071-3272-2 (cloth : alk. paper)
1. Humphrey, William—Correspondence. I. Crowder, A. B. II. Title.
PS3558.U464Z48 2007
813'.54—dc22
[B]

2007001095

The paper in this book meets the guidelines for permanence and durability of the Committee on Production Guidelines for Book Longevity of the Council on Library Resources. ♾

For my son, Ashby

citoyen du monde
cetatean al lumii
citțâdino del mondo
weltburger
гражданин мира

Contents

Acknowledgments

A number of institutions and people have proved essential to the completion of this project. The Harry Ransom Humanities Research Center, University of Texas at Austin (especially Thomas Staley, Pat Fox, Margaret Tenney, Victor Hauser, Richard Workman, Lisa Richter, Steve Mielke, and Debra Armstrong); DeGolyer Library, Southern Methodist University, Dallas (especially Kay Bost and Cynthia Franco); Princeton University Library; John Davis Williams Library, University of Mississippi, Oxford (especially Sharron Eve Sarthou and Debbie Lee Landi); Hornbake Library, University of Maryland at College Park (especially Beth Alvarez); University of Reading Library, England (especially Michael Bott and Verity Andrews); University of Sussex Library, England (especially Elizabeth Inglis); Manuscript and Rare Book Library, Columbia University, New York City; and Editions Gallimard, Paris, France—all these institutions have provided letters and materials from their collections, and I am grateful to the staffs who assisted me. Friends and family of William Humphrey have also shown remarkable generosity in providing letters. Theodore and Renée Weiss allowed me access to their Humphrey letters before they were given to Princeton University Library. Pierre Affre of Paris, France, dug out all of his letters from Humprhey for my benefit. Don Emery of Clarksville, Texas, sent me letters that Humphrey had written to family members and others in his hometown. At his country house in Souvigny-en-Sologne, Lamotte-Beuvron, France, Jean Lambert, in the days just before his death, opened for my use a cabinet full of letters received over a period of thirty years. Jean Rose, library manager of Random House Archive and Library at Rushden in England, made available the letters to Secker and Warburg, Humphrey's second English publisher. Barbara Dupee lent me letters that were excluded from the Dupee collection at Columbia University. Harding Lemay posted to me the Humphrey letters that he still held in his file and that were not part of the Knopf Collection in Austin. Bert Almon, author of the first book on Humphrey, sent me a copy of a letter that he once received from Humphrey, and the Reverend James Elliott Lindsley did the same. Harry Grabstald generously gave me the use of all the letters he had received over a period of fifty years. Antonia Weidenbacher, William Humphrey's stepdaughter, not only provided me with letters and other manuscript materials left at the Humphrey house in Hudson when her stepfather died but has generously given me permission to publish all of these letters.

Peggy Morrison at the Hendrix College Library has assisted me by securing interlibrary loan materials and by contributing to the notes. The staffs of the Little Rock Public Library and the University of Arkansas at Little Rock Library have also been helpful, Jennifer Flaxbart of the Perry-Castaneda Library at the University of Texas at Austin as well. Others who have kindly assisted me in various ways, directly and indirectly, are Kevin Asman, Michael Bright, Charles Chappell, William Bedford Clark, Robert Compton, John Easterly, George Gladney, Gina Goad, Jason Hall, Fred Hobson, W. Donald Kay, John Krebs, Terri Lewers, Marylou Martin, Zbigniev Maszewski, Garrett McAinsh, Keeley Murry, Wayne Oudekerk, Pat Preston, George Roupe, Michael Slater, David Teague, Bill Topich, and Francis Warner. My wife Lynn has been an excellent reader and proofreader and advisor throughout the process. Without her keen and loving eye this book would not be so presentable as it is. My son Ashby has proved to be the most necessary help with many annotations and translations. I am grateful to all the good-hearted people, some very close to me and some whom I have never met, who helped me with this project.

Quotations from some of the letters of Leonard Woolf to WH are from *Letters of Leonard Woolf*, ed. Frederig Spotts (New York: Harcourt Brace Javanovich, 1989).

The American Philosophical Society (through a Franklin Research Grant), the Mellon Foundation (through the Harry Ransom Humanities Research Center), and Hendrix College have generously given financial support that has made my research possible, and Hendrix provided the year-long sabbatical leave that gave me the time to do it. A Senior Fulbright Grant in the following year (2005–2006) put me at the University of Lodz in Poland, where I was able to complete the project.

Abbreviations

ALS	Autograph letter, signed
ALU	Autograph letter, unsigned
TLS	Typed letter, signed
TLU	Typed letter, unsigned

CU	Manuscript and Rare Book Library, Columbia University, New York City
EG	Archive of Éditions Gallimard, Paris, France
HL	Hornbake Library, University of Maryland at College Park
HR	Harry Ransom Humanities Research Center, University of Texas at Austin
LC	Jean Lambert Collection, Souvigny-en-Sologne, Lamotte-Beuvron, France
PH	Privately held
PU	Princeton University Library
SMU	DeGolyer Library, Southern Methodist University, Dallas, Texas, A1994.1973C
UM	John Davis Williams Library, University of Mississippi, Oxford
UR	University of Reading Library, England
RH	Random House Archive and Library, England
US	University of Sussex Library, England

Chronology

1924 William Joseph Humphrey born to Clarence and Nell (née Varley) Humphrey, on 18 June in Clarksville, Texas.

1937 WH's father fatally injured in a car wreck on the fourth of July. He and his mother move to Dallas.

1941 WH attends the Dallas Institute of Fine Arts and Bryant Technical High School, from which he is graduated in February. He enrolls in Southern Methodist University, Dallas.

1942 WH transfers to the University of Texas at Austin and joins the Young Communist League.

1943 WH returns to Southern Methodist University but leaves before being graduated, goes to Chicago, and works in a defense factory.

1944 WH returns to Dallas, writes a play entitled "Ambassador Ben," works for the *Southern Weekly*.

1945 WH leaves Texas for New York City and soon after, in Woodstock, meets Dorothy Feinman Cantine, whom he later marries.

1947 WH is a farm worker in Brewster, New York, and begins to write, getting his first story, "In Sickness and Health," published in *Accent*.

1949 WH begins teaching in the Literature Division at Bard College, Annandale-on-Hudson, New York, in September.

1950 WH meets Katherine Anne Porter. He and Dorothy marry on 10 October in Brooklyn City Hall.

1953 *The Last Husband and Other Stories* published.

1958 *Home from the Hill* published to overwhelming critical praise. WH leaves his teaching position to live in England, France, and Italy.

1959 WH wins the Texas Institute of Letters Award for the best first novel by a Texan *(Home from the Hill)*.

1960 Hollywood issues a film based on *Home from the Hill* starring Robert Mitchum and Eleanor Parker.

1963 WH is Visiting Glasgow Professor at Washington and Lee University, Lexington, Virginia, during the fall semester. The National Institute of Arts and Letters gives WH an award of $2,500.

1965 *The Ordways* published and receives the Texas Institute of Letters Award for best book of fiction. The Humphreys buy a farmhouse built in 1795 near Hudson, New York, and WH teaches both semesters at Massachusetts Institute of Technology in Cambridge.

1966 *The Ordways* wins the Texas Institute of Letters Award for best fiction book.

1968 *A Time and a Place,* a collection of stories, is published.

1969 WH awarded honorary doctorate by Southern Methodist University.

1970 *The Spawning Run* published.

1973 *Proud Flesh* published to a chorus of negative criticism.

1976 WH is Elizabeth Drew Professor of English for the fall semester at Smith College.

1977 *Farther Off from Heaven* and *Ah, Wilderness! The Frontier in American Literature* published.

1978 WH wins the Texas Institute of Letters Award for best work of nonfiction *(Farther Off from Heaven).*

1978 *My Moby Dick* published.

1981 WH visiting professor at Princeton University for fall semester.

1984 *Hostages to Fortune* published and wins the Texas Literary Festival Award for the outstanding work of fiction, given by the Southwest Booksellers Association and the *Dallas Times Herald.*

1985 *The Collected Stories of William Humphrey* published.

1986 *Open Season: Sporting Adventures of William Humphrey* published.

1989 *No Resting Place* published.

1992 *September Song* published.

1996 WH receives the Lon Tinkle Award for Continuing Excellence in Texas Letters from the Texas Institute of Letters.

1997 In April, WH diagnosed with an undifferentiated cancer extending into his esophagus. On 20 August he dies at home.

FAR FROM HOME

[INTRODUCTION]

> Your letters from Italy to Alfred are so much more entertaining than most of what we publish today. . . .
>
> —HARDING LEMAY to Humphrey, 27 February 1963

At his death on 20 August 1997, William Humphrey had traveled a long way from his beginnings—not just in miles (he had moved from Clarksville, Texas, to Hudson, New York) but also socially and psychologically. Born to dirt-poor and uneducated parents who month after month could not pay the rent when he was a child, he had by the late 1950s joined America's glittering literati and been featured in *Vogue* magazine's "gallery of international charmers among men," together with Marlon Brando, Sir Edmund Hillary, Leonard Bernstein, and John F. Kennedy. From shooting squirrels and stripping their pelts in the swamps of Sulphur Bottom in East Texas, by the 1960s, he strode onto the hunting fields of Columbia County, New York, looking as though he had just emerged from the pages of an Abercombie and Fitch catalog (that is how Hilary Masters, a member of his social and literary circle, saw him). In a deeper sense—and one related to the fiction he wrote—Humphrey had made the long journey from being an unreconstructed southerner to being an unabashed critic of his native land: he considered foolish the South's regard for an idealized past and its myth of the heroic, star-crossed struggle to preserve what never was. Perhaps his traveling and living abroad gave him the disinterested perspective that let him step outside the shadow of the Confederate memorial in the town square of his hometown. He saw clearly the chilling effect that the dead hand of the southern past could have on subsequent generations. This theme would dominate Humphrey's Texas fiction.

We see this view of the South in Humphrey's first three novels—*Home from the Hill* (1958), a tragedy; *The Ordways* (1965), a comedy; and *Proud Flesh* (1973), perhaps best described as a tragicomedy. During his long career he also wrote three volumes of short stories (*The Last Husband and Other Stories* [1953], *A Time and a Place* [1968], and *September Song* [1995]), a memoir (*Farther Off from Heaven* [1977]), two fishing books (*The Spawning Run: A Fable* [1970] and *My Moby Dick* [1979]), and two additional novels (*Hostages to Fortune* [1984] and *No Resting Place* [1989]). In 1996 the Texas Institute of Letters gave its highest recognition to Humphrey: the Lon Tinkle Award for excellence sustained throughout a career. This award was the fourth from the Texas Institute; previously he had received "best book" awards in 1959, 1965, and 1978. In 1963, the National Institute of Arts and Letters had given him one of its yearly awards "in recognition of [his] creative work in literature."

Throughout Humphrey's long career, critics greeted his books with unrestrained approval, the single exception being *Proud Flesh,* though even it was well received in France. Sometimes the praise was ecstatic, as when Irish novelist Elizabeth Bowen, responding to his first book, *Home from the Hill,* declared its author a "genius" and his novel a "tragic masterpiece." In reviewing Humphrey's last book, *September Song,* Jonathan Yardley summed up Humphrey's career: "[H]e has dedicated his life to his writing with a fidelity all too rare in a culture that encourages facile success and empty honor. Utterly devoid of fashionable glitz, his books are made of durable stuff that will secure his reputation long after those of the day's 'hot' writers have settled into oblivion."[1]

Before the end of his senior year at Southern Methodist University in Dallas, Humphrey walked away from Texas and went to work in a defense factory in Chicago. He quite possibly wrote no letters home, for his mother had married for a third time and he was made to feel unwelcome in the new family. He did not stay in Chicago long but returned to Texas briefly and then was off to New York City early in 1945—and it is from there that we have the first letters of William Humphrey. They were written to his college friend Harry Grabstald, an army surgeon, after Humphrey had fallen in love with Dorothy Feinman Cantine (1916–2003), with whom he lived (they would eventually marry) for the rest of his life. The earliest letter is dated 13 May 1947, when he was twenty-three years old, struggling to keep Dorothy and her daughter Antonia and himself fed, clothed, and sheltered. During this rough time Humphrey turned to his friend Grabstald for financial assistance, and Grabstald was his main correspondent throughout the late 1940s. He wrote to his friend not only

1. Elizabeth Bowen, "Texas Beyond the Oil Wells," *Tatler and Bystander,* 12 March 1958, 506; Jonathan Yardley, "Harvest of the Years," *Washington Post,* 5 July 1992, Book World Section, 3.

about his dreams of success as a writer but also about practical matters. Once Humphrey had gained a position with Donald Peterson (producer of *The Ave Maria Hour* and other radio programs) as a goatherd, gardener, and handyman in Brewster, New York, he was able to make time for writing. When he finished a story, he mailed it to Grabstald in Baltimore, and Grabstald subsequently posted the story to the magazine that Humphrey had designated. This procedure was intended to hide Humphrey's whereabouts, because he and Dorothy had furtively taken Antonia from Dorothy's husband and mother-in-law. Though Humphrey was having some success with little magazines, there was no reason to think at this point that he would become a writer of any distinction, and so there was no reason for Grabstald to save those letters other than affection for the one who wrote them. Years later Grabstald's first wife threw away many of Humphrey's letters, but Grabstald did preserve over a hundred.

Humphrey secured a position at Bard College, Annandale-on-Hudson, New York, at the end of 1949 and began to gain some standing as a literary figure; after that he wrote less frequently to Grabstald. He turned his epistolary attentions to Katherine Anne Porter, who took an early interest in her fellow Texan. She became his main correspondent in the early 1950s. And when the poet Theodore Weiss and his wife Renée left Bard for an extended sabbatical, they became important correspondents and remained so for the rest of Humprey's life.

Humphrey's letter writing shifted into high gear after the publication of *Home from the Hill* in 1958, when he and Dorothy left for Europe, where they remained for several years. Humphrey kept his former literary colleagues at Bard and elsewhere apprised of his progress and frustrations with his second novel, *The Ordways.* His letter to Alfred Knopf, urging him to get off his back and not rush what could not be rushed, is the kind of letter many writers would like to write to their publishers if they had the courage. He also wrote wonderful "travel" letters about the places he and Dorothy lived and visited. His minute account of life in Biot, France, to which they resorted in 1959, captures the place for all time, but it was his excitement over the little towns on Lake Como in the Italian Alps, which prompted him to write "The Mountain of Miracles," published in the *New Yorker* (29 October 1960), that led to his most exuberant personal letters praising the blue lake and white mountains and marking the place he was sure he wanted to retire. Also conveyed in vivid detail in a letter to Knopf is Humphrey's pleasure in "lovely Perigord" and Illiers, Marcel Proust's fictional Combray, where he and Dorothy toured Aunt Leonie's house. Just as forcefully, his disillusionment with all of Spain comes through in letters written during a too-long sojourn in that country, cut off, in his view, from the rest of Western civilization. Humphrey's disgust with Spain, his letters imply, was owing mainly to the offending and ubiquitous *tricornio* of the Guardia Civil, the Franco regime's face to the world. But Humphrey was not in Europe mainly to travel: that came only as a brief reward at the end of long months of writing and trying to write.

After nearly eight years in Europe, Humphrey returned to the United States in 1963 and went almost immediately to Washington and Lee University for a semester as Visiting Glasgow Professor. He was shocked to be once again among people who clung to the pieties of the Old South, which in Lexington, Virginia, "the shrine of the South," were more ingrained than they had been among the inhabitants of East Texas he had run away from almost twenty years earlier. Humphrey was vexed by a people who had set their clocks back a hundred years, and he wrote some telling observations of southern culture to his northern and English friends. The traveling in Europe resumed at the beginning of the summer of 1964 for a short time, and then he and his wife settled down in the Hudson Valley of New York and joined the literati of Columbia and Dutchess counties.

Perhaps the most significant of Humphrey's letters are those describing and analyzing his fictional methods, especially those letters focused on *The Ordways*. Though he is obviously not a disinterested critic, Humphrey's astute commentaries on his own work, as insightful as James Dickey's on his own poetry, constitute a valuable example of literary criticism. We realize from these letters, if not from elsewhere, that his was a remarkable intelligence.

Humphrey was not all seriousness. Playing the raconteur, he gives an account of Christmas dinner with Robert Lowell that is a comic gem. His funny story about trying to say hello to Claude Gallimard, his portrait of the Jewish carpenter he had hired, his rendition of how Cyril Connolly was nearly arrested at the Gotham Book Mart in New York City, and many other portraits and anecdotes need to be preserved as examples of American humor writing. His hair-raising tragicomic account of losing and finding the only manuscript of *The Ordways* on an Italian train is in its own special category of letter. Alfred Knopf once wrote to Humphrey: "Your letters are always a delight" (11 August 1961). These funny letters certainly are.

Not humorous but painful are those letters that record his feelings of despondency following Christopher Lehman-Haupt's 1973 pummeling of *Proud Flesh* in the *New York Times* and the piling on by the rest of the critical gang. Humphrey's response to his book's being blasted away was to feel as if it "were a varmint on literature's manicured front lawn," as the *Times Book Review* recently characterized another disfavored novel.

Humphrey never expected his letters to be preserved. Except in a few rare instances, he never saved copies of any of the letters he sent. In his last decade he wrote to Jean Lambert, his French translator: "What a chore it would have been for me to keep copies of all my letters to people! Besides, I've never been conscious of any future biographer. Certainly I would never do anything to help one. Quite the contrary" (27 October 1990). In fact, Humphrey had nothing but scorn for a self-promoter like E. B. White, who, Humphrey felt, wrote letters not just to "the person to whom they were addressed but to the world at large." To Nick Lyons, a friend who had recently purchased the *Letters of E. B. White,* Humphrey wrote, "Even as he wrote them he was seeing them in print—not the way to write to a friend. Indeed, it is using a friend for self-promotion. . . . No wonder you were disappointed in them; real letters are addressed in intimacy and written with private passions to their recipients; the E. B. Whites of this world are writing only to themselves. Dead letters. Junk mail" (29 December 1976). Although Humphrey did not save his letters, those to whom they were addressed did save them, and they are real letters and sometimes very intimate—thus to Norah Smallwood, president of Chatto & Windus after Ian Parsons, "Now this is strictly between you and me" (10 October 1978).

The nature of the letters—all written far from his childhood home—changed over the years (as the circumstances of Humphrey's life changed), but as a whole they reveal a man devoted to writing. No one can read these letters without recognizing their author's deeply felt commitment to making a lasting contribution to American literature. The letters are sometimes erudite, sometimes deeply sad, sometimes witty, sometimes full of outrage. As William Bedford Clark says, "[T]hey not only present us with a dynamic and compelling portrait of the man, in all his weaknesses and strengths, but they are filled with keen critical judgments on the work and worth of Humphrey's contemporaries and offer frequently sophisticated theoretical (and practical) insights into the art of fiction and the nature of the writerly vocation." Some of them secure significance through the eminent literary figures who were his friends: Katherine Anne Porter;

Leonard Woolf, the husband of Virginia Woolf; and Theodore Weiss.[2] His correspondence with his publishers, Alfred A. Knopf, Ian Parsons, Norah Smallwood, and Seymour Lawrence, is also significant, for these letters are not the usual kind of business letters. Humphrey's relationship with his publishers was always personal and intimate. He wrote to them not only about arrangements for the publication of his books but also about particular frustrations and problems during the writing process, his reasons for specific fictional techniques, his views on the state of American culture, and his personal affections. Yet even the letters to his uncle Bernard Varley, a Clarksville barber, and to other hometown people reveal the certain connection between his fictional world and the hardscrabble Texas life from which he emerged.

On 14 November 1962, Alfred Knopf wrote to Humphrey: "You are a wonderful letter writer, and if you don't in the course of time give me the novels I want, I shall rush into print a volume of your letters." Humphrey did, eventually, produce those novels. But now that there will be no more novels, it is fitting that the volume of letters Knopf envisioned appear in print. These letters—in which he writes about his work, his travels, his friends and acquaintances, and his disappointments, and in which he remarks on society and politics—are an achievement complementary to Humphrey's fiction and form a significant chapter in America's literary record.

The guiding principle for the selection of letters for this edition is, broadly speaking, interest. I chose letters because they contribute to the portrait of the man (or to that of the correspondent), or because they contain keen critical insights into his own or others' writing, or because they contain insights into the vocation of the writer, or, finally, because they are examples of Humphrey's felicitous writing style. The letters are presented chronologically so that their biographical significance might be apparent. Parts of some letters are omitted for two main reasons. If a passage is trivial, it is left out. For example, sections of the letters Humphrey wrote to Theodore Weiss when Weiss was on sabbatical leave from his position as head of the Division of Literature at Bard College are left out because they contain detailed attention to events and academic politics at the college

2. Eudora Welty's papers in the State Archive of Mississippi in Jackson probably contain letters from Humphrey, but this collection is unavailable at this time.

or mundane matters related to the publication of the *Quarterly Review of Literature (QRL),* neither of which would be of interest to an outsider. In the letter to Theodore and Renée Weiss of early September 1953, I omit a passage about disagreements among Bard faculty on rent owed on the Weisses' apartment and the use of their telephone and about a bill for the registration of Renée's car. Another example of an omitted section is in a letter of late September 1953: a brief and confusing paragraph pertaining to the *QRL* ending with "I hope you know what I'm talking about—I don't. I have accepted nothing for the magazine." The second reason for omission is to avoid repetition. When Humphrey was abroad and writing to friends in the United States, he would sometimes include the same material in more than one letter. Such repetitions are excised. I have given a brief description of the contents of omitted passages. I occasionally omit a word that WH inadvertently repeated in the typing. These I have simply indicated with an ellipsis. Because Humphrey sometimes used ellipses himself, I bracket mine. All of the multiple-dotted ellipses between paragraphs are Humphrey's. I assure the reader that I have kept no secrets, and generally the texts are reproduced in full. Humphrey's habits with respect to italics (he rarely underlines the titles of books, for example), punctuation, and spelling are followed. My few editorial corrections are bracketed.

When Humphrey wrote on aerograms (air letters), he often omitted paragraphing in order to get as much in the limited space as possible. I have divided such letters into their natural parts, providing the paragraphing that Humphrey most likely would have furnished were he not cramped for space. Sometimes in those air letters he indicates paragraphs with the word "paragraph," at other times he notes them with ellipses; in those cases I have omitted the word or ellipses and recorded the paragraph.

The annotations follow each letter for the convenience of any reader wishing to identify allusions, people, places, objects, and events. For identifications following an item's initial appearance in the letters, the reader can use the index as needed to locate information. Obvious references to Shakespeare are not noted; otherwise I err on the side of completeness. Head notes, when deemed appropriate, provide the context of a letter.

[STRUGGLING IN NEW YORK]

1947–49

TO HARRY GRABSTALD

[Early in 1945, WH left Texas for New York City and quickly fell in with a crowd of Greenwich Village bohemians. Having gone to Woodstock with the anarchist and pacifist poet Jackson Mac Low (1922–2004), he met Dorothy Feinman Cantine (1916–2003), a painter and model, and shortly thereafter they ran off together, she leaving not only her husband, Holley, but also her young daughter. In a few months' time, the couple "kidnapped" the daughter, Antonia. Because they could not afford a flat, Dorothy moved in with her parents, Tilly and Louis Feinman, who lived in Brooklyn, and Bill found a bed in the janitors' quarters at the Marine Hospital on Staten Island.

Grabstald (1922–) was WH's friend from the time they were undergraduate students at Southern Methodist University in 1941. He went on to be graduated from Southwestern Medical College, University of Texas at Dallas, in 1945. Later he became a distinguished professor of urology at Cornell University Medical School and Mt. Sinai Medical School in New York City. In 1947, Grabstald was briefly assigned to the Merchant Marine Academy sick bay in Pass Christian, Mississippi.]

ALS/PH [New York City
May 13, 1947]

Dear Harry,
I am sorry I have not written. I just didn't want you to know how hard up I was. I have exactly 44¢. My rent is paid up till Saturday. I have sold all the books I had in New York with me and sold everything else I own. For the last 2 weeks I have lived on one meal a day. There seems to be absolutely

no hope of a job in the country. I gave that up long ago. I have been turned down by every hash house[1] in New York, Staten Island, and Brooklyn. I have a job in Doctor Mahoney's V.D. lab[2]—but it doesn't begin until July 15th—for they have overshot their appropriations for the fiscal year ending that date and can't hire anyone until then. Have a job on the staff of "Time" magazine[3] as a research asst.—that pays $65.00/week—can't begin until July 1st. In the meantime Dorothy's mother threatens to expose her to Holley[4] if she doesn't either give me up or get out of her house.[5] Wrote my mother—not one cent could she dig up. Sold her car, hocked her silver, fur coat, everything she owns to support her child while her drunken husband has been out of a job for months.[6] Will go tomorrow to try to sell a pint of blood—doubt they'll take it—I am skin and bones.

Auden[7] promises me he'll have me living off my writing in two years—if I can just manage to stay alive for the next 6 months. He is trying to get me a job. No luck.

Even in 1930[8] you could get a day's work as a bus boy. Not now apparently.

I am ready for the East River. So is Dorothy. It seems a pretty good idea. I am not being dramatic, purely pragmatical.

Be thankful you are down there. The depression hit New York first and worst in 1929. It's bad.

Don't worry. I'm not. It doesn't do any good. One may as well starve without worry as with it.

God, what a world! What a civilization.

Yours,
Bill

1. A cheap eating place.

2. In the United States Marine Hospital on Staten Island, where WH had worked as a librarian for a short time in 1946.

3. Perhaps a fabrication.

4. Holley Cantine, Dorothy's husband, a painter and coeditor of *Retort: An Anarchist Review,* published between 1942 and 1951.

5. The Feinmans lived at 65 Fort Green Place in Brooklyn.

6. WH's mother was in her third marriage, to a man named Butch Troughton, and she had a son, Tommy.

7. The poet W. H. Auden (1907–73), who then lived in New York City.

8. During the Great Depression.

TO HARRY GRABSTALD

ALS/PH

[New York City
late May 1947]

Dear Harry,

I got your check. Thank you, Harry. I haven't had to use it yet, though—for I got a job the next day. I am working in a book-store—the Gotham Book Store[1] (most famous book-store in the world since 1920—very avant-garde—my kind of literature). Pays me 40 a week. Promise of $10 week and 10% of profits after 3 months. Only one catch—the woman is insane. She has had over 400 employees come and go in last 2 years. She is a legend. So far I have got along with her—but, have a tempting promise of a better job in another book store beginning in 2 months. Maybe it will come through—if it does—$75 per week!!!

Now we have joined the legion of apartment hunters. Do you remember anybody on Staten Island who might help?

Gee, if only you could get back up here! We could rent a place together. Wouldn't that be wonderful?

Do you have any civilian clothes to spare? The old blue suit of yours has fallen completely to pieces after being worn night and day for the last three months. And the old blue suit of mine is much too small. I have borrowed a suit from Dorothy's younger brother (a very nice fellow) because I must look presentable for this job. But I can't keep it too long and Dorothy and I are going to need every damned penny for a while. I won't be able to buy much of anything. It is impossible to imagine anyone so completely naked as I am.

Boy, am I lucky to have a job. Today's headlines in the times: 400,000 out of work in N.Y.C. alone during last month! The depression. Financial writers for the times have now lost the old glibness—even the most optimistic now admits the depression is here. Most say that 1930 is nothing compared to what this is going to be.

Next letter I'll tell you about what Randall Jarrell[2] has promised to do for me. He is one of the most respected of the younger generation of poets (from University of Texas, where I knew him slightly). Saw him (by appointment) in New York last week. Very encouraging he was—but haven't time now to tell all about it. Let it wait till next letter.

Dorothy sends her love and Toni sends love to Uncle Harry.

Yours,
Bill

1. A literary bookstore then at 41 West Forty-seventh Street, New York City, founded in 1920 by Frances Steloff; see letter of 5 November 1968 to Porter.

2. Randall Jarrell (1914–65), a southern poet who had recently published *Little Friend, Little Friend* (1945) when WH met with him.

TO HARRY GRABSTALD

[During the third week of September 1947, WH and Dorothy moved to Brewster, New York, where he did farm work for Donald Peterson, who produced and directed The Ave Maria Hour *and other radio programs for WMCA. WH earned twenty-five dollars a month (after rent) for doing basic chores, and he could do additional day work for eight dollars a day. On 1 November 1947, WH wrote to Grabstald, who was then a resident at the United States Marine Hospital in Baltimore, Maryland, to enquire about where Dorothy might obtain an abortion. Apparently Grabstald suggested a doctor in New York City, but his fee was four hundred dollars, more than the couple could afford.]*

ALS/PH [Brewster, New York November 1947]

Harry—

What in the world are you thinking of? How can you suggest such a thing as giving away the child if we should have it? I don't want one and Dorothy doesn't want one—but, holy God!—do you think we could give it away? The only thing I can think is that you must have been more excited in your letter than I was in mine. As for my being hysterical, no doubt I was, but I certainly can't see that I was more hysterical about our problem than you were in your proposed solution. I wonder—I just wonder if you yourself would be cold-blooded enough to do, if you were in my position, what you suggest I do. I can't believe you would. And don't you see—it's just that that makes our position so very imperative. After what Dorothy went through I'd give anything now to have the baby. But if we did we'd never be able to get custody of Toni when the business with Holley and his mother[1] finally does come up—as it must eventually and not too far away. If now we could find someone to do the thing for $200 or even $250 I'd borrow the money from Peterson (I think he'd probably let me have it, and work it out to pay it back.) But it's got to be done—if I have to get out my Cunningham[2] and do it myself. But please—no more letters about giving the child to a Jewish home[3]—particularly *Jewish*. But surely someone connected with the hospital must know someone. Only it's got to be done soon—or no one will handle it. Now don't think I'm hysterical. I'm anxious, of course. That seems permissible enough under the circumstances. But you're our only hope. You've got to help us.

Bill

1. Josephine Arosamena Cantine; see note to letter of January 1948 to Grabstald.

2. An anatomy text.

3. Dorothy and Grabstald were nonpracticing Jews.

TO HARRY GRABSTALD

[In order to prevent Dorothy's husband Holley Cantine from tracing his address, WH arranged to send his stories to Grabstald, who in turn would submit them, with his own return address, to magazines.]

ALS/PH

[Brewster, New York
December 1947]

Dear Harry,

Thanks for forwarding the "Voices." So happy you liked my contribution.[1] This is a manuscript of a story.[2] I don't want it to be postmarked "Brewster" so mail it from there for me. Read it if you like. Be sure to leave the return envelope (the folded one inside)—by some impossible chance they just might reject it. I've only put in 8 months work on those 13 pages!

Forgive me for not writing more, but yesterday was the first day Dorothy has been up and off [e]rgotrate.[3] Until tonight she has not bled from her getting up. We're keeping our fingers crossed. God! The trouble we've had with this thing. I've cooked 3 meals a day now, cleaned the house, washed clothes and dishes for 3 weeks. You may imagine I'm pretty tired of it. And the snow! Well you must have read all about that by now. It's incredible.

I have to go soon. Bedtime. You must try to get up before May—if, as you say, it's only for a week-end. You could leave on Friday afternoon and get back Monday night late. We'd have a good time. But May is a long time off.

Toni will be starting school in less than 2 weeks now. It's hard to accustom oneself to that reality. We're looking forward to the freedom it will give us, I must say. The poor kid is getting horribly neurotic and blabs to her make-believe friends without interruption all day. Maybe meeting a lot of real children will straighten her out.

I'll be getting back to work soon (haven't had much time to while D. was sick). I'm in good health—in fact, I get better by the hour. My mental outlook is pretty good. I get a little more satisfaction from my writing now—what little time I have for it—and that helps keep up my spirits.

Let me know how you like my little take-off on anarchists (specifically a slightly touched-up picture of Holley's mother). The reference on page 5 is to: Thoreau[4] was jailed for non-payment of property taxes. R. W. Emerson[5] paid him a call, said, "Henry! What are you doing in there?" Replied Henry, "What are you, R. W., doing out there?"

Yours,
Bill

P.S. Don't seal the envelope for Sewanee—just fold the clasp. Saves postage that way.

1. The only review WH is known to have written, "The Poets Coming Toward You," *Voices* 132 (Winter 1948): 45–7.

2. "In Sickness and Health," WH's first short story to be published.

3. A uterine stimulant given to stop excessive bleeding after an abortion.

4. Henry David Thoreau (1817–62), New England writer and transcendentalist, author of *Civil Disobedience* (1849) and *Walden* (1854). He spent a day in jail for not paying his poll tax as a protest against the Mexican War.

5. Ralph Waldo Emerson (1803–82), American transcendental philosopher and poet.

TO HARRY GRABSTALD

ALS/PH

[Brewster, New York
(?) January 1948]

Dear Harry,

I am enclosing a letter which I wish you would mail for me—don't use a hospital envelope, though, I guess.

I have really nothing to tell you. What with this depressing rainy weather we've been having my thoughts turn rather naturally to unpleasant things and I've been very sad and discouraged lately about not being able to get anything accepted anywhere and having to sit here and not hear anything from any of those damned editors. "Partisan Review"[1]—for example. That thing's coming out *monthly* now and yet it must be two months at least since you sent them that story of mine. And, "Accent,"[2] well, it must be three months since they received Grogon[3]—if they did.

I finished the story I read you part of when you were here.[4] But instead of sending it to you for you to forward I mailed it direct to "Sewanee"[5] from Danbury. I gave it a lot more going over and I believe the ending was good. Well, you can judge for yourself—you'll be getting it back without doubt—though it'll probably take that schmeckel Palmer[6] 6 mos to read and reject it. When he does I'll send it to Virginia Quarterly Review[7] (although I'm not absolutely certain that this magazine still functions).

So, as if I didn't have trouble enough getting a short story printed, I have begun breaking ground on a novel.[8] God knows it couldn't be any *harder* to get published than a short story.

What I'm going to do is this: After being turned down by two or three other people I am going to write Katherine Anne Porter[9] and ask her to let me send her some stories of mine. Do you remember when I came back to Dallas from Chicago and went to work on "The Southern Weekly"[10] for five months before I left and came to New York for the first time? The editor was a funny old bird, named Peter Molyneaux. He had been managing editor of the Fort Worth Star years before. He liked me very much. Well, he claimed to have practically raised Katherine Anne. At the time that didn't make much impression on me. I'd never read any of her things. But Molyneaux assured me she was not only a good writer but a very nice person and with a reputation for helping young writers. Maybe she'll write to some editors (as I have heard Randall Jarrell say he had done for Robert Lowell,[11] who wasn't able to get a poem of his accepted anywhere until Jarrell did this for him, and then, once he was in print, became the rage and even won the Pulitzer Prize) or, if she doesn't like my stuff well enough to do that, then maybe she'll criticize it for me. At least, it can't hurt to ask her. But so many subsequently famous writers have tried for so much longer than I have yet to get published that I hate to ask her for a while more.

Then if she refuses there are two or three others I might try.

At least it's one more recourse.

Well, that's enough about my troubles.

I was very glad to hear about your "promotion." I guess that must look pretty good to be the head of the urology dept. there, doesn't it? I mean prestige value.

Toni gets out of school this week.

When are you coming again?

Bill

1. This influential literary journal with a political edge was founded in 1934. WH had sent a story about a pregnant woman with an anarchist mother-in-law, obviously based upon Dorothy and Josephine Arosamena Cantine, who, along with her son Holley, was a leader in the pacifist-anarchist movement of 1940–50. This story was never published and is not among WH's papers.

2. *Accent: A Quarterly of New Literature,* founded in 1940, was the first to publish stories by WH.

3. The family name of the married couple in the short story "In Sickness and Health."

4. "Man with a Family."

5. The oldest literary magazine in the United States, *Sewanee Review* emphasizes British and American fiction and poetry and carries reviews and literary criticism. It was founded in 1892 at the University of the South, Sewanee, Tennessee.

6. WH uses a Yiddish term of abuse meaning "little prick" to refer to John E. Palmer (1913–), editor of the *Sewanee Review* from 1946 to 1952.

7. *Virginia Quarterly Review* is a national journal of literature, social sciences, and politics, founded in 1925.

8. "Commuting Distance," the outline of a novel that WH turned into "The Last Husband," the title story of his first volume.

9. Katherine Anne Porter (1890–1980) was a Texas writer. Her major works are *Pale Horse, Pale Rider* (1939), *Old Order* (1955), and *Ship of Fools* (1962).

10. A Dallas publication, formerly the *Texas Weekly,* edited by Peter Molyneaux (1882–1953) from 1928 until his death.

11. The poet Robert Lowell (1917–77) is best known for his *Life Studies,* which won the National Book Award in 1960.

TO HARRY GRABSTALD

ALS/PH [Brewster, New York 1948]

Dear Harry,

Well, your guess is as good as mine what Palmer meant. It's just words—something to show that he has considered the thing[1] gravely, don't you know. Revision! What gall: *him* telling *me* to *revise* something. What did he ever write that he should sit up and tell somebody to *revise* something. Not one single line!!!

Well, I'll be done in about a month with a beautiful story.[2] Jesus, it's good—much better than either of the other two,[3] good as they are. You'll like it very much I'm sure. And so I'll give him one more chance to be the first to publish me, then strike him off my list. He won't publish it and he'll have an easy excuse: it[']s about three times as long as Grogan—around 11–14000 words—about 30–35 pages in his magazine.

Well, anyhow, we'll try *Accent* with this now. You'll see I had to type it over again (only about 5 hrs. work—of a kind I hate) because that schmeckel ruined my manuscript so. There's some stamps here and will you have the thing checked once again before mailing it from Baltimore to be [sure it's] enough. And then when you get it back, don't send it to me. Keep it. That is unless it's so banged up it needs typing again, but maybe it won't be since I've put it in a folder. Just keep it and when I decide when to send it next I'll send folders and stamps and the address.

Well, the new thing I'm working on is so good I'm really unable to be discouraged about Palmer.

Dorothy is very disappointed that you're not coming because she was anxious to get a start on your portrait. Her painting is going very well.

Listen, you said you might find some of those nice notebooks around the hospital. Look into that[,] will you[?] I could use them, as many as you can get, and when I fill them up I'll give them to you and one day your grandchildren will be wealthy. Also paper, all you can get. I'm using bushels of it. Going like wildfire. We saw *Treasure of the Sierra Madre*[4] in Danbury last night. It was hard to judge it. I suppose it was a good movie as movies go but it was such a disappointment after reading the book. Buy it—it only costs 25¢.

I'm sorry to hear about your mother. Of course, there's no sense my being hypocritical about it and I must admit that she's done little enough for you that you should get so upset. But, little as I think of my own, I suppose I'll feel just as bad when she gets bad sick.

I have to eat my lunch now and get back to work—spading up Peterson's garden.

Write often—
Yours—
Bill

1. "Man with a Family."

2. "The Hardys," which *Sewanee Review* did accept on 18 November 1948.

3. "In Sickness and Health" and "Man with a Family."

4. Directed by John Huston and starring Humphrey Bogart, this 1948 Warner Brothers film was based on a novel of the same title by B. Traven (1890–1969), which was first published in the United States in 1934.

TO HARRY GRABSTALD

ALS/PH

[Brewster, New York
early April 1948]

Dear Harry,

Dorothy was in New York last week for Easter and we are just getting settled down again. I rewrote the story that Sewanee rejected[1] and am sending it to you tomorrow to forward to Kenyon Review.[2] I've used all the stamps we had in the house, so when you get ready to send it on have it weighed (at the hospital P.O.?) and see if the 12¢ is enough to cover it (it must go 1st class); if not will you put some more on it (probably not more than 1 or 2 cents more) and don't forget to add the same amt. to the return envelope inside. I have already begun another story[3]—about farm people in Texas—which I am pretty well into now—and which so far promises to be better than either of the other two. I am constantly working toward perfection of my style. Eventually I want a style which will be more convoluted, long flowing sentences, but I feel that I won't really know how to do that properly until I am able to write simply. It is like modern painting in which the artist does not feel able to progress to abstraction until he has mastered realistic painting. I'll have the new thing finished (I see it as rather long) by the time you're up again and will enjoy very much reading it to you.

Before I forget—Dorothy would like more vitamin capsules like you sent before—if you can manage it.

I have just got over a rib contusion—sustained from the fall of a tree I was chopping. Very painful when I coughed and sneezed. Now I'm feeling very fit—and a good thing, too, for beginning a few days ago Peterson came out of hibernation to begin gardening and he's mocking [the] hell out of me!

Toni goes back to school tomorrow after a 12 days vacation during which we, of course, have managed to do almost no writing or painting.

Hurry with "Pale Horse, Pale Rider"[4] [because] I need it in my work. You may be interested to know that Dorothy and I read The Treasure of the Sierra Madre (Pocket Books—25¢)[;] it is wonderful! We read Traven's—"Bridge in the Jungle"[5]—which she brought back from NYC—very good, too, but not so good as Treasure.

I have to write my mother tonight I suppose and I'm not looking forward to that at all. So—I'll start now working up courage.

Yours,
Bill

1. "Man with a Family."

2. A journal of literature, culture, and art founded by John Crowe Ransom (1888–1974), Fugitive poet and New Critic, in 1939 at Kenyon College, Gambier, Ohio.

3. "The Hardys."

4. Short story collection published by Katherine Anne Porter in 1939.

5. B. Traven's novel published in 1938.

TO HARRY GRABSTALD

ALS/PH [Brewster, New York 1948]

Dear Harry,
Here's another one[1] for you to forward for me. God! What are they doing with my stories? Why don't we hear from Accent? Can't figure it out. It's been nearly four months with them and 2 months with Partisan. Now Sewanee has had the last one[2] nearly a month. It's driving me out of my head.

I don't know anything to tell you. I'll write when I'm not so depressed.

I hope everything goes all right in your new job. Write me often.

Bill

1. "Man with a Family."

2. "The Hardys."

TO HARRY GRABSTALD

[WH gives an account of opening Grabstald's letter to learn that his short story "In Sickness and Health" had been accepted. This first story of WH's to be published appeared in Accent *(Winter 1949): 91–101.]*

ALS/PH [Brewster, New York 1948]

Dear Harry—
Well, we made it, didn't we? I must say I don't even regret the abandon-

ment of our little book project.[1] I waited this morning until long after the postman had come and gone. I didn't see much point in going down. I did and found your letter, but as I had had one only the day before, I figured you were probably writing mainly to say there was no news, or that I shouldn't fly off the handle and write Palmer a nasty letter, or something. So—I tucked it under my arm and read Peterson's copy of Time all the way through. When I was done with that I started back up the steps and opened your letter. I began yelling for Dorothy, got tangled in my bedroom slippers, lost them both, fell down and nearly broke one of my fingers and haven't calmed down yet. Said to hell with work, packed a lunch, went picknicing [*sic*] and spent the day lying under a shade tree laughing and giggling and smiling. It plumb wore me out. Gee, how we missed you. You and Dorothy, the only ones I want to share it with.

Happy as you are I don't think that even you realize what this may mean, can mean, has meant to others, actual, demonstrable cases. I'm hoping (*I'm* pretty sure, in fact) it will get reprinted either in the O. Henry collection[2] of best stories of the year or the Martha Foley collection.[3] There's more money. It means I can get accepted other places, and when you've been accepted by a couple—Partisan, Kenyon, Sewanee, you can easily get some of that big luscious "Harper's Bazaar" money or "Mademoiselle"—neither of which places you need feel ashamed of appearing in. Then comes collection of stories in book form—then, a Guggenheim.[4] Then, a job teaching creative writing in some little university. All these things have happened from just such a little start—not once, but many times, believe it or not.

Don't say—There goes Billy again. If it doesn't happen that way—other nice things can come. I know of a little schlemiel[5] who printed, somehow, in Partisan Review, one of the worst pieces of dreck[6] you ever read. Immediately he received offers from two publishers of advances on his first novel!

Well, we'll see.

Don't worry about me writing Mr. Shattuck[7] that he has no right telling me to make revisions. I will. He's right.

In fact, from now on, don't worry about anything. I'm started now and I can't let anything stand in my way. Not Holley—not the army—not my ulcers—not nothing.

Come as soon as you can and we'll celebrate all over again.

Forward the two letters enclosed for me. If we don't hear from Partisan

Review pretty soon—we will certainly *not* send them another letter, still nastier and I'll tell you why. Night before last I wrote Accent a real stinger, saying they had had my story 4 months and my letter inquiring after it for six weeks and that seemed long enough to me. I got much nastier. I was going to mail it yesterday but Dorothy said, wait one more day. I nearly put it in the box this morning. The postman would have picked it up and then left the letter from you containing the letter from Accent. So, we'll let Partisan keep it a while.[8] I don't care—and maybe—well, I guess that would be expecting a little too much, though, wouldn't it?

Yours—
Bill

P.S. I'm not sending out any of the old manuscripts anymore until this one appears in Accent, ie—Man with a Family[9] and the one Partisan has. Send Man with a Family home to me. I can't make head nor tail of my copy anymore and I want to do more work on it. I'm working on a new story for Sewanee.[10] It should be done in a couple of months. I'll send it for you to read as soon as I'm satisfied with it.

1.WH had been designated to write a fifteen-thousand-word essay for a book of fifty to sixty plates on the career of the painter Will Barnet (1911–), to have been published by Press Eight.

2. *First Prize Stories,* published yearly.

3. Martha Foley (1897–1977) was editor of *The Best American Short Stories,* published every year.

4. The John Simon Guggenheim Memorial Foundation, established in 1925, grants money for scholarly research and creative endeavors.

5. A "loser" in Yiddish.

6. "Crap" in Yiddish.

7. One of the editors of *Accent,* Charles Shattuck (1910–) was on the English faculty of Vassar College.

8. See note for letter of January 1948 to Grabstald.

9. "Man with a Family" was accepted on 6 July 1949, and the story was published in *Accent* 9, no. 4 (Summer 1949): 179–201.

10. "The Fauve."

TO CRAIG WYLIE

[Apparently the Houghton Mifflin Company had seen one of WH's short stories and expressed an interest in his first novel. The "novel in progress" was "Commuting Distance," which WH eventually turned into the long title story of The

Last Husband. *On 20 June, Wylie responded to the following letter, writing, "We cannot at this time undertake any such advance as you require, but I think our Fellowship competition, of which I enclose a description, should fit your bill fairly closely."]*

TLS/HR

Brewster, N.Y.
June 14, 1949

Mr. Craig Wylie
Houghton Mifflin Company
2 Park Street
Boston, Mass.

Dear Mr. Wylie:
Thank you very much for your letter. I am pleased that you liked "The Hardys."

I have not heard from Mr. Dale Warren.

Yes, I have plans for a novel and I thank you for your interest in that. But you ask to read it when it is completed. I do not say this out of arrogance—but the publisher who reads it when completed will be the one who has made it possible for me to write it.

Macmillan is interested in it and William Morrow and Co.[1] has come reasonably close to the advance I asked for.

However, I have not yet reached any agreement with either of these companies.

It may seem strangely presumptuous of me to state the terms I want in any contract for my book before you know if you like it, or indeed, have even seen it. But as these are the only terms under which I should begin more concerted work on it at the time, it may be as well, for both you and me, to discourage you at the start, if you are going to be discouraged.

I want $500 on acceptance of 10M words and $100 per month for at least a year, preferably 18 months.

If that seems to you too much for a first novel—regardless of how you like it—I shall simply have to wait until you or some other publisher is impressed enough with my name as a writer of short stories, to feel it is right.

You see, for two years I have been working as a farmhand. That has left me little time to write. More than I ever managed from any job I was able to get in the city, but not much. Well, even that job is running out now.

I have an offer from Bard College[2] to teach creative writing next year. It's far from what I want, but I have a wife and child.

You will understand that I tell you all this not to impress you with my misfortunes and obligations, but only to explain the reasons for my demands.

So . . . although I have voluminous notes for my big book, many little scenes written, the major characters minutely documented, a well-defined outline, I'm not going to begin putting it all together until the conditions are right.

If you have not lost interest by now, I'll be glad to send you a brief outline of my book and, if you like, one or two of my shorter pieces that have not yet appeared.

Thank you again, and Mr. Warren, for your interest.

Sincerely,
William Humphrey

1. WH never developed a relationship with the publishing firm of Macmillan (established in 1843), but William Morrow and Company published his first book of short stories, *The Last Husband* (1953).

2. A liberal arts college in Annandale-on-Hudson, New York, founded as St. Stephens College in 1860 by the Episcopal Church. WH taught there from 1949 to 1958.

[PROFESSOR OF NO DEGREE]

1950–58

TO KATHERINE ANNE PORTER

[WH joined the faculty of Bard in September 1949. At the beginning of his second year, he invited Porter to speak informally to the English students. She not only accepted the invitation but also went on at length about how she admired WH's stories: "When I think how long it has been since I first read and admired so much your stories, it seems a little late to be saying so." She then discussed how she planned to help his career. "Help helps," she insisted (26 September 1950).]

TLS/HL

[Bard College
Annandale-on-Hudson, New York]
September 28, 1950

Dear Miss Porter,

First let me try to tell you how much the part of your letter that deals with me means to me.

I spent a good while trying to learn how to write, and did many foolish things without learning from any of them; I aped Henry James' late manner[1] and set out to rewrite Finnegans Wake.[2] Reading you was my great revelation; I knew then what I wanted to do. You were my one teacher. When I wrote I had copies of Old Mortality and Noon Wine and The Cracked Looking Glass and The Old Order[3] open on my table at favorite paragraphs. I stole my first printed story completely from A Day's Work[4] (as you no doubt know). I wrote for you. You were the only person whose approval I wanted, and my wife and I asked each other constantly, "Do you think *she* has seen it? Do you think she will like it?" At one time I was barely persuaded by my wife not to impose on you by sending you everything I had done, to ask you whether the editors were right, or whether I should go on. I asked everyone [*sic*] of the literary people I began to meet after I started printing if he knew you, what you were like, and I worried deeply when I heard once that your health had been poor lately. I bought every piece of your uncollected writing I could and when this job came along I taught you, you and more you. I admired you as a critic almost as much as a writer, having my students read the Stein piece,[5] and revealing to them that you were the one person who ever succeeded in making [T. S.] Eliot—as he so richly deserved—look downright silly.[6]

Your praise, and the knowledge that you worried yourself over me, is the most rewarding thing that I have ever known. (It might amuse you to know also that your being from Texas was very important for me: it had always seemed to me that a *writer* had to be from England, or France, possibly from New England, but I thought that being from Texas ruined my hopes. You were a blessing to me, then, in more than one way.)

Now about Bard. I feel terribly ashamed to offer you no money. What money we have comes out of the students' entertainment fund. The literature club gets *somewhat* less than the dance committee. Can't you, if we don't announce it, accept fifty dollars above your expenses? That is what we have, and if you don't take it, someone infinitely less deserving will. In any case, we have two dates we can grab away from the social scientists and other campus enemies—Wednesday, December 13th, and November 28 (Thursday).[7] Would either of these be possible for you? If you're willing it might be nice if you'd talk on the craft of the short story, and illustrate your talk with your own work. But we'll listen gladly to anything you might like better to talk about. Suit yourself entirely in this, only let us know so we can make posters with the title of your talk. If these dates neither suit you let me know and I'll demand another that does. You have been offered a very sumptuous room in the home of the president, another in the home of the dean. I very much hope that you will decline both of these and accept a much less sumptuous one at my place. Though here again please feel completely free to do what will be more comfortable for you.

You must pardon me if I go on and on, but I have been waiting for this chance to talk to you for a long time. To my great delight, I see that you're to have a story in the coming Harper's.[8]

You know now, I believe, with what eagerness I shall look forward to hearing from you. Thank you again, for everything.

Yours,
William Humphrey

1. The style of Henry James (1843–1916) found in *The Wings of the Dove* (1902) and *The Golden Bowl* (1904): It is complex, ambiguous, elliptical, and embellished. An American writer, James became a naturalized British subject in 1915.

2. By James Joyce (1882–1941), Ireland's most famous fiction writer, *Finnegans Wake* (1939) is an experimental novel depicting a dream world and the unconscious.

3. These stories were published in *Pale Horse, Pale Rider* (1939), *Flowering Judas and Other Stories* (1935), and *The Old Order: Stories of the South* (1941).

4. Porter replied, "I did notice that your first story ["In Sickness and Health"] was something on the order of A Day's Work, yet, the theme is certainly in the public domain, and the human situation was happening any where, to all sorts of persons: why should I have been the only one to write about it?" (30 September 1950).

5. "Gertrude Stein: Three Views," reprinted in *The Collected Essays and Occasional Writings of Katherine Anne Porter* (New York: Seymour Lawrence / Delacorte, 1970), 251–70.

6. T. S. Eliot (1888–1965), author of *Prufrock and Other Observations* (1917) and various books of criticism, was a modernist poet about whom WH often thought but did not respect. In "On Criticism of Thomas Hardy" (*Southern Review* 6 [1940]: 150–61), Porter defends Hardy against the priggish criticism of Eliot found in *After Strange Gods* (1934); she says that Eliot "need[s] to be reminded of the individual dignity and importance of the country people."

7. The twenty-eighth was on a Tuesday.

8. "The Prisoner," an excerpt from the yet-to-be-published *Ship of Fools* (*Harper's*, October 1950, 88–96).

TO KATHERINE ANNE PORTER

[Porter invited WH and his wife Dorothy to dinner in her New York City apartment on 15 October 1950.]

TLS/HL

[Bard College
Annandale-on-Hudson, New York]
October 19, 1950

Dear Miss Porter,

I've tried about seven times this week to write telling you how much the evening meant to me.[1] But you must know. You must have finally met someone you had worshipped and not been disappointed but even more rewarded than you had hoped to be. That is how I feel and that evening will always be one of my most important. Thank you for everything, for the trouble you went to, cooking and cleaning up after us (it struck me in the middle of the night: Katherine Anne Porter has got to get up in the morning and wash *my* dishes! My God!) and thank you for your patience with my stories[2] and for all you had to say about them. I'll work more on both of them and hope they'll please you later. Thanks too for being so handsome, and if you can find that photograph you promised me please send it soon.

I'll send you a train schedule[3] right away and we can make our plans. Meanwhile, without doing anything for which I shall reproach myself that it is interfering with your work, won't you please write.

Yours,
Bill Humphrey

1. For a different perspective on this evening, see WH's letter to William A. Owens, May 1988.

2. "Report Cards" and "The Fauve."

3. Because Porter was to be lecturing at Bard.

TO KATHERINE ANNE PORTER

TLS/HL

[Bard College]
Annandale-on-Hudson, New York
December 2 [1950]

Dear Katherine Anne,

I feel bad, asking this,—but would you read this story[1] again and tell me if it's so bad that fourteen editors are right in turning it down. Of course, they've turned down almost fourteen revisions of it. I've done some things to it since you saw it last and I do believe that though there are many things wrong with it, it has moments of pleasure. It's been a long time since I had anything in print, and my job here depends in large measure on my keeping myself before some kind of small public. So I would like to get this thing printed, or to do whatever is needed to it to make it publishable. If you think well enough of it, would it be too much to ask you to plead with Harper's magazine to reconsider it (it was submitted to them a year ago, in quite a different version, by my then agent, Diarmuid Russell).[2] Or else offer me your suggestions. Thanks, in either case.

Yours,
Bill

1. "Report Cards." WH had received an encouraging letter from Pearl Kazin of *Harper's Bazaar* on 10 October 1949 saying that the magazine might consider this story.

2. After author Eudora Welty (1909–2001) wrote to Diarmuid Russell of Russell and Volkening Literary Agents recommending that he take on WH, he approached WH on 16 September 1949, and their brief relationship began.

TO KATHERINE ANNE PORTER

[Porter answered WH's letter of 2 December on 6 January 1951, explaining that she had been in the hospital for bronchitis. About his story, "Report Cards," she wrote, "I am shocked beyond words to know that you have re-written your story every time it was refused, trying simply not to make it a good story, something you must write of your own in your own way, but to meet the demands of some editor who has a special kind of public, or thinks he has, and wants something written to order for it."]

TLS/HL

[Bard College
Annandale-on-Hudson, New York
8(?) January 1951]

Dear Katherine Anne,
I had no idea it was anything as bad as having to go to a hospital. I now feel guilty for having even suggested your coming up here, and added to your strain. And now you've got me worried by the program you've outlined for yourself. Having just got over this, don't you think that a working day beginning at five a.m. is a little steep[?] I understand your impatience to finish up the big book.[1] But you must not put yourself back in the hospital by spring. I'm sure I make you feel ever so much better by these bleak cautions! Forgive me. But I know what an exhausting thing writing is for me, especially when I'm on the last lap of a piece (I can only imagine my state when within sight of the end of a *Novel*!) and I feel you ought to be careful. And so I see I've forgot the important thing, and that is to tell you how glad I am that you are better. I approve completely of your determination to keep the world locked out (Only do relent enough to make one evening for me before you go to Chicago (and let me know which evening I may have). If you're going to Europe from there—and I wish you wouldn't, considering the state of things European[2]—who knows when I'll get another chance?)

Now I have to disabuse you of a couple of things. I see so well how I have misled you about these two things, and how in so doing I have caused you a lot of quite unnecessary worry over me, and over the state of things, too, if my case (or what I've led you to think of my case) is indicative of the state of things. I was hasty in one letter and led you [to] believe that this was the kind of pressure I lived under: that knowing I had to publish in order to keep my job, every rejection slip has terrified me into trying desperately to revamp the story to fit the prejudices of the next editor it was tried on, or the same editor again. (Now don't think I repudiate with anger or scorn the charge that I've tried to tailor my stories to a certain market.) I'm not editorially astute enough to know what any individual editor wants. Moreover, I make this admission with neither pride or shame, I don't read the fiction in any magazine unless I already like the author, so I don't know what the fiction aims of any magazines are. Moreover, if anything, I sin in the direction of refusing to take any constructive suggestions for my work, being the most bull-headed person I know, so much so that when I've been contemplating a certain change in one of my stories I refuse to make it for the longest time if someone else suggests it. Myself, my wife, and you are the only three people in the world I will listen to for criticism. Moreover, not to draw this out, I've never received any constructive criticism from an editor: they all just say no thanks. The reason, then, that that little story[3] was so often done over was that each time it came back I myself saw some little way to improve a paragraph or two (which gives you some idea how ill-equipped it was when it began its travels.) My method is different from yours (and much inferior, I know very well, though there seems to be little I can do about it.) I don't keep a story as long as I should before sending it out. I have made a New Year's Resolution though.

And really, Katherine Anne, I'm quite grateful for this job. It doesn't exert all the pressure on me that you think. I take it no more seriously than to consider it a way of making a living. I've been in it long enough already to see people (former writers) who make a Cause of it—who tell themselves they haven't time to be writers because of their teaching commitments, and who must therefore see teaching as a very worthy Endeavor. I'm not in any danger of that. I grant you that the best kind of teacher is one who never wanted to do anything but teach. (No, on second thought I don't grant that: even with my more or less cynical attitude toward it—and I feel I just reel my class room stuff off the top of my mind—I'm still a better teacher than the professional teacher. Students get something extra from listening to someone to whom literature is a living thing. But this is all by the way[.]) The point is that it beats anything I ever did to make a living in the only way that matters (aside from giving me more money, by about three times, than anything else I ever did. For I get $2800 dollars a year. My last job brought me seven to nine hundred a year) . . [.] the only thing that matters: time and freedom from anxiety to write. It takes about 25 hours a week and I get 4 and a half months vacation a year. Now the situation is, I don't have any degrees. This makes me a special case. I can't bring any credit to the place as a scholar and am not expected to. But unless I bring some kind of credit then that lack of degrees is something of an embarrassment in the eyes of the world. So, I am The Writer of the place, a situation not nearly so bad as I see you imagining. They leave me alone, don't care what I write—don't read what I write, for that matter—and don't care where it's printed, but would like something to come out every once in a while with a note in the contributors' column saying that I teach here. Don't think that I live in agony for fear of not being reappointed. However, I am pretty sure now to be reappointed for next year. I would like to hope that that will be my last year teaching—not because I find teaching so awful, but simply because there is something I would rather do: farm. In another year, if I can persuade some publisher to do a book of my stories and to give me an advance on the novel I mean to tackle as soon as a book of stories is finished, then I'll take off to Vermont. They almost give old farms away there, and though they're not much good, they'll do for what I have in mind. I want to raise a kitchen garden, a cow, two pigs, two dozen chickens and some rabbits and do whatever I have to do to bring in about nine hundred dollars a year, and I'm set for life. These are things which I like to do, can do, and have done for other people to make my living. Just don't have fears that I'm going to be seduced into thinking that teaching is the important thing. I could never. I'm too crazy to be anything but a writer. I really am sorry to have caused you all this concern over me. But really and truly, Katherine Anne, I'm not "at a crisis." If I ever should be (and my ego is so vast that it's unlikely that anything external could ever so penetrate as to bring me to a crisis) I'll be honest enough to admit it to myself and the second person I shall tell will be you. Okay? (Selfishly, I must admit a certain amount of pleasure in having caused you some concern over me. You'll forgive me for that though.[)]

Well, I hope you don't go down for this until your working day is over.

I'll do what you say to the story. You're quite right, of course. But I'll send it back to you only if you assure me that to send it out is not going to interfere with you longer than to lick a stamp. Promise to tell me truthfully about this. You MUST not write a volume to recommend it to an editor. Take care of yourself and write me as often as you can honestly spare the time. Thank you again for thinking of me.

Love,
Bill

P.S. If it will further calm your fears for me, I'm in the middle of the best story I've had.[4] It's a beaut![5]

1. *Ship of Fools.*

2. Could WH have in mind the resurgence of conservative governments across Europe in reaction to the leftist governments that had emerged after World War II?

3. "Report Cards."

4. Possibly "The Shell" or "Quail for Mr. Forester."

5. Postscript added by hand.

TO IAN PARSONS

[Chatto & Windus would publish The Last Husband *on 17 November 1953. Ian Parsons (d. 1980) was president of the London firm until his retirement in 1974.]*

TLS/UR

Rhinebeck, N.Y.[1]
July 27, 1953

Mr. Parsons
Chatto & Windus, Ltd.
40–42 William IV Street
London, W. C. 2

Dear Mr. Parsons,
I have your name from my friend Joseph Summers,[2] whom you saw in London a few weeks ago. He has told me that you spoke very kindly of my short stories at that meeting. Thank you very much.

I am writing also because having your name gives me someone at Chatto to thank for the firm's interest in my work. I am very happy that you are to be my publishers in England. Of course, I am happy simply that my little book is to appear there. But I have always regarded Chatto & Windus as the best publisher in England (and isn't that to say in the world?) and I am more honored by your acceptance of the book than by all the other things that have ever happened to me as a writer. I know that your imprint on the book will assure me the most serious readership, and that as one of the writers sponsored by you I shall keep the best literary company I ever could. Thank all of you very much.

Sincerely,
William Humphrey

1. The Humphreys had recently moved from barracks housing on the Bard campus to nearby Rhinebeck.

2. Joseph Summers (1920–2003), a member of the literature division at Bard College, had met with Parsons in connection with Summers's book *George Herbert: His Religion and Art,* which was published by Chatto & Windus in England and Harvard University Press in the United States in 1954.

TO THEODORE AND RENÉE WEISS

[The poet Theodore Weiss (1916–2003) was head of the literature department at Bard College. When he was on sabbatical leave during the 1953–54 academic year, WH was acting head of the literature division and was put in charge of tending to the daily business of the Quarterly Review of Literature, *the influential journal for poetry, fiction, and criticism founded in 1943, which Weiss and his wife Renée edited. WH had just returned from visiting his mother.]*

TLS/PU

[Bard College
Annandale-on-Hudson, New York
early September 1953]

Dear Ted and Renee,
Please forgive me for waiting so long. I got back from Cleveland and spent three days sleeping to catch up. Then I started writing and have not caught my breath until today. You know, I figured I had about as much again of that story[1] to write during the field period—another 7,000 words—and I thought I must might [*sic*] be able to finish it. Well, I've finished it already. I wrote as much as 1,4000 [*sic*] words a day—as much as I ever wrote in a month before. I am extremely anxious for you to hear it. I'll begin where I left you. Saw my agent that day—he said we'll give up Viking, let everything wait until I have the book of stories entirely finished. The days of 3,000 dollar advances on first serious novels are over, he says. He can't sell the Report Cards story—Atlantic Monthly, Harpers magazine and Harpers Bazaar have turned it down. Mademoiselle had it when I saw him

and since I haven't heard from him yet I presume they too have turned it down. God knows who will take this new one—it's over 14,000 words. It'll have to wait for a book.

I've been sending out a few E. P. issues of the magazine—not many though. I sent the three to W. C. Williams.[2] Vivian [*sic*] Koch's book on him[3] arrived yesterday—a big fat volume full of fat claims, with which you will agree and I won't. [. . .]

My mother doesn't know what she had, but I do—unhappiness. But I had a good trip and enjoyed her for the first time in my life. We spent all day five days reminiscing over my little home town and exchanging Southern gossip. My little brother[4] gave me a very queer feeling—in the first place he look[e]d a lot like me. And when she spoke to him my mother used a tone of voice and certain words that I hadn't heard from her since I was five and cracked certain jokes that she used with me. It was a little disturbing, yet pleasant too. He is a bright kid, and his case is hopeless. He'll be a football player for sure and go into a bank or be an attorney—he'll also be very much an Irishman, and probably Catholic—his father.

Meanwhile a scandal has broken out on the campus—not official but personal—and yet I'll only tantalize you and say not a word more now. There has been no mail I thought worth sending or even mentioning. I'm sending out no subscriptions to the mag. And have so far deposited no checks but will in a day or so. The weather here is astounding—mostly warm rain, cold for the last day or so in the morning and evening but warming up beautifully midday—very sunny, never a cloud.

We are offered Dylan Thomas[5] for an evening for 100 dollars. Shall we accept?

A gentleman writes: ["]Dear Sir, please send me any information you may have appertaining to creative writing fellowships at Bard, as I am desirous of ascertaining what this information may be." I guess I needn't feel so ashamed of my lack of education.

I'm sure you'll be glad to know the dean is back—spent his vacation in bed with flu, but recovered. Trustees meetings every day. Life at Bard. Will write soon.

Love,
Bill, Dorothy, Toni

1. "The Last Husband," fourteen thousand words, the title story of WH's first collection (1953).

2. William Carlos Williams (1883–1963), American poet and fiction writer. His epic poem *Paterson* was in process in 1952 (it was published in five volumes between 1946 and 1958).

3. Vivienne Koch's book *William Carlos Williams* was published by New Directions in 1950.

4. Tommy Troughton became an alcoholic in his thirties and preceded WH in death.

5. Dylan Thomas (1914–53), Welsh poet who had recently published his *Collected Poems* (1952).

TO THEODORE AND RENÉE WEISS

TLS/PU

[Bard College
Annandale-on-Hudson, New York]
Monday [late September 1953]

Dear Weisses,

Your letter came today. What a good life it sounds! Tell us more about Scotland. Meanwhile, excuse the delay in my writing. My typewriter has been in repair shop for a month. We have had a thousand droppers-in-upon, and I worked so damned hard on my book[1] I got up reeling and staggering from the desk at night. Then I went to New Hampshire (caught nothing) for a week just before school opened. And school did open, and so it's just now that I am able to get you a line. [. . .][2]

I am sorry to report that you have received three rejection slips—from Accent, Partisan, and Poetry.[3] No point in copying out their polite formulae. You might be pleased to hear of the plight of both Accent and Partisan—"overstocked on creative work, need criticism." This age of encroaching creativeness!

School began. We have no students in literature. The admissions people seem to have realized their (and S. Hirsch's)[4] ambition to destroy that vicious notion that Bard is an arts school—14 freshmen, 5 seniors. Well, we'll not be overworked. Except Bellow and Botsford, that is. What with the Book of the Month club, Bellow is all the rage,[5] and we've all advised students to take French while the cat, I mean the mouse, I mean the rat is away.

What shall I say about the new people. Botsford is what I expected and more—a dostoevskian [*sic*] pathological liar, and a little boy. Ludwig[6] is another one—a defensive little boy—every other word is a hard word and usually fuck or shit. He apparently resents all the rest of us very much because he has not published any creative work. Perhaps not a bad sort under this. Bellow is another little boy. In fact, it's one big bunch of pushing little boyish egos. But Bellow is more complicated. In fact, you know him less the more you know him. I've read his book—it's trash I think. So far

I've said nothing to him about it, let him think I hadn't had time to look at it. In another letter I began writing you Saturday before your letter came I used the very word you did—pointless. Well, I'll have to speak to him about it soon, and I gather that he is accustomed to hearing no less than that it is just about the biggest book since Leo Marcel Herman Charles Ernest F. Scott Shakespeare God.[7] A very self-regardful man. And yet, a generous man in many ways too. Not simple enough to say one thing about him, without having to qualify it immediately. He won't be with us after this year—he's already told me as much.

Warren[8] I like—very much. And by the way he has read me 50[-]odd pages of his new novel. It is very good. Much better than anything in the published one. His wife Marjorie is very nice. Well, for one thing, they are someone to talk with about you-all! [. . .][9]

Nothing to tell you about us. Well, we paid our visit to the Summers[10] at long last. Ye Gods, that is the most horrible place I've seen since Texas. If you ever hear me complain about Bard again, just whisper, Storrs. He was sick with the flu, looked awful. We went and came back same day. He was the same old Joe. I felt very sorry for him. Living conditions very sordid. He told me his G. Herbert book is being brought out in the mother country by Chatto and Windus and here afterwards by Harvard U. Press. So I suppose he'll be able to go back home—into the Ivy League, that is.[11]

Your abode sounds delightful, and I am pleased to hear that you are reading some novels, A Room with a View is something less than either The Longest Journey or Howards End, so you have the best Forester ahead of you.[12] As for Dickens, you have all of him ahead of you—Nick Nickleby is one of his worst. Read Great Expectations, Our Mutual Friend, Little Dorrit—even the Old Curiousity Shop, which though it has Little Nell also has Dick Swiveller.[13] You'll be a convert then. As for me, I'm reading Thackeray,[14] and liking it. Reading also Hazlitt[15]—your Hazlitt, and liking it better than I deduce from the lack of Weissian marginalia than you did. He can write. Dorothy is reading George Meredith.[16] God help her.

Will you look out for any announcements of my book.[17] If you're ever in London will you ask them for me whenever it is to appear. I hear nothing from them.

Rewrote the first 100 pages of my novel[18] this summer (have all told about 160 pages now) and I believe it's pretty fair—at least it's more dramatic. I'm going to be taking it to a publisher soon and try for an advance on that much. I hope Morrow turns it down. I'll go to Harcourt or Viking.[19]

The American literary scene is full of Mr. Robert Penn Warren at the moment. In the Times, Mr. R. Jarrell tells us that Brothers to Dragonflies[20] contains the two most memorable characters in American literature, and Miss Babble-ette Douche in the Herald Tribune devotes a page to Mr. Warren as the new Milton, only (with a bow to those behind hand moderns who have not heard of Mr. Eliot's latest essay on J. M.) better than Milton.[21] I suppose that otherwise the biggest thing on the colonial literary scene is the adventures of Augie March.

Book list—get me any or all of these you can, good used if you can: A North's Plutarch.[22] Prestley's The English Comic Characters.[23] Yeats Autobiographies (this [is] new—just came out).[24] Collected Poems of T. Hardy.[25] Dostoevsky by N. Berdyaev.[26] Flaubert's Three Tales translated by Frederick Whyte.[27] F. M. Ford The Good Soldier.[28]

Yours,
B-D-+T[29]

1. *Home from the Hill.*

2. A paragraph on a vague matter pertaining to *QRL* is omitted.

3. *Poetry: A Magazine of Verse* was founded in 1912 by Harriet Monroe.

4. "Steph" Hirsch, a Bard College administrator.

5. Saul Bellow's comic novel *The Adventures of Augie March,* published just before he came to Bard College to teach, was an alternate choice of the Book-of-the-Month Club in 1953. Bellow (1915–2005) taught at Bard College during the 1953–54 academic year. Keith Botsford, on the Bard faculty from 1953 to 1956, was a fiction writer and playboy; he became Bellow's lifelong friend.

6. Jack Ludwig, on the Bard faculty from 1953 to 1958, was a Joycean. He adored Bellow.

7. WH is invoking the Christian names of authors Tolstoy, Proust, Melville, Dickens, Hemingway, and Fitzgerald.

8. Warren Carrier, on the Bard faculty from 1953 from 1957, published his first novel, *The Hunt,* in 1953.

9. A paragraph on Bard academic gossip is omitted.

10. Joseph and U. T. Miller Summers (see note 2 on letter of 27 July 1953 to Ian Parsons) had moved to Storrs, Connecticut, when he took a post in the English Department at the University of Connecticut.

11. Summers, a graduate of Harvard, returned there to teach. Later he became a distinguished authority on Renaissance literature and retired as Roswell S. Burrows Professor of English at the University of Rochester.

12. In his 11 September 1953 letter, Weiss had remarked that *A Room with a View* was "successfully slight (I do not use the word slightingly)"; WH advises that the other novels by E. M. Forster (1879–1970) are more substantial.

13. The novels WH mentions are some of the most famous by Charles Dickens (1812–70).

Dick Swiveller is the light-hearted, feckless, and convivial friend of Fred Trent, the brother of Nell, the heroine of *Old Curiosity Shop* (1841).

14. William Makepeace Thackeray (1811–63) shared the English literary spotlight with Dickens in the Victorian period.

15. William Hazlitt (1778–1830) wrote elegant essays on miscellaneous subjects.

16. George Meredith (1828–1909), Victorian poet and novelist.

17. *The Last Husband and Other Stories* (Chatto & Windus, 1953).

18. *Home from the Hill.*

19. Viking was the publisher of Bellow's *Augie March.*

20. WH's jazzed up title for Robert Penn Warren's *Brother to Dragons: A Tale in Verse and Voices,* reviewed by Randall Jarrell in the *New York Times,* 23 August 1953, 3. The poem is about Thomas Jefferson and his criminal nephews, who butchered one of their slaves on a meatblock. Warren (1905–89), poet and novelist from Kentucky, was one of the Fugitives (a group of writers and poets who founded the *Fugitive,* a literary journal) at Vanderbilt University in Nashville, Tennessee, in the 1920s and 1930s.

21. WH's version of Babette Deutsch, who reviewed Warren's verse drama in the *New York Herald Tribune Book Review,* 23 August 1953, 3. T. S. Eliot in 1936 denounced John Milton (1608–74) as one whose sensual capacities "had been withered early by book learning," but in 1947 he recanted his low opinion.

22. Sir Thomas North's translation of Plutarch's *Lives* was published in 1896.

23. First published in 1925, this book is by J. B. Priestley (1894–1984), English novelist and playwright.

24. The Irish poet W. B. Yeats (1865–1939) had just published *Autobiographies.*

25. *The Collected Poems of Thomas Hardy* was published in 1930.

26. *Dostoevsky's World Conception* (1923) by Nikolai Berdyaev (1874–1948).

27. First published in 1877 by French writer Gustave Flaubert (1821–80).

28. *The Good Soldier* (1915) by Ford Madox Ford (1873–1939) is that English writer's most famous novel.

29. Bill, Dorothy, and Toni.

TO THEODORE AND RENÉE WEISS

ALS/PU

[Bard College
Annandale-on-Hudson, New York]
Monday, 19th October [1953]

Dear Ted and Renee,

I have been remiss not only about writing but about tending to the QRL. At last, a month late, I have got the envelopes off to the Orange Print Shop. I have been sick with a cold—and Dorothy has been engaged—consequently me too—on a program of entertaining all the college worthies old and new whom we've owed dinners for the last two years. Between this and teaching and being depressed, I've been a very bad magazine business manager. I'll try to do better on the next issue. (Meanwhile—one item of magazine business—please write Random House, and let them know what issue you mean to run William Carlos Williams' Theocratic poem in.[1] They say they'll bring out a volume of his verse in the spring that will include that poem and they can't schedule publication until the magazine publication.[2] One other item: I have a letter from the advertising firm representing the Bollingens requesting tear-sheets of their ad—but I never have received the ad,[3] or the plate for it. What do I do?)

Whitney Bolton[4] is in England and wants me to send him your address. Shall I?

What to tell you about the college? The Literature weekend is taking shape—what kind of shape is another matter. Topic: The Arts of Narrative. Hoo-ha! Mr. Bellow's suggestion. Speakers? Well, so far John Berryman[5] has accepted. Suggestion of Mr. Wanning.[6] James Gould Cozzens[7]—my suggestion—refused. Invited and refused—suggestion of Mr. Wanning, unanimously, but for that eternal nigger in the wood pile yours truly, seconded by the division: Monsieur Georges Simenon,[8] creator of that eternal character, Inspector Maigret. Next on the list to be invited—also unanimously seconded by division (I for fear of being called a Southerner, kept quiet.) that great American novelist, and friend of Mr. Bellow, Ralph Ellison[9]—whom I tried to read—worse piece of crap I've seen in years, and I felt like saying that being a Negro does not insure that a man can write. Also invited, not yet replied, Mr. Robert Penn Warren. It ought to be a lovely time for all.

My writing is going badly or not at all. Just now 150 pages of the novel[10] are at Morrow and I haven't heard yet though they've had it two weeks. Meanwhile, they've sent me the first royalty reports on The Last Husband, and I can understand from it why they've not been hastening to give me the [advance] on the promise of the novel. I won't tell you the numbers of copies The Last Husband sold. Not a happy number. Meanwhile the Adventures of Augie March has 26,000 copies in print and yet I like Bellow.

You're doing about as well as I am, I'm sorry to say, and just got a rejection slip from the Sewanee Review. No doubt they consider you too well established, like me.[11]

I really ought to stop this letter now. Somehow I am getting bitterer by the minute.

Would you like a report on the over all literary scene? Well, in the current Kenyon there is a short story by F. Scott Fitzgerald—no! By golly, it's by Authur Mizener. I *thought* it was rather poor Fitzgerald.[12] There is a verse play by Leslie Fiedler,[13] and in a review entitled Prose Genius in Verse, Mr. Robert Lowell tells us that in Brothers [*sic*] to Dragons "Warren has written his best book. [It] is as though Professor Babbitt had begotten Rousseau[14] or a black minerva dancing in Congo mass. Warren has written a big book; he has crossed the Alps and, like Napoleon's shoeless army, entered the fat, populated river bottom of the novel."[15] I assure you it makes just as much sense out of context as it does in, lovely style, too, ain't it? The current Partisan has the long poem, called Homage to Mistress Bradstreet, the labors of composition of which kept Mr. John Berryman from our conference on Shakespeare, you remember. Fifty-seven eight line stanzas.[16] I can't understand one word of it. The Hudson Review[17] is interesting, as always, this issue. My God why try?

Hope you are well and having fun. I've got papers to grade now. Write often.

Yours,
Bill

[R]eason for the lousy script—my typewriter broken down again.

1. "Dactyls—from Theocritus, Idyl I" was put in *QRL* 4 (1954): 255–60.

2. "Theocritus: Idyl I" was incorporated into *Paterson V*, published in 1957.

3. The regular advertisements for the Bollingen series in *QRL* appeared without interruption in 1953 and 1954.

4. Perhaps the author of *The Silver Spade: The Conrad Hilton Story* (New York: Farrar, Strauss, and Young, 1954).

5. John Berryman (1914–72), American poet best known for Pulitzer Prize–winning *The Dream Songs* (1964), in which he speaks of his life, especially the death of his father, through a character named Henry. Berryman's long confessional poems have the reputation for being disorderly.

6. Andrews Wanning (1913–97), a scholar of seventeenth-century prose, taught at Bard College from 1951 to 1977.

7. James Gould Cozzens (1903–78), American novelist best known for *Gaurd of Honor* (1948), which won a Pulitzer Prize in 1949, and *By Love Possessed* (1957).

8. Georges Simenon (1903–89), Belgian-born author of crime fiction, created the famous investigator Detective-Superintendent Maigret.

9. Ralph Ellison (1914–94), black American novelist, author of *Invisible Man* (1952).

10. *Home from the Hill.*

11. Monroe K. Spears, the new editor of *Sewanee Review,* in turning down WH's application for an *SR*-sponsored writing fellowship, had written on 18 June 1953, "[W]e felt that we ought to help other young writers who are less well established [. . .]."

12. F. Scott Fitzgerald (1896–1940), regarded as one of America's best twentieth-century novelists. Arthur Mizener (1907–88) was a Fitzgerald specialist at Cornell University.

13. Leslie Fiedler (1917–2003), famous for his *Partisan Review* essay "Come Back to the Raft Ag'n, Huck Honey," was another literary critic who dared also to write belles-lettres.

14. Irving Babbitt (1865–1933), a professor of French literature at Harvard, is author of *Rousseau and Romanticism* (1919). Jean-Jacques Rousseau (1712–78), a novelist and philosopher born in Geneva, is considered the most important writer of the Enlightenment. He argued that civilization has led to the degradation of humanity. The central concern of his work is liberty: "Man is born free but everywhere is in chains" (*The Social Contract* [1762]).

15. The quotation from Lowell's review reads as follows: "That Warren, one of the bosses of the New Criticism, is the author is as though Professor Babbitt had begotten Rousseau or black Minerva dancing in Congo masks. Warren has written his best book, a big book; he has crossed the Alps and, like Napoleon's shoeless army, entered the fat, populated river bottom of the novel" ("Prose Genius in Verse," *Kenyon Review* 15, no. 4 [Autumn 1953]: 621).

16. Berryman's tribute to the Puritan poet was published in book form in 1956.

17. The *Hudson Review,* a quarterly magazine of literature and art founded in 1947 in New York City by Frederick Morgan.

TO THEODORE AND RENÉE WEISS

TLS/PU

Bard College
Annandale-on-Hudson
New York
Sat. Morn. [late November 1953]

Dear Ted and Renee,

I'll begin this letter now and finish it Monday. Dorothy has a duck in the oven to take with us in a hour or so up to our friends Dr. and Mrs. Elliot from Brewster[1] to their country house in Hillsdale.[2] So I'll write for a while. The magazine[3] came at last. I'll send copies to you Monday. I read Wilbur's poetry conference speec[h][4] last night and I thought it was really fine. No doubt you like W. C. Williams[5] better. That's all I've had time to read so far, but the issue looks good. Meanwhile, really it's not my cantankerousness—but no manuscripts have come in worth looking at. The poetry has been especially bad—silly stuff, old ladies poetry—doggerel. The short stories [are] all about children. I do think you'd have liked none of it any better than I.

Well, I saw my publishers[6] over the 150 pages of my novel. They didn't like it. I was in no very strong arguing position, because I liked it less than they did. So now I'm starting it al[l] over again. Warren[7] has finished his novel—writing time a little less than 3 months. I haven't seen the last half of it, but as I told you, I like the first half a good deal. Meanwhile, Warren has come to like Bard somewhat less than he did—not enough to want to go away, but he has lost that skeptical look when he hears me gripe now. That's natural, I guess. I like it somewhat less, too.

Case[8] is not speaking to me, again. I got up at the last faculty meeting and said I thought there were too many administration people on the personnel committee in proportion to the faculty. Then he in that suffering Jesus on the cross attitude you know so well made this all personal, and said he hoped no one meant to suggest that the aims of administration were not the same as those of faculty, and hoped no one meant to imply that administrative duress had been used et-shitera [*sic*]. And so now he ain't speaking. I have a notion he's gonna really try to fire me this time, now that you're away. I saw Poppsy[9] the other day to air my feelings about our people. I recommended everybody but Botsford (not that there was any real question about him, but Pop[p]sy said, suppose Artine[10] decides to stay another year. I said I'd even tolerate Botsford for that. Yes, I recommended everybody—in lukewarm tones, except Warren. Poppsy made it plain that it didn't really matter what I said me not being on tenure, and that he was asking me really just so I wouldn't feel slighted. I recommended Wanning for tenure, which he would have got anyway. He's getting better, you know. He tells Case where to get off. He takes a very angry hen with her brood attitude about the division. I having hired them as asst profs thought we ought to wait another year. Meanwhile Mssrs. Hecht,[11] Ludwig, and Bellow have formed themselves into a little literary B'nai Brith,[12] or really a Love Saul Bellow committee[.] With Hecht I believe it's sincere. With Ludwig, something else again. I understand that Ludwig is going to drive Bellow to Reno during the field period[13] to get his divorce.[14] For which Bellow is taking Ludwig's writings to Viking (his writings! Oh, my god, he read a story at the lit club recently. I was never so ashamed. However I rather think the guy is a pretty good teacher.) So these three are having little to do with us goyem.[15]

By the way, were you aware that Botsford is an Italian count?[16] Or rather, that he would be if his mother had not married a commoner and lost her title? So his wife told Marjorie Carrier. He is having a novel published by Harcourt Brace this spring. Unfortunately, no one will know about it. It has to be published anonymously, for his wife's family does not approve of writers and do not know he is one. She is heiress to the

Cunard steamships, you know. So he said, and I guess he ought to know. This boy is mad.

By the way, I'm beginning to get passionate letters from Katherine Anne Porter again, and she just wrote telling me to apply for a Guggenheim[17] instantly. I haven't got the forms yet, though I know it is supposed to close Oct. 15. She feels you can be a little later than that. Will you write for me? You don't have to do it beforehand, but after I give your name. It may be too late, and you won't have to.

Yours,
Bill

1. The town is about thirty miles north of New York City; WH was a farm worker there from September 1947 to August 1949.

2. A hamlet in the east of New York's Columbia County with far-reaching views of the Berkshires.

3. *Quarterly Review of Literature*.

4. Richard Wilbur (1921–) spoke at a poetry conference on "Experimental and Formal Verse" held "some years ago at Bard College," according to *QRL*. Wilbur's speech, "The Bottles Become New, Too," *QRL* 7 (3): 186–92, defends traditional rhythms, stanza forms, and rhyme—all the elements that Williams had attacked.

5. In his speech at the conference, "Some Hints Toward the Enjoyment of Modern Verse," *QRL* 7 (3): 172, 173, Williams holds that poetic tradition is "the resort of a cowardly disposition"; he advocates "structural imagination."

6. William Morrow, which published *The Last Husband* (1953).

7. That is, Warren Carrier.

8. James Herbert Case Jr., president of Bard from 1950 to 1960.

9. Perhaps the academic dean.

10. Artine Artinian, on the Bard faculty the entirety of WH's tenure.

11. The poet Anthony Hecht (1923–2004), a Bard graduate, returned to teach at the college from 1952 to 1967; his first book of poems, *A Summoning of Stones*, was published in 1954.

12. A secular Jewish association interested in advancing the rights of Jews in cultural and educational activities, founded in 1843; the name is Hebrew for "Sons of the Covenant."

13. The term at Bard College for the long vacation between semesters.

14. Bellow divorced Anita (née Goshkin) to marry Sondra Tschacbasov.

15. "Gentiles" in Yiddish.

16. Botsford claimed that he was a direct descendant of Machiavelli.

17. WH's application was not successful. Weiss had warned in his 12 December 1953 letter: "We know how madly unpredictable KAP is; she'll lead someone to water, then drown him in it."

TO THEODORE AND RENÉE WEISS

TLS/PU

[Upper Hook Road]
Rhinebeck, New York
Sunday [24(?) January 1954][1]

Dear Ted and Renee,

The letter that went astray to France has been returned to me. The bill from the printshop is $349.89. I am enclosing the other things that were in that letter, things which as I said, I didn't know what to do with. There is no other pressing news of Quarterly Review that I can think of. No manuscripts. No fiction comes at all, and the verse is mostly of this quality: He ca[m]e to me for such a little while. / He left and made an awful empty place. / It was not love I felt behind his smile / And yet I long once more to see his face. Close quote. I am returning this one, I should add. Really, I've no news of any kind to give you.

My publishers in England[2] have sent me a couple of reviews. I see you have not been making many friends for me over there—I thought you would have buttered up every reviewer in old Zealand[3] by now. The man in the London Times—ouch![4]

Well, I am writing.[5] It's not very good I'm afraid, but it's the best I seem able to do. More and more I come to realize that the only way to learn to live with the knowledge that you're not and not going to be a great writer is to work hard and honestly and try not to care.

Meanwhile, I get more sour on the literary situation in these United States all the time. It's set in now like a real illness with me. It used to exercise me a little, give me a kind of workout, now it saddens me, scares me, and makes me feel terribly alone in a very real and unhappy way. I wish the Quarterly Review didn't have exchange subscriptions.[6] That's what's got me reading the little mags, I guess. Anyhow, I've just gone through the current Partisan, Hudson, Kenyon and Sewanee. There is no hope. I think I told you that in the current Partisan Delmore Schwartz[7] says that Augie March is superior to Huckleberry Finn. Did I also mention Mary McCarthy's story—if I did, you see then by this repetition how the thing eats at me. I must quote you a bit from Mary McCarthy. Her story (piece f[ro]m a novel) is called, Dottie Makes an Honest Woman of herself.[8] [WH then quotes a passage describing in great detail a girl's learning to squat, part "the labia majora with the left hand," and insert the "pessary" that she has been fitted out with and to give herself a douche. The passage ends with the following:] "She had no wish ever to see Dick again, but the possession of all this machinery left her no choice. She sat down on the park bench with her two parcels beside her. Her underwear felt sticky from the lubricants the doctor had used and this soiled nasty sensation trickled into her very soul." The only thing I know of worse is the pieces (very long) of Randall Jarrel[l]'s novel (yes) *about* Mary McCarthy which appear in (yes) the current Kenyon and the current Sewanee.[9] He is a worse bitch about her than she is about her sweet little subjects.

Mr. Monroe K. Spears has lowered Sewanee from heights never breathtaking, and I assure you I do not say it because he rejected me for one of his fellowships.[10] This issue brings us an article called Between the Numen and the Moha (sic) or Notes Towards a Theory of the Novel, by R. P. Blackmur.[11] If I tried to give you his explanation of those two terms you'd be no better off than you are now. We have also an article in which Mr. Bon-ami Dobree tells us that in The Confidential Clerk Mr. Eliot has established himself as the Tourneur or Kyd of his time.[12] A great work, says Mr. Dobree, and compares its versification (which as he says is so good it doesn't sound like poetry at all) to the versification of the Shakespeare (the Eliot of his time) of Measure for Measure, instancing the similarity of this line of Shakespeare's: Stank like the forfeits in a barber's shop, to this one of Eliot's: and lock the gates behind you. From The Tempest he chooses: And makes my labours pleasures, to compare with, That was a nearer guess than you think. My God, you think you're losing your mind, reading such stuff. Sewanee brings us also an essay on Shakespeare's The Comedy of Errors by Frances Fergusson,[13] and for creative work, one of the most tasteless, untalented, ridiculous things I ever read, by Richard Eberhart, with a note in which he tells us how it came to be written, in course of which he says he thought "America deserved the opportunity to listen to serious poetic notions."[14]

Kenyon gives us an article on Conrad's politics by Irving Howe,[15] one on Scottish poetry by Stanley McTavish Hyman,[16] an article on George Orwell[17] (Oh, well!) and poems by Hecht, Josie Miles, Richard Wilbur, and Marianne [M]oore,[18] and the funny [thing] is, they all sound like they were written by the same person—John Crowe Donne.[19] Well, more than enough of this.

I was about to forget to say that I received the English Comic Characters. Thanks very much. I'll share it with you—I know you like it, because you were the one who told me about it. Only I'll pay for it. Only tell me how much, and how much for the Hardy Poems.[20]

Let me interrupt to release a cry from the soul: Jesus, I wish you-all would come home. How'm I gonna get through another half of it?

Love,
Bill

1. Weiss answers this letter on 4 February 1954.

2. Chatto & Windus.

3. England.

4. WH must have meant the *Times Literary Supplement,* which Weiss had quoted from in his 24 January 1954 letter: "[T]he unspoken competition between the generations comes through rather too often in this author's writing, weighing it down in a depressing manner. His style still seems not quite formed. [. . .] The majority of these stories do not really hold the imagination, for the dialogue and observation are not sparkling or sharp enough to redeem somewhat drab atmospheres."

5. On *Home from the Hill.*

6. In his 4 February 1954 reply, Weiss wrote, "(We are sorry to have left you all those deep-freeze mags, the worst part of your inheritance. But jiminy do you have to read them?)" WH refers to the Autumn 1954 issue of the *Hudson Review,* edited by William Arrowsmith and Joseph Bennet.

7. Delmore Schwartz (1913–66), poet, short-story writer, playwright, and translator, was an associate editor of the *Partisan Review;* he reviewed Saul Bellow's *Adventures of Augie March* (1953) in the January–February 1954 issue ("Adventure in America," vol. 21, no. 1, pp. 112–5).

8. "Dottie Makes an Honest Woman of Herself," an excerpt from *The Group* (1963) by Mary McCarthy (1912–89), was published in *Partisan Review* 21, no. 1 (January–February 1954): 34–52.

9. "Book III: Miss Batterson and Benton," an excerpt from the novel *Pictures from an Institution* (1954) by Randall Jarrell, was published in the *Kenyon Review* 16, no. 1 (Winter 1954): 81–123. WH is mistaken in saying an excerpt from this novel was also published in the *Sewanee Review.*

10. Monroe K. Spears was editor of the *Sewanee Review* from 1952 to 1961. On 18 June 1953 Spears informed WH that his application for a writing fellowship was unsuccessful.

11. R. P. Blackmur's essay appears in the *Sewanee Review* 62, no. 1 (Winter 1954): 1–23.

12. Bonamy (WH spelled the name like the brand name of a once-popular household cleaning product) Dobrée, "The Confidential Clerk," *Sewanee Review,* 62, no. 1 (Winter 1954): 117–30. This play by T. S. Eliot was published in 1954. Cyril Tourneur (1575?–1626) was the English dramatist who wrote *The Revenger's Tragedy* (1607), and the Tudor playwright Thomas Kyd (1558?–94?) was author of *The Spanish Tragedy* (1594).

13. Francis Fergusson, "*The Comedy of Errors* and *Much Ado About Nothing,*" *Sewanee Review,* 62, no. 1 (Winter 1954): 24–37.

14. "Preamble II, *a poem,*" *Sewanee Review* 62, no. 1 (Winter 1954): 84–100. The offending comments by Richard Eberhart (1904–2005) are on page 99.

15. Irving Howe, "Joseph Conrad, Order and Anarchy: The Political Novels," *Kenyon Review,* 15, no. 4 (Autumn 1953): 505–21; "Joseph Conrad III: The Political Novels (Continued)," *Kenyon Review* 16, no. 1 (Winter 1954): 1–19.

16. Stanley Edgar Hyman, "The Language of Scottish Poetry," *Kenyon Review* 16, no. 1 (Winter 1954): 20–37.

17. Philip Rieff, "George Orwell and the Post-Liberal Imagination," *Kenyon Review* 16, no. 1 (Winter 1954): 49–70.

18. Anthony Hecht, "Upon the Death of George Santayana," 75; Josephine Miles (1911–85), "Barge," "Belief," "Find," "Bush," and "Height," 76–78; Marianne Moore (1887–1972), "Fables by La Fontaine, translated," 71–74—all in the *Kenyon Review* 16, no. 1 (Winter 1954).

19. That is, John Crowe Ransom, founding editor of the *Kenyon Review;* WH is playing on the name John Donne, seventeenth-century English poet.

20. See notes for letter of late September 1953 to the Weisses.

TO THEODORE AND RENÉE WEISS

TLS/PU

Rhineback, New York
March 15 [1954]

Dear Ted and Renee,

Sorry to have been so long about writing, but since before my last letter to you and until a week ago I have been sick. I had three colds right after each other—my usual lavish productions—one complicated by bronchitis that kept me coughing all night, consequently sleep-walking all day. After that it was a combination of school, and of trying to get my novel[1] (I now have 254 pages) retyped to show an agent—whom I didn't like. Now the novel is being formally considered by Morrow, and I have a bit of time. (Am hoping Morrow[2] rejects me). [. . .][3]

I am sorry Chatto was so unpoetic. I rather thought they'd be hospitable. They told Joe Summers they expected to lose money on me. But maybe they *have* lost so much on me they don't trust any of my poet friends. Perhaps you'd have done better if you hadn't told them you knew me. But the anthology of American poets sounds like a good idea. Do you mean to go ahead with it, or drop it?[4]

Oh—I just thought of some more Quarterly business. There has come in some rotten in my opinion translations of Martial epigrams[5] by Deadly Fitts.[6] He being such a famous name, I hesitated to send him your routine see-us-next-August slips. What shall I do? Send them to you, or send them back to him? And, there has come in a translation of a long, hitherto unpublished in America story of Italo Svevo[7] by that guy who's been doing Svevo here and there and mostly in The Hudson Review, named Ben Johnson.[8] I haven't read it, but it *is* by Svevo, so I thought you might like it sent on. Trouble is, it's thick and heavy. Was sent in by Marc Slonim of Sarah Lawrence,[9] *for* Johnson, who, he says, is in Italy. And, one last bit of QRL, I shall make a long overdue deposit of money day after tomorrow, at the bank.

I'm glad to hear that you feel kindlier towards your poems now than you did when you wrote last. I remember the old gardener lady[10] with much warmth and affection—even if I did argue with you over the worms like luxury[11]—and would like to see it now—because seems to me too that you had your hands there on as promising a mine of stuff as could be. As for me, though [I] carefully hoarded what tiny little bit of life was in me for each day, and did manage thereby to do a little on my novel on each of my sick days but one, now that I'm well I've slowed down. Writing about love is hard for a sour bastard like me—one from that puritanical southern tradition I'm in. But, though slowly, it does come. I hope someone likes it, but I rather doubt that many will—I doubt you will—you don't like Hardy—he throws a dark shadow over this book, I fear.[12] Oh, well, it's only a book. [. . .][13]

Do something for me before you leave England: look up the address of the Sasieni pipe company (tobacco-pipes). I mean, of course, in London. O.K.? And if you're in London with a few minutes for one last time would you go into some respectable looking pipe shop and price for me Meerschaum pipes[14] with clear amber stems in leather cases, by any of the following makers: Dunhill (this will probably be a fortune), Sasieni, or G.B.D. (yes, that's a trade name) or any other of similar quality the names of which I don't know. I'm sending you an ad from an American catalogue to give you an idea of prices here and shapes of pipes.[15]

Yours,
B

1. *Home from the Hill.*

2. This publishing house had the right of first refusal on WH's first book after *The Last Husband.*

3. A passage on academic politics at Bard and one on *Quarterly Review* business are omitted.

4. Weiss eventually dropped plans for the anthology.

5. Marcus Valerius Martial (A.D. 38–103) was a Latin epigrammist who wrote twelve books that capture early imperial Roman life in vivid detail.

6. Dudley Fitts (1903–68), an American poet whose first serious poetry was published

in *Hound and Horn,* with which he was associated his entire life, was mainly known for his translations from ancient Greek.

7. Italo Svevo (1861–1928), Italian novelist, author of *Confessions of Zeno* (1923).

8. Ben Johnson, together with P. N. Furbank, would also translate *Further Confessions of Zeno* (1969).

9. Mark Slonim was a Russian specialist at Sarah Lawrence College, Bronxville, New York.

10. Weiss's poem "The Generations" begins with "(An old woman working in her garden.)" and was published in *Outlanders* in 1960.

11. The word "worms" must be WH's and Weiss's argot for "an improper word." The usage that WH must have objected to is the following from "The Generations": "sweat glistening like luxury in the dirt" (Theodore Weiss, *The World Before Us: Poems, 1950–70* [London: Macmillan, 1970], 90).

12. Hardy's *Tess of the D'Urbervilles* (1891) and *Jude the Obscure* (1896) are obvious influences on *Home from the Hill.*

13. A passage on road works in the Hudson Valley and another on Bard politics are omitted.

14. Tobacco pipes, whose bowls are made of meerschaum, the popular synonym for sepiolite.

15. WH inserted in the margin: "let me know in L s d" (pounds, shillings, and pence).

TO KATHERINE ANNE PORTER

ALS/HL

[Rhinebeck, New York
summer 1955]

Dear Katherine Anne,

Your odd Belgian[1] cards reached me today at the old address you know. I'm delighted to hear that you're in the country, where, however, you're no doubt feeling the season's difference, and I don't mean the icy fang and churlish chiding of the winter's wind. A little of that *would* be flattering [illegible].

Now tell me more than the small blank spaces provided by the Belgian postal authorities will allow. Where is Southbury, inland or coastal, and what brought you there and where, besides Belgium, were you before that? What have you there? A farm? Friends, or alone? A job or leisure? But you did say the important thing, that you're well and hopeful.

As for me, still a college prof[2]—now on summer vacation and getting very little accomplished of all I'd promised myself, a not unusual development. Have 300 pages of a novel,[3] or rather it has me, and having all sorts of trouble killing off three people and driving another convincingly crazy—hard work in this heat. Reading meanwhile for the courses I'll teach in the fall—all new to me. Going over the nineteenth century

Americans, and suffering. I just mange to tolerate Hawthorne, can't Melville, and Whitman is the writer of all times and places I despise most. But of course there are compensations: Thoreau, Twain, James, Crane.[4] Will also try to show our supercilious students who think that literature began with Eliot and ended with Dylan Thomas that the Edwardians[5] are not all that bad. By the way, have you ever read a novel called *The House with the Green Shutters* by George Douglas Brown?[6] No doubt you have, probably everyone has. But you know how it is when you happen on a good book for the first time: think you own it, almost think you wrote it. Preparing also to teach the Italian novel, now in Manzoni[7] and looking forward to Verga[8] again. It's the one fun of teaching, getting paid to read.

My house is in a photographic turmoil. Dorothy, a painter since she was a child prodigy at it, has turned photographer. Professional, that is—or it is hoped, will be, and so indeed it does seem to promise. This began some six months ago, and the clothes that were taken out of the downstairs closet to make a darkroom still repose in the corners of the various rooms where tossed. Hypo Hall we call the place. I myself have been bitten (though I haven't quite decided to give up my job) for I'm very Sternian[9] about hobbies—I have hobbies the way other men have worries for which they need a hobby, though I did drop one recently—my ambition to play the jazz clarinet, and the house is at least quieter.

Write and tell me what your life there is like and what your plans are.

Yours,
Bill

1. Using Belgian post office change-of-address cards, Porter informed WH that she had moved to Southbury, Connecticut.

2. At Bard College.

3. *Home from the Hill.*

4. Nathaniel Hawthorne (1804–64), Herman Melville (1819–91), Walt Whitman (1819–92), and Stephen Crane (1871–1900). WH often refers to Mark Twain (1835–1910) as the American writer to whom he was most indebted, especially to the style of *The Adventures of Huckleberry Finn* (1884).

5. British writers in the early years of the twentieth century.

6. George Douglas Brown (1864–1902); the novel WH mentions is the only one for which Brown is remembered.

7. Alessandro Manzoni (1785–1873), Italian novelist, dramatist, and poet.

8. Giovanni Verga (1840–1922), Sicilian novelist, dramatist, and writer of short stories.

9. Perhaps an allusion to Laurence Sterne (1713–68), who neglected his duties as an Anglican clergyman in order to pursue his interest in writing satires.

TO HENRY C. CARLISLE JR.[1]

TLS/HR

[Upper Hook Road
Rhinebeck, New York]
Monday [28 August 1956]

Dear Henry,

Excuse the silence. I've been in bed all week and dizzy with cortisone and sedatives. Have just today more or less returned to living. Bad back. Doctor says it came from too many hours in the same position (this position) through the summer.

Many thanks for the good day.

Needless to say, the book[2] is no further along than when I saw you and I'm still not sure that this week coming up—my last of summer—will be saved. And so I now formally request a postponement of my deadline.

I think you've made me understand that deadlines are not lightly to be put aside, that they involve much planning and strategy, and that postponements, especially just now, cost money. And so I am genuinely sorry to request this now. But I do hope I persuaded you, and that without too much embarrassment you will be able to persuade your associates, that is was not that I took our previously agreed upon date lightly, nor that I did not work hard or achieve little this summer. In fact I may say that never have I worked so hard or so well in a comparable time period, and that I think you will agree that the time-consuming changes I made in the book were worth it. To help allay any fears you may have that having defaulted once I might get the habit, let me just say I think I'm as eager as anyone involved to get the book finished.

School starts in just one week and the first couple of weeks of it are a time when I can give no attention at all to my manuscript. I put in a total of 14 hours a week at school, have a weekend from Thursday afternoon to Monday morning (and don't go to Sunday school). However, there are papers to grade and, having done absolutely nothing this summer by [way] of preparation for my courses, I'll have a lot of rereading along to do (and the Victorians and the Edwardians wrote, you know, even more lengthily than I). Considering these things and the present state of the book and this lost week and this uncertain one just ahead of me, and allowing for the opening weekend of duck season and a day of utter mindlessness for the national elections (and another for grieving, considering the side I'm on)[3] and then adding still a safety factor so I won't have the humiliation of asking for yet another postponement, I suggest January 15. That's a time, you'll remember I told you, when again (December 21–February 22) I am out of school, and so I can then spend any amount of time with you on final revisions. I think that for me this is a practical date; I hope it is not too impractical for you.

Think I'll lie down again. It's been quite a comfort to me all this past week to know that when I got up again I didn't have to deal too much with that little bastard Brucie.[4] Thank you for putting the kibosh[5] on him. Thanks too for all the other good suggestions.

Yours,
Bill[6]

1. Along with Herbert Weinstock, WH's editor at Knopf.

2. *Home from the Hill.*

3. Republican Dwight D. Eisenhower (1890–1969) ran for reelection after his first term against Adlai Stevenson (1900–1965), the Democratic candidate for president. Stevenson carried only seven states.

4. The child of Opal Luttrell in the novel.

5. "Restraint" in Yiddish.

6. In pencil on the verso WH scribbled: "What do you think? Would Mrs. H—on seeing the Captain lying dead on the floor—conclude that Theron did it?" "Mrs. H" refers to Hannah Hunnicutt, wife of Capt. Wade Hunnicutt and mother of Theron, characters in *Home from the Hill.*

TO ALFRED A. KNOPF[1]

[On 31 July 1957, returning to the United States on the Mauretania, *Alfred Knopf read the proofs of* Home from the Hill *and wrote to WH: "It is a magnificent work [. . .]. It is a pleasure and a privilege to be able to publish so distinguished a novel [. . .] ," and then Knopf invited the author and his wife to lunch or dinner "some weekend."]*

TLS/HR

Upper Hook Road
Rhinebeck, New York
August 2, 1957

Dear Mr. Knopf,
I think I'll never get over being somewhat amused at the idea of anyone reading something I've written. I was quite tickled to think of my novel keeping you company on the deck of the Mauretania out in the middle of the Atlantic. It was a little like hearing that a child of mine, without my

knowledge but—after the fact—with my approval, had gone off on an adventure. I am delighted that you found "him" good company. Thank you for all that lavish praise.

Of course my wife and I would like to come to Purchase.[2] Can it be on one of the days of the weekend of August 10–11, or August 31–September 1. And please tell me how one gets there.

Thanks again.

Sincerely,
Wm. Humphrey

1. Alfred A. Knopf (1892–1986), a leading twentieth-century publisher in the United States (with his assistant Blanche Wolf, whom he married in 1916), founded Alfred A. Knopf, Inc., in 1915. A firm with high standards, it remained independent until 1960, when it was sold to Random House, though the Knopf imprint was retained. Knopf became chairman emeritus in 1972.

2. Village in Westchester County, New York. On 5 August 1957, Knopf invited WH and Dorothy for 11 August (a Sunday).

TO PETER CALVOCORESSI

[Calvocoressi, a director and WH's editor at Chatto & Windus Publishing House, London, acquiesced to the following plea that Anglicanisms not be substituted for Americanisms in the English edition of Home from the Hill.*]*

TLS/UR

[Upper Hook Road
Rhinebeck, New York]
October 24, 1957

Dear Mr. Calvocoressi:

Here is the set of page proofs, corrected.

I have, as you see, indicated in the margins my preference for the original in those instances in which you have substituted Anglicisms for Americanisms, namely: pp. [*sic*] 5: streets for walks; p. 7: bonnet for hood (twice); p. 11: pavements for sidewalks; p. 156: margarine for oleo; p. 208: pavement for sidewalk; p. 209: hairdresser's shop for barber's shop (about this one I feel very strongly; here, a hairdresser's shop is strictly for women, and while I know that your edition is meant for British readers for whom this meaning does not exist, nonetheless I cannot reconcile myself to Capt. Wade's going to be shaved in what, to my mind, is synonymous with a ladies' beauty parlor); p. 282: pavement for sidewalk. I may well be quite wrong, but it seems to me that in each case the American word is common enough, and the context unmistakable enough, that the British reader would not be put seriously off his stride by it. Moreover, in my opinion, the atmosphere of the original should be attractive for him, as the atmosphere, reflected in the style and the vocabulary, is one of the charms of English books for us here. Please, at least, give my plea a hearing.

Now to your reader's queries: pp. 91–92: spade-shaped snout: tapered snout. I visualized a popular kind of spade, rather long of blade, blunt at the end, tapered on the sides, used principally for digging postholes. I see no contradiction in the two descriptions. Pp. 103. stet. The idea is that he sensed he was alone where he stood in the large room, his mother at the opposite end, his father still at the door. Pp. 284: I don't understand the question. Is this word not used in England? It's common here. Webster: spat: a brief, petty quarrel. Pp. 285: comeuppance. Webster: deserved punishment, retribution. See clipping from this last Sunday's N.Y. Times Book Review. Pp. 312. chopper. A chopper is simply one who chops—in this case one who is chopping cotton. One plants the seed of the cotton much too profusely; after germination one thins out the plants. Negroes do this work, with hoes, chopping out the unwanted profusion and leaving plants evenly spaced in the rows. You may, if you think it will help the sense, change it to read cotton-choppers (which term is often employed).

Please note my change on page 302. This is important to me.

....

I am extremely pleased with the look of the book. I like the type and I like the size of the page.

Knopf's edition is now finished and they announce publication date of January 13, 1958.[1]

Yours,
William Humphrey

1. The formal copyright date was nonetheless 13 December 1957 in the United States and Canada.

TO KATHERINE ANNE PORTER

[On 12 January 1958 Porter wrote to WH: "I despair of even beginning to tell you what a strange sort of life I lead, a constant exhausting breathless struggle to maintain working hours and strength against the incessant pulls and pressures from every direction of—well, I suppose its just Life with a capital L, hu-

man affairs and needs and demands which I feel I cannot side step or deny, yet none of it seems to have one smallest thing to do with me, that is, with what I am really doing; and it is this continual and repeated pulling apart from the center that does wear me out, simply. I am talking in generalities because it is not permissible to give particulars, too personal, too confidential." She then went on to praise WH's "impressive performance" in Home from the Hill: *"[Y]ou have really brought back to life a full entire society and way of thinking and feeling, customs, speech, motives, everything breathing and moving—even a stranger who never heard of the south or read a book about it would realize at once that he was in a living country, a real one."]*

TLS/HL

Upper Hook Road
Rhinebeck, New York
1/15/58

Dear Katherine Anne,

First of all, don't feel you have to reply to this. You have distractions enough. I understand without your going into details: "human affairs and needs and demands": that's particulars enough. Still, I must write, because I must try to tell you a little what your letter has meant to me. Help helps, I remember your writing me once,[1] and your letter comes at a time when I need all the help I can get. It is a trying time. A little, in a small way, like I suppose a mother must feel as she waits to be told whether the child's normal or anomolous [*sic*]. To know that you found things to like in the book, well, that helps more than anything. I don't want to embarrass you further, but your good opinion is the one I have always wanted most. I'll just leave it at that.

Of course I want to hear what more you have to say about the book—but don't take time now. When we meet. There is Faulkner in the boar hunt, of course—ah, if that were the worst that the reviewers might say![2] Not that I care what reviewers say. Except that I would like to sell a few copies so I could for a year give up the easy job of teaching and devote myself full-time to the slavery of writing. Because I'm involved with another novel.[3] The reviews are, by the way, on the whole most heartening.[4]

I am really distressed to hear that you've had a time of crises lately. But I won't dwell on it because you don't and I'm glad to hear that it's over, and gladder still to hear that you feel a good writing time coming on. I know that feeling you describe; it's [*sic*] announcement is never to be mistaken. So do give yourself to it, don't let life interfere. I expect to receive one of the first copies of *Ship of Fools,* and to see you just as soon as it's finished. Meanwhile I shall, as always, pray for you.

Yours,
Bill

1. See editor's note for letter of 28 September 1950 to Porter.

2. Porter had written: "[K]eep your shirt on when reviewers begin to compare the boar hunt by the boy with the hunt in Faulkner's The Bear. . . . It is in no sense an imitation, but wonderful in itself." William Faulkner (1897–1962) is the southern fiction writer whom critics were forever identifying as an inescapable influence on WH. Some reviewers suggested that *Home from the Hill, The Ordways,* and *Proud Flesh* were trapped in the manner and substance of Faulkner's *Sanctuary, The Unvanquished, As I Lay Dying,* and "A Rose for Emily."

3. *The Ordways.*

4. One of the first reviews of *Home from the Hill* said that the "dark and beautiful first novel" with its "pure narrative magic" conveys emotion and love that is "tender and genuine" (Taliaferro Boatwright, *New York Herald Tribune,* 12 January 1958, 1).

TO HERBERT WEINSTOCK[1]

[In this letter WH reacts to Mary Elizabeth Edes's notice in the "Fiction Forecast" column in Publishers' Weekly *(16 December 1957). He exaggerates her "offence": After saying only that "Knopf has a very exciting new author in Mr. Humphrey," she goes on to praise the novel, which "is very likely to command respectful attention" (50).]*

ALS/HR

Upper Hook Road
Rhinebeck, New York
Sept. 23 [1958]

Dear Herbert,
Today the college librarian showed me a little notice about my book in The Publisher's Weekly. It said, "*Home from the Hill,* by Wm. H., a first novel by a new writer of promise."

Possibly the editors of the magazine are responsible for that wording, but will you please see to it that from Knopf's end I am not spoken of in any future publicity as a new writer, or one of promise. There is always something condescending in that term "promising"—at my age it is even less welcome. I don't enjoy being thought of as a rookie—even a promising rookie. Will you tell Mr. Cole, or whoever is responsible for releases, and whoever else is concerned, please to use some other tone about me and Home from the Hill. After all, though I've filled no five foot shelf, I published my first story in Accent in 1949, have since published another in Accent, two in The Sewanee Review, one in The New Yorker,[2] Harper's Bazaar,[3] The Quarterly Review of Literature,[4] Prize Stories of 1950 (The O. Henry Awards),[5] A New Southern Harvest, ed. By R. P. Warren and Albert Erskine,[6] and a volume of stories[7] published in 1953 by Wm. Morrow and Co[.] and Chatto and Windus.

I'll appreciate your making my feeling about this known in the offices.

How are things?

Yours,
Bill

1. Herbert Weinstock was one of WH's editors at Knopf; he resigned in 1959.

2. "Quail for Mr. Forester" was published in the *New Yorker* on 11 October 1952.

3. "Sister" appeared in *Harper's Bazaar* in the May 1950 issue.

4. "A Fresh Snow" was published in *QRL* 7, no. 1 (1953): 39–43.

5. *Prize Stories of 1950: The O. Henry Awards,* ed. Herschell Bricknell (Garden City, N.Y.: Doubleday, 1950).

6. *A New Southern Harvest* (New York: Bantam [1957]), which contains "The Hardys."

7. *The Last Husband.*

TO ALFRED A. KNOPF

[WH responds to Knopf's essay in Atlantic Monthly, *January 1958, 63–7, on the Polish-born English novelist Joseph Conrad (1857–1924), author of* Lord Jim *(1900) and* Heart of Darkness *(1902). Knopf calls the "remarkable correspondence" of Conrad "heartbreakingly tragic."]*

TLS/HR

[Upper Hook Road
Rhinebeck, New York]
February 28, 1958

Dear Alfred,

I've just read your latest Atlantic article, about Conrad, and I find it very touching. How belligerent he had become. How irritable and suspicious and arrogant. Do you know Robert Penn Warren's introduction to Nostromo[1] (my favorite Conrad)? Warren says, "When we read parts of A Personal Record we see the image of the false Conrad conjured up by reviewers long ago, the image that William McFee[2] complained about: 'a two-fisted shipmaster' telling us simply how brave men behave. And we realize how far this image is from the Conrad who suffered from gout, malaria, neuralgia, dyspepsia, insomnia and nerves; . . . who suffered 'moments of cruel blackness'; who, on occasion, years later, had two doctors attending him, each unaware of the other, and who at the same time emptied all the medicine into the slop."

I wonder how much this came from what Gustav Morf[3] called (rather convincingly documenting his case, I believe) Conrad's sense of guilt for betraying Poland and his heritage from his father of Polish nationalism? How much from those awful lonely hours as the captain on the deck? How much from that unbelievable anom[a]lous position: being a master of an alien tongue? How much simply from the popular neglect in his adopted country of his books? I hope you got to him in time. That is, in time to reach him still, before he became too bitter to care. For that can happen. He was, wasn't he, through your efforts, much more popular here than he ever became in England?

Well, you were lucky. To have known and been able to help such a man. Because all the others are just deck hands compared to him. Recently I taught a course in English novels of the period 1900–World War I, and we read Bennett[4] and Lawrence[5] and Forster (all good writers, don't mistake me) and Joyce, and then we came to Conrad. That's quite an experience, reading Conrad and Joyce together, for you know that for the past twenty-five years Joyce has been top dog. We read A Portrait of the Artist as a Young [M]an (I was brought up to believe that this was, next, of course, to Ulysses, the greatest twentieth[-]century novel in English, and indeed that it set a standard of judgment, and that other novels that were different from it in kind were thereby bad.) Well, we read it, as I say, and then Conrad, and I suddenly realized that in A Portrait nothing ever happens except people go for walks. On the walks they talk about art. In Conrad people suffer and live. The difference is as simple as that.

Well, it was a very interesting article.

. . . . .

Many thanks, if you're still with me after all this tedious length, for the other evening. Segovia[6] was wonderful and the dinner fit for an evening of him.

Yours,
Bill

1. In the Modern Library edition of *Nostromo* (1951) by Joseph Conrad (1857–1926).

2. William McFee (1881–1966), a British writer who provided the introductions to various editions of Conrad's work.

3. Gustav Morf is the author of *The Polish Heritage of Joseph Conrad* (1930).

4. Arnold Bennett (1867–1931), realistic English novelist famous for *The Old Wives' Tale* (1908).

5. D. H. Lawrence (1885–1930), English novelist and poet, author of *Sons and Lovers* (1913), *The Rainbow* (1915), *Women in Love* (1923), and *Lady Chatterley's Lover* (1928).

6. Andrés Segovia (1894–1987), Spanish musician, the foremost guitarist of his time.

TO PETER CALVOCORESSI

[Calvocoressi passed the following letter on to his colleague Ian Parsons. On 25 March 1958, Ian Parsons, who knew E. M. Forster, sent a copy of Home from the Hill *to him with a note saying "how much both [WH] and we would value your opinion of it." There is no record of Forster's responding.]*

TLS/UR

Upper Hook Road
Rhinebeck, New York
March 15, 1958

Dear Mr. Calvocoressi,
Will you please do me this favor: have a copy of *Home from the Hill* sent with my compliments to Mr. E. M. Forster. Since he is my favorite living writer, I should like very much to have him like my book. Needless to say he will not even read it, since he never heard of me, and since he must receive books from strangers rather too often anyhow. Still, I shall have done my best to bring the book to his attention. Thank you very much. Bill me for the copy, of course.

Sincerely,
William Humphrey

[UNSETTLED YEARS, MOSTLY ABROAD]

1958–63

[On 24 July 1958, supported by the proceeds from Home from the Hill, *WH and Dorothy set sail for Europe. The first stop was a brief one in London, and then they settled down in Wareham, Dorset, remaining there until October. Then the couple went to southern France and Italy before returning to New York in September 1959, but by the end of the next year they were back in Italy.*

After their marriage in 1949, Dorothy's daughter Toni was legally in their care; she remained with her mother and WH while he taught at Bard College, but the fifteen-year-old girl was not welcome on their European sojourns. She was left behind in boarding school and in the care of friends during vacations. Toni and her mother and stepfather were estranged for many years; they disapproved of her marriage to William Weidenbacher, and after that time the parent-child relationship did not improve.]

TO IAN PARSONS

TLS/UR

West Mills Farm
Wareham, Dorset
August 6, 1958

Dear Mr. Parsons,
I've been so long in writing because only today have we found an address that bids to be of any permanence. We arrived in this very popular resort town on the worse weekend of the year, never having heard of a Bank Holiday.[1] Or rather, associating the phrase with one of the most sinister events in American history—the bank failures of 1933 in the U.S. I now personally think the English Bank holiday is almost as sinister. The proprietor of the Black Bear took us in on a kind of day-to-day sufferance. That was Friday. Since Friday we have walked all over Dorset—we began

to feel like characters in a Hardy novel, and not to like the feeling one bit, I can assure you. Picturesque charming old English cottages standing empty with signs on them reading: For let, only American novelists need apply, are becoming increasingly scarce hereabouts. And so last night we arranged for the taxi man to pick us up and get us to the morning train to London and it was, and I am quite serious, a toss-up with us whether to go on to France or take the next plane back to the US. And now, to cut short this tale of woe, we are very happily settled in a couple of rooms in a farm, and life looks quite rosy again. We shall be here for a[t] least the next two weeks, so will you please tell your receptionist to forward any mail that may have accumulated, and which may come in.

Sincerely,
Wm. Humphrey

1. A general holiday, when banks are closed.

TO ANNIE LAURIE WILLIAMS[1]

TLS/CU

West Mills Farm
Wareham, Dorset
August 9, 1958

Dear Annie Laurie,

Your letter just came this morning. I am so sorry not to have called that last day, but there were a million changes in our plans at the last minute, and needless to say it never occurred to me that you'd be getting a frantic call from Hollywood that very last day. Mr. Vaughan[2] did not reach me. Do I want to identify the picture with Clarksville, Texas? I don't care one way or another. That should depend on the picture people, seems to me. If they want to go down and have a look at Clarksville and decide whether it looks good through a lens, that's what they should do, seems to me. And I am afraid I can't tell them much more about the place than you can. It is twenty-one years since I left Clarksville, so I am not sure I'd recognize the place if you set me down there. As to the weather and the crops, tell Mr. Vaughan to read the book. It was cotton and corn and sorghum when I was a boy. Red soil and sometimes black soil. Hot from March till November. Rainy then until the next March, and cold. Sulphur Bottom is (was in my time, and I can't believe they have changed such a big thing) a real place, and is called that. I believe I heard that it is now entirely the property of one man, a big insurance broker, who lives in the town of Annona, some fifteen miles from Clarksville. If it's at all like it was when I was a boy, however, they'll need army tanks to get in there with a camera crew. And they will have to bring their own wild boar—so far as I know there was never one in Texas: poetic license on my part altogether, or as I have one red necked character say, to protect myself, "Musta strayed ovah f'um Loozyanner."[3]

I have packed away the letter from the Clarksville Chamber of Commerce (not the Mayor) and it is somewhere in one of about sixty cartons in the barn in Brewster. But it was signed by Mr. A. N. Quarles, it was a request to me to invite the motion picture people to shoot the film there (though Mr. Quarles was a little confused and had the idea that it was a film biography of me) and it was a most urgent and cordial invitation.

I remember Clarksville with much affection. The square was not picturesque part by part, yet the total effect was picturesque. The courthouse, which was not in the square, but a block north, in a square of its own, was very nice—sort of Texas Gothic Revival, with a tower (all of yellow stone) about four or five stories high with a four[-]faced clock that bo[o]med every quarter hour. It's rather a prosperous town, but the houses of even the citizens of quality were without much distinction. It's Texas, after all, as you must remind Mr. Vaughan, and there are no FFV[4] mansions with porticoes and Spanish moss (that's the stuff out of which they make the wigs for the darkies who serve the mint juleps). Clarksville is one of the oldest Anglo-Saxon (as distinct from the Spanish) towns in [Texas], and was the port of entry for nearly everybody in the US, including Davy Crockett and Sam Houston.[5] And so it's not quite so raw as some of the western Texas towns. It is, as I am constantly telling everybody, a Southern town, not a Western town, and I never saw a cowboy in my life. Tell Mr. Vaughan that I think of myself as a Southerner, of my characters as Southerners, not Westerners, and this is what he can expect to find in Clarksville. I still have people down there. My uncle, my mother's youngest brother, is the town barber, named Bernard Varley. He has lived there all his life, knows everyone, is a hunter himself, and is a likeable fellow who would I'm sure be glad to help anyone who came down there on any business connected with his nephew—despite the fact that I haven't been back there in twenty-one years. So tell Mr. Vaughan any of this you think relevant, and tell him to write me here if he wants to know anything more. This address will last us until the first of October.

We're in just about the most incredibly beautiful spot you ever imagined, a town on the south coast of England in Dorsetshire. Two churches in town, one founded in 785 A.D., and the other an upstart that came along in 810. The town is surrounded with earth works put there for protection against the Danes. Over the way are the ruins of Corfe Castle, pulled down by Cromwell. The houses are all 14th and 17th century and roofed with stone—not slate, but slabs of marble. We have a couple of rooms in a farmhouse—cows and chickens and pigs in the front yard outside as I write, and alongside the house is a disused old mill and stream, called the Piddle. Our car[6] not being ready, we've rented bicycles and are seeing the countryside a-pedal. I'm getting fat on Mrs. Mears' (that's our landlady) cooking, and I am writing about as well as I ever did in my life. I see I'm running out of space and before I do I want to thank you again for the lovely flowers. They brightened that otherwise rather drab stateroom all the way over, and I put one in my buttonhole as we left the ship and it lasted for another couple of days. Our best to Maurice[7] and to everyone else in the office.

Yours,
Bill and Dorothy

1. The New York agent who sold WH's *Home from the Hill* to Metro-Goldwyn-Mayer (MGM), the American motion picture production company founded in 1924.

2. James T. Vaughn, a unit manager at MGM.

3. An innacurate quotation from *Home from the Hill* (New York: Knopf, 1958), 80.

4. First Families of Virginia.

5. Davy Crockett (1786–1836), frontiersman slaughtered at the Alamo; Sam Houston (1793–1863), the first president of the Republic of Texas.

6. The Morgan, a two-seater sports car, which WH had ordered before sailing from the United States, was delivered on 1 September. When he went to London to pick up the car, he met Ian Parsons for the first time.

7. A. L. Williams's husband, Maurice Crane, also a literary agent.

TO BLANCHE AND ALFRED A. KNOPF

[In October 1958 the Humphreys traveled from Wareham to Paris, where they spent two weeks. At the end of the month they went on to Provence, first to Grasse, then to Nice, and finally to Biot, a town in southern France about two miles from the Mediterranean and twenty miles east of Italy. There they lived until almost the end of January.]

LTS/HR

Les Jardins,
Biot, Alpes-Maritimes
November 2, 1958

Dear Blanche and Alfred,

You may know Biot. It's about halfway between Cannes and Nice just behind Antibes, and it's where we'll likely be staying the winter. We've no visa, and at the end of the three months permitted tourists must leave France, if only for a few minutes, and will probably go then for a week or so to Venice, and from there possibly for a day or so to Vienna, meanwhile keeping the place here. Which is an apartment on the top floor of a house having railed balconies and a little courtyard with a big palm tree and mimosa in bloom and against the wall of the house an orange tree laden with fruit.

In case you do not know Biot, it's a quiet little pottery town perched on a mountain, as yet, as they say, undiscovered, though this is a state soon to be deflowered. For they are building here the Musee Fernand Legee[1] [*sic*] (of all the modern French painters, the one I despise most) and it will open next year, is now three-quarters done, with one wall a mosaic après le maitre[2] like something on a pavilion in a world's fair, or like a billboard advertising plumbing fixtures, as all his things look. But meanwhile Biot is very tiny, very sleepy, very steep. We live in the valley just below the southwest side of the town proper. [. . .][3] The people are warm and helpful and friendly, and I could sometimes cry with vexation that I cannot understand or speak to them.

The language barrier is sometimes amusing, as when, in Aix-en-Provence, having made the pilgrimage out to Cezanne's studio,[4] I found myself saying to the custodian, pointing to a paint-box, "We are the veritable brushes of the master, are we?" But most of the time I am just so completely stultified and helpless that I could scream. There are the urgent practical things that cannot get done, as when yesterday in Nice[5] I tried to explain to the mechanic what was wrong with my voiture,[6] and there is the sense that this is the most intelligent country in the world, and one cannot make contact. Boulangeries[7] alternate with libraries in Paris, I see a weekly newspaper called ARTS, with interviews with E. M. Forester and reviews of an exhibition of rococo art in Munich and of all the hundreds of concerts that apparently go on all the time in Paris; I go to an opening of an exhibition of young painters and you have to queue up; and I struggle to recall the future tense, second person plural of voir.[8] Bad enough for anyone, but for a man who makes his living by, and lives for, talking, it is really something almost tragic. Dorothy knew rather a lot of college-classroom French before coming, but in the strain of trying to listen and understand and respond, it deserts her.

There is nothing to tell about our time in Paris, really. We were there two weeks, and so was the rain. Being both mad about painting, we spent all our time in the museums, where of course we could see almost nothing, since they depend not on Edison but on his predecessor in the lighting field, and He often shuts off His current. Nonetheless we managed to discover a great painter we had never liked before, Poussin.[9] We have never talked much about painting, have we? You know, Dorothy was a painter, and in fact, has gone back to it since we came to Europe. I wanted to be a painter and studied very hard at it when I was young, gave it up when I acquired enough taste to see that I had not enough talent, and it was a very bitter thing, and I really think I still care more for it than even for literature. Does it mean much to you?

Aside from that we called on M. Gallimard,[10] and that story might amuse you. I had written ahead from Wareham, reminding him that I had been supposed to meet him at your luncheon back in June or whenever it was, and saying just when I would arrive and that I would call on him. We went, and in our execrable French told the snooty girl at the switchboard that we wanted to see M. Gallimard. You never saw such consternation. We were asked to deposit ourselves in the waiting room and soon another girl came out and we explained ourselves, and you would have thought we had asked to see Le Grand Charlie lui-meme.[11] Aping our revolting accent, and looking at us with that wilting scorn of which, I think, only French women are capable, she slowly said, "*You* want to *see* Monsieur *Gallimard*! I will send you our foreign editor." Came the foreign editor, who informed me with what seemed like genuine pleasure, that he had never read my book, then introduced me to a colleague who was equally pleased with himself at never having heard of me, as he said. We chatted very brokenly for a few minutes. We went home. Three days later to the hotel comes a note from M. Gallimard, saying he had been in a most important conference and could not be interrupted. If I should happen sometime to find myself in the neighborhood of his office, he hoped I would drop in. I was in the neighborhood, all right, but I did not drop in. I called Mrs. Bradley,[12] as you, Blanche, had suggested; but she was, as you know, in New York. It was lonely knowing no one in Paris and it is going to be lonely here too; we shall miss you both even more than before, so please do write. Let us know what you are doing and what the talk is in the literary world, and say, do you think I stand any chance, especially after the sensation of Lolita,[13] for one of the prizes? And if you have friends in this part of the world, English speaking friends, that is, do write and tell them to get in touch with us. I am afraid that, without substituting French, I shall forget English.

I am reading the letters of Vincent Van Gogh. There is a new edition out, the first complete one in English, and, Alfred, you should own it. It is published, the copy I bought in England at any rate is, by someone calling themselves Thames and Hudson, but I think I remember hearing that the Graphic Arts Society was to do it at home. It is well made, contains excellent reproductions of all the drawings that he made in his letters to Theo. I think it is one of the great books.[14] I like letters, and van Gogh was in the company of Keats and Madame de Sevigne[15] as a letter writer. The common picture of him as a kind of inspired idiot is entirely wrong. As a matter of fact, though painters are usually illiterate if not downright imbecilic, van Gogh was extremely intelligent and, in a home-made way, well educated. His letters are one of the great autobiographies, wonderfully candid, wonderfully graphic, and heartbreaking. If you read the book, and I urge you to, don't be easily discouraged: the first two hundred pages are a bore, for they are of the period of his life when he was fanatically religious. But get over that, and there is a change as dramatic, as, say, the break in the career of W. B. Yeats.[16] You should, in fact, bring these letters to a wider audience, a selection, say, in the Vintage series. In any case, do read it. The little line counter at the top of the machine tells me that that is all. Please say hello to Pat[17] for me and tell him I'll write him soon. The best of everything to you both.

Yours,
Bill

1. Fernand Leger (1881–1955), French painter, an early Cubist exemplifying the machine aesthetic.

2. After the master.

3. WH then, in the omitted passage, describes the women doing laundry, also contained in the letter of 27 November 1958 to Ian Parsons.

4. Aix-en-Provence is the southern French city that is the birthplace of Paul Cézanne (1839–1906), French postimpressionist painter.

5. City in southeastern France on the Mediterranean, twenty miles from the Italian border.

6. Car.

7. Bakery shops.

8. The future tense, second-person plural of *voir* is *verrez.*

9. Nicolas Poussin (1594–1665), seventeenth-century French painter.

10. Claude Gallimard was head of Éditions Gallimard, the distinguished publishing house in Paris that published the French editions of all of WH's books.

11. The Grand Charles (de Gaulle) himself. De Gaulle (1890–1970), a military leader during World War II, was first elected to head the French government in 1945.

12. Virginia Bradley (1886–1983) was WH's literary agent in Paris; she had represented Joyce, Hemingway, Gide, Sartre, Proust, and others. Her husband had established himself as a literary agent in Paris in the 1920s, and she took over upon his early death.

13. This novel by Vladimir Nabokov (1899–1977) was published in 1958 by Putnam. Praised by many, *Lolita* attracted an unusually strong measure of indignation from those reviewers who denounced it as immoral. It did obtain *succès de scandale* and much critical acclaim.

14. Vincent van Gogh (1853–90), the most significant Dutch painter after Rembrandt. Theo was Vincent van Gogh's brother. *The Complete Letters of Vincent van Gogh* was published in three volumes by Thames and Hudson in 1958; the New York Graphic Society published the letters in the United States the same year.

15. Many regard the letters of John Keats (1795–1821), English romantic, as equal in value to his poetry; they record his rapid development as a poet. Madame de Sevigne (1626–96) is famous for letters that provide a vivid picture of life in seventeenth-century France.

16. Yeats's breaking away from his romantic moorings to embrace modernism is signaled by the poem "A Coat," published in 1914.

17. The son of Alfred and Blanche, Alfred A. Knopf Jr.

TO JEAN LAMBERT

[Jean Lambert (1914–99), the son-in-law of André Gide (1869–1951), was a travel writer, fiction writer, literary critic, and biographer; he was to translate all of WH's books into French.]

TLS/LC

Les Jardins
Biot, A.M.
November ? [*sic*], 1958

Dear M. Lambert,

Thank you for that very friendly letter of yours. It has made me regret all the more that I did not—and apparently won't—get to see you. We were in Paris two weeks, and with nothing to do on those days when the sun didn't shine and you could see nothing in the Louvre,[1] and I'd have written in hopes of seeing you; but not knowing the places of the departments[2] of France, I had no idea you were so near.

But if you spend as much time in America as your letter indicates, and since we are apparently both part-time members of the same profession (I am a college professor too) we will no doubt meet there some day. I hope it will not be long. Is there no chance of your coming to this part of France before your departure?

We've come to Biot in search of a little sunshine, after two months of England. Perhaps you know Biot? I gather that in summer it swarms with tourists and types from the 6th arrondissement,[3] but now it's very quiet and sleepy and rustic, and the sun does shine. Two miles away is the chemin au bord de la mer,[4] and I find it inexpressibly vulgar and mercantile (Nice is one of the most hideous towns in my experience) almost as hopeless and dreary as New Jersey, which is au bout du monde.[5] But tucked away in here just two miles off the road one is centuries away from all that. We have a house, or part of one, the rest of it empty, and in the yard a persimmon tree, a palm tree, an orange tree. . . [.]

One is also, alas for me, a long way from anyone who speaks English, and so we are reduced to monosyllables and signs. One feels like what one is, a barbarian. I could go to Italy and not be shamed of not speaking the language, or Spain (German I do know a bit, and have no desire at all to go to Germany). But of course it is shameful not to know French, and I am now completely discouraged. It's like waiting until too late in life to begin a musical instrument. And so we sit inside all day, me at work on a new book,[6] my wife painting, and outside there goes on a very intense and seemingly happy village life from which we are excluded, and in Antibes[7] I see papers on the stands such as could never exist in America, weekly papers devoted to serious arts, serious political things, matters of the mind, and I realize that I am obviously in the most intelligent country on earth, and I can't appreciate it. It is very disheartening.

. . .

I do not envy you the task of trying to find French equivalents for the two kinds (white and Negro) of southern dialects. Do you know anything about the patois[8] French spoken by the so-called Cajuns of Louisiana? They are, as you know, a mixed people: Spanish-Negro-French, and their language is very colorful.[9] I do not really know it, but I have heard it spoken many times, and it seemed to me that it is Negro-French much like Negro-English. But I'm not at all sure whether it isn't too exotic to be understood by the average French reader—and besides, if you do not already know it, it would probably be a study in itself. Anyhow, a more practical suggestion comes to mind: What are the French translations of Mark Twain's Huckleberry Finn like? Are they good? He was the greatest master of dialects—and of the subtle nuances in the dialects of the different races of the same region—that American literature has had. So if he has been well done in French, you might profit from studying them. Do not be offended by this suggestion. After all, he helped me write it;[10] why shouldn't his translators help you translate it? As to the names of the various breeds of hounds—I don't have a copy of the book with me, but as I remember (I finished the book two years ago, and am beginning at last to forget it) it was quite a long list, and those breeds of dogs probably don't exist anywhere outside the South. So that poses a problem.

Do please call on me for any assistance that you think I can give you. It will be a pleasure.

I shall write your mother-in-law[11] at once, and hope to go and visit her, and not just wait until I find myself in that neighborhood.

I wish you great success with you reminiscences of Gide.[12] I wish I could read it, but I shall have to wait until you translate it into English.

I look forward to hearing from you again.

Sincerely yours,
William Humphrey

1. National museum and art gallery in Paris.

2. France is divided into eighty-seven departments, comparable to counties.

3. The artsy quarter of Paris, including Saint-Germain and the Latin Quarter.

4. Path by the sea.

5. The very worst in the world.

6. *The Ordways.*

7. Town on the Côte d'Azur (French Riviera).

8. Dialect.

9. The Cajuns of southern Louisiana are descendants of French colonists expelled from Nova Scotia by the British in 1755. Their French includes words from English, German, Spanish, and various American Indian languages. The Cajuns' culture has been influenced by their black Creole neighbors.

10. *Home from the Hill.*

11. Madeleine Rondeaux, who married André Gide, one of France's most distinguished writers, in 1895.

12. *Gide Familier* (1958).

TO IAN PARSONS

TLS/UR

Les Jardins, Biot,
Alpes-Maritimes, France
November 27, 1958

Dear Ian,

It may amuse you to know that I am now speaking French. Doesn't sound so very amusing? Well, that's because you haven't heard me. But, though I don't like to plume myself, I must say I think it's pretty good to carry on conversations with one's voisin[1] on the following topics: mushrooms, Picasso, American farm price subsidies, the hydrogen bomb, snails and Charlie Chaplin,[2] all with the present tense third person of three verbs and the past participle of four others. As to the nouns, my recipe is this: take an English word which you think, remembering your one year of it in high school, is from the Latin, lengthen the vowels, swallow the consonants, end up as if you needed to blow your nose, and the chance is about 50-50 that it's French. Often it's pretty damn rattling good French, at that. As to the le and la problem, just act as if, being Anglo-Saxon, the whole thing embarrasses you somewhat, and, really, you would rather not say. That's all there is to it. And so me and my voisin meet over the back mur[3] and have about a fifteen-minute causerie[4] per day. When we are done, we shake hands extremely vigorously and part in the friendliest frame of mind imaginable. He doesn't know what I've said and I don't know what either of us has said. I have seldom met a fellow I liked more. Franco-American relations should be entrusted to us two. I do think, however, that I made a mistake in going first to England; I find it almost impossible to remember that beaucoup[5] is not pronounced beecham.[6] A language is like a doe: you have to walk right up to it and look it in the eye.

Biot is a little dream town. We're outside the walls and to go into the village, which we do every morning to shop, we climb at an angle of about 80 degrees up steps intended to discourage any invaders. We pass the outdoor laundry basins—of stone, naturally, but with chromium taps and hot water—where the women, most of them over 100 to judge by their looks, are busy beating their clothes with bats and talking a *bleu*[7] streak. Us they greet with this one word—joursieretdame.[8] Everybody has a bonjour for you and for everyone else and the best comparison I can find is that they are as friendly as the English! The streets of town are covered for a great part of their distance, covered by rooms of the houses on either side, and just about wide enough for two cats to pass. Up in town is the inevitable Place de Gaulle,[9] where on Sunday comes a traveling dry-goods store to spread itself, and a fish vendor, and where the men play boule[10] with steel balls. In one of the bars there is a shelf of books devoted exclusively to the history of painting for the patrons to dip into; I think of the bars in America! Oranges grow everywhere and just now the mimosa is beginning to bloom and the olives just coming ripe. The sides of the hill on which the town is perched are terraced entirely and covered with vines, flowers, persimmon trees, bamboo. The hills beyond are wild—dry, bare, rocky, red, with sage and cacti and aloes and stunted evergreens. And the food! Especially the fruit, my god how good! And whatever we praise, the people say, yet but wait till you see Italy! They are all of Italian descent here, for Biot was decimated in the sixteenth century by a plague, and the town was given by the French government to 16 Italian families (thus the name 2 (bi) times whatever is the Italian (ovvatto?) for 8), and speak an Italianate French. Not that I can tell that, but so I'm told. We shall get our first peek at Italy sometime soon—it's just some twenty miles away, the frontier marked most conspicuously these days by one solitary majestic snow-capped peak.

Our apartment is in a house otherwise unrented at this off-season and thus very quiet. We've not much of a view, though there is much interesting activity outside and we sit on the balcony in our shirtsleeves (it's zero centigrade in Paris today, I read) and watch the farmers till their fields of grapes and roses and twice a day there goes [*sic*] by the town shepherd and his flock of broken-nosed, corked-horn sheep (which also seem to speak French). He looks like something out of a painting by Velasquez[11] and the other day as he came by I remarked on the enormous size of the champignon[12] he was carrying. Please take it as a gift he said, I don't like them, but I saw this one and I picked it thinking I might meet someone who would want it. I think this is what he said, anyhow I took this mushroom and now I have another good friend.

Dorothy is painting exotic still lifes and I am writing, though not on the same book I was working on in Wareham,[13] having laid it temporarily aside and started a little idyl about incest and infanticide.[14]

This is no doubt the busiest time of your year, but do write when you find a moment. Give our best to Mrs. Smallwood[15] and Mr. Calvocoressi.

Yours,
Bill

1. Neighbor.

2. Chaplin (1889–1977) was a subtle comedian of silent film, especially known for his role as the "little tramp."

3. Wall.

4. Chat.

5. Much.

6. WH is apparently thinking of the English surname and village name Beauchamp, which is pronounced *beecham.*

7. Blue.

8. The greeting "good day, sir and madam," in a slurred manner.

9. Many French towns and cities have a square named in honor of Charles de Gaulle.

10. Ball.

11. The Spanish painter Diego Velazquez (1599–1660) had a genius for capturing the dignity of everyday subjects.

12. Mushroom.

13. *The Ordways.*

14. Perhaps a story that WH discarded, though he might have once considered including incest and infanticide in *Proud Flesh.*

15. See editor's note to WH's letter to Smallwood on 7 June 1972.

TO F. W. AND BARBARA DUPEE

[F. W. (Fred) Dupee was a Henry James scholar on the English faculty at Bard College before he moved on to Columbia University. Barbara (Andy) was his wife. They were longtime friends of the Humphreys, lasting even into the Dupees' retirement.]

TLS/CU

Les Jardins,
Biot, Alpes-Maritimes
France
January 7, 1959

Dear Fred and Andy,

[. . .][1]

We're still here too. We'd planned to be in Italy by now, but Dorothy got a pain in her back (pas grave,[2] said the doctor, but when he said it was a calcification of the os,[3] I thought that sounded pretty grave). And then as she was taking a shower one day (during the recent floods) to go to the doctor, she was asphyxiated by the gas water heater in the salle de bain.[4] I caught her and got her to a bed and revived her and ran for the doctor and it was, I gather, a close call. Well, that's over now, and the back seems to be pas grave sure enough, so we're knitting. We'll stay here until the end of

January, then Italy for three weeks or so I guess. We're thinking of Spain for a few weeks after Italy.

We have been taking the most wonderful rides in the mountains back of the coast here. We've two friends, the agent and his wife who found us our apartment, and just about every Sunday we pile into his old Citroen limousine and head for the hills. She's Parisian but he's a native of Biot, and since we have trouble enough understanding Jeanne, we get about one word an hour of Henri's. Nonetheless, he is a very sweet and a wonderful guide and has shown us the most unexpected countryside. Unexpected to us, at least—really wild, almost undiscovered looking: snow-covered ranges of mountains and below the snow volcanic lava and vast valleys with little streams and on top of rock abandoned and ruined villages and monasteries and little lost villages, like one called Cannaux of last Sunday's outing perched upon its hill overlooking valleys of pasture, a town with a chapel (on the wall of which is the town boite de poste)[5] and four houses—that's all. Everywhere we go we have no sooner parked the car than someone calls out, "Henri!" and we are then invited into the house to drink the new wine, look at the family photo album, and be jabbered at in Provencal-Italian-French.

We enjoy so much the rustic simplicity of these people: for example, our prochain voisins:[6] the mere[7] of the family, a shrill old peasant girl with a mouth full of blackened teeth, whose at-home son has greenhouses in which he raises roses for sale. The house and land, however, instead of passing down to them through the centuries, were, as we've learned through our agent friend, bought for them just a short time ago in payment by Jean Cocteau[8] for their other son. Now the old gi[r]l seems to be bargaining for her pretty daughter with someone who stops by in a chauffeur-driven Bentley.

Hope you're beginning to be able to live in your house instead of for it, though of course in a different and better sense it is the kind of house one lives for.

No other news. We lead such quiet lives here that nothing happens. Not even able to say what we've read, for although I found the English-American Library in Nice the only thing I've taken out is Huckleberry Finn. Started Dr. Zhivago[9] but couldn't stand it and quit.

Write when you can. This address will hold for the rest of the month.

Yours,
Bill and Dorothy

1. The opening paragraph of this letter is omitted; it refers to a lost clipping from the *Paris Herald Tribune,* and the paragraph has no meaning in the absence of the clipping.

2. Not serious.

3. Bone.

4. Bathroom.

5. Post office box.

6. Next-door neighbor.

7. Mother.

8. Jean Cocteau (1892–1963), a filmmaker (director of *Orphée* and *La belle et la bête*) and prolific French writer who distinguished himself in poetry, fiction, theater, and the essay.

9. The novel *Doctor Zhivago* helped author Boris Pasternak (1890–1960) win the 1958 Nobel Prize.

TO ANNIE LAURIE WILLIAMS

[Toward the end of January 1959, WH and Dorothy, their French visa about to expire, moved on to Italy—first to Florence, then to Rome, Siena, and Arezzo, then back through Florence to Venice, and finally to Lugo di Farda and Lugano. About the first week of March, they settled in Lenno, on the western shore of Lago di Como. There he worked on The Ordways *until the end of April.]*

ALS/CU

Albergo Brentani
Lenno (Lago di Como)
Italy
March 5, 1959

Dear Annie Laurie,

Delighted to hear from you. [. . .][1]

Somebody sent me a clipping that said Robert Mitchum[2] is being considered for a role in our movie. What role, it doesn't say—but that's hardly necessary. With those sleepy dope-filled eyes, he's just what I had in mind for Deuteronomy, the lead hound-dog. If they don't get started pretty soon it's going to be a costume-piece.

Yes, I got the receipt for the deposit. The delay was caused by my bank—as I knew it was.

So you've been to the Nat'l Book Awards shindig. Who got it? My own guess is Malamud.[3] What an affair that must be! Have you ever seen a TV production called Queen for a Day? I saw it once. They bring 6 or 8 old broken-down charwomen out and each one tells her tale of wretchedness. When all are done one is chosen by applause meter to get all the loot. All the rest drift offstage—presumably to return to their drunken husbands and crippled children and wretched lives. That's how I visualize the authors waiting for THE ANNOUNCEMENT at the Nat'l Book Awards Dinner. Glad I wasn't there.

Glad, in fact, that I'm right where I am. Outside there is snow on the mountain tops across the blue lake and sun on the leaves in the trees down here. I'm studying Italian, trying my best to learn to be a through and through dago.[4]

As to Pamela[5] and the Virgin Island, tell her not to go. In 1959 there is no longer any such place on the map with a name like that.

Yours,
Bill

1. A brief paragraph is omitted on movie business, the context of which is not clear.

2. Robert Mitchum (1917–97) played the role of Capt. Wade Hunnicutt in the film *Home from the Hill.*

3. Bernard Malamud (1914–86) won the National Book Award for *The Magic Barrel.*

4. Disparaging slang for an Italian.

5. Pamela Barnes, an agent at Annie Laurie Williams, Inc.

TO THEODORE AND RENÉE WEISS

ALS/PU

Lenno,
Lago di Como
Italy
April 17, 1959

Dear T. + R.

I 'spect this'll be my last from Italy. We leave a week from today, and after much indecision *are,* after all, going to Spain—for a couple or three weeks only. Then back to Paris for a few days and to St. Malo for the ferry to England. And much as we're looking forward to Spain and pleasant as our memories of England are, we hate leaving Italy. Our time here seems to have flown. [. . .][1]

I don't remember who the poetry editor of The Nation is, but whoever he is, by all means use him and try Macmillan again, and I think you're right to edit the book. Good as everything in it was, it was, from the publisher's point of view[,] just too expensively fat, I'm sure.[2] I know your feeling about anemic poets who print skinny little volumes—but let a skinny one be the thin edge of a fat wedge if it can!

Did you read about the bust-up at AAK, Inc.[3] speaking of publishing. Pat (AAK, Jr.) after years of being the somewhat overlooked son of vigorous parents, has bursted loose and he and Hiram Hayden and Simon Michael Bessie are starting a new publishing house.[4] And though there's no connection Herbert Weinstock has resigned from Knopf to write and travel. I don't know what all this means but changes should occur that's for sure. In all the time we've been abroad I've heard not a word from Harry Ford[5] so where he stands in all this—or in anything—of course I don't know.

I must tell you of the grand prize I won! For you won't have heard of it otherwise. I have been deemed by the Texas Institute of Letters[6] (pres. J. Frank Dobie)[7] to have written the Best First Novel by a Texan in 1958.[8] The competition, as you can imagine, was fierce! I didn't know that I'd won this honor until it was too late to refuse it, for Alfred went to Dallas to be the principal speaker at the ceremonies (at which Lon Tinkle was awarded the prize for having written the Best Book by a Texan) and accepted my garlands in my name.[9] The book I wrote, according to a Texas press clipping I've just received, was Home on the Range. So you see I am indeed *The Home-r of Texas.* Whoever said that a prophet is without honor in his country was thinking of countries that had a little choice amongst its prophets. But the eyes of Texas have been upon me,[10] and word just comes that I've been awarded the title Most Distinguished Ex-Student of the University of Texas of The Year (I went there for one year: made 2 C's two D's, two F's)[11]—which *is* a distinction! And now comes word that a Hollywood crew has moved in on Clarksville![12]

We are studying Italian hard, and making some progress now. It's not an easy language but after French it's a snap. The verbs are mostly very proper and well-behaved and the pronunciation, again unlike French, at least looks attainable. And, again unlike the French, the Italians don't look at you as if you should drop dead when you misuse their mother tongue. We practice mostly on our friend the fascist count who takes his meals here, and who tells us stories, in Venetian dialect (which has snob value and is the most un-understandable of all Italian dialects) about being D'Annunzio's aide in Fiume.[13] But it is a beautiful language—and it would be nice to read Petrarch and Verga[14] and others in native dress. In Biot I got the feeling that I was too old to try to learn a language. Now I've decided oh, well, why not?

My writing has gone fairly well here in Lenno. But the book[15] which was to have been a nice little novella has become (in my head, not yet on paper, needless to say) as big as all outdoors—which, I suppose, is what it's about. I'm not sure. I'll have to put it aside again when we hit the road, but hope for another quiet and settled time in England, and I'll come back with about 150 finished pages, which I guess isn't too bad for someone who's meanwhile been seeing Europe for the first time.

If you write soon, address c/o Am Ex. Paris from May 15 to June 7. After that we're going to Cornwall but I don't know for just how long, so will write.

Meanwhile, Love
Bill and Dorothy

1. Two paragraphs follow on academic politics at Bard.

2. Apparently WH is referring to the anthology of American poets that Weiss first proposed to Chatto & Windus (see WH to the Weisses, 15 March 1954).

3. The Alfred A. Knopf Company.

4. Pat Knopf (Alfred A. Knopf Jr.) and two friends, both editors and publishers, founded the Atheneum Press in 1959. Knopf was chairman of the board for more than twenty years.

5. Harry Ford (1918–99), poetry editor at Knopf and designer of the firm's edition of *Home from the Hill.*

6. An organization founded in 1936 to promote Texas writing.

7. J. Frank Dobie (1888–1964) was a western writer and Texas folklorist. Among his many books are *Vaquero of the Brush Country* (1929), *Coronado's Children* (1931), *The Voice of the Coyote* (1949), and *Up the Trail from Texas* (1955). WH was probably not aware at the time that Dobie was an outspoken critic of some of the features of Texas culture, especially the bragging Texan.

8. *Home from the Hill.*

9. In fact, WH and Alfred A. Knopf had corresponded on the issue; on 1 April 1959, Knopf advised WH, "Take the cash and let the credit go. You can afford to be magnanimous about such things." The cash amounted to $250. The novelist Lon Tinkle (1906–80) received the award for *Thirteen Days to Glory: The Siege of the Alamo* (1958). He was WH's first mentor at Southern Methodist University in 1941; later on he wrote a column for the *Dallas Morning News.*

10. "The Eyes of Texas" is the official alma mater of the University of Texas, written in 1903 by John Sinclair.

11. The Texas Exes (the ex-students' association) gives only one award, the Distinguished Alumni Award. It was first given in 1958, but WH never received it.

12. To film *Home from the Hill.*

13. Gabriele D'Annunzio (1863–1938), Italian poet, novelist, and dramatist, was an early exponent of Mussolini's fascism. In 1919 he led an invasion of the port city of Fiume, claiming it for Italy.

14. Petrarch, a fourteenth-century Italian poet and humanist, wrote a long series of sonnets to Laura; Giovanni Verga (1840–1922) was a Sicilian novelist, dramatist, and writer of short stories.

15. *The Ordways.*

TO ALFRED A. AND BLANCHE KNOPF

[The Humphreys left Italy for Britain in June 1959, arriving in Cornwall on WH's birthday, 18 June. After a few weeks, they visited Alfoxton in Somerset before returning to London and then departing for the United States on 12 September. They lived about a month in New York City.]

TLS/HR

c/o Mrs. Main
The Mill House
Tressider near St. Buryan
Penzance, Cornwall
July 17, 1959

Dear Alfred and Blanche—wherever you are,

We, as you see from the above, are in England once again, rather world-besotted, as Yeats put it.[1] When we finally tore ou[r]selves away from Italy we drove across southern France and, leaving our car in Perpignan,[2] went by train to Barcelona. In Barcelona live the 1 million big thieves for whom the other 40 million Spaniards toil. Very chic. Makes St. Honore[3] look like 14th Street.[4] Extremely dull. What we should have done was turn around right then and head back to civilization, to the 20th century; what we did was buy railway tickets worth 1700 miles, and went to Madrid, Toledo, Seville, Granada, Alicante, Valencia, and back to Barcelona.[5] Have you ever ridden a Spanish train? Well then, have you ever ridden a dromedary (isn't that the camel with only one hump?) You can't see all those places in under two weeks, though we tried. The train only gets up to five miles an hour downhill; besides, eager as you are to get out of each of those holes, you dread so much what you will find in the next one that you hesitate to move on. I had expected to dislike the evidences of the state in Spain, and did; I also came to feel that if any nation deserves such a government it's the Spaniards. A cheerless lot, sour, dour, bigoted, backward, unhandsome, unmusical and suspicious. And ignorant. No, for me the bell did not toll.

Then we went through lovely Perigord,[6] (saw Lascaux[7]—marvelous!) and then wandered up the ugly Loire valley being shown boring chateaux by bored guides, and came at last to Illiers[8] which as you know is Proust's[9] Combray. There is an old man named M. Larcher in Illiers who is dedicated to restoring Aunt Leonie's[10] and Proust's garden with the famed aubepines and researching all the things of that temps perdu,[11] and he has Marcel's[12] magic lantern[13] with the slides of Genevieve de Brabant and Golo,[14] but the nicest thing of all is Mr. Larcher, who guides you through the house dressed in morning costume of third republic cut and quotes relevant passages from le maitre[15] and who is just as conscious as you are that he is a Proustian character himself. A lovely town, rather poor and a little sad, and quite unconscious of its fame. We of course walked out Swann's Way, and the Geurmantes [*sic*] Way.[16] Spent three days there, and even the prospect of Chartres,[17] which is only ten miles away, was hardly enough to draw us on.

Met Mrs. Bradley. Which is a bit like saying you passed by the Grand Canyon. She should be put in the guide bleu,[18] along with Pont Neuf and Saint Chapelle,[19] as one of the landmarks of Paris which are not to be missed. Her flow of talk was as endless and vast as the waves that come in against these Cornish coasts, and just as fascinating, and just as salty. In short, we loved Mrs. Bradley. She took us to dinner one night at Quasimodo's,[20] and just as we finished eating, a rocket burst over Notre Dame[21] and showered it with falling gold. Instantly thereupon liquid strains of music floated up, and from down below, as if the Seine itself were geyser-ing, great spumy jets of water arched into the sky, veiling the lighted dome of the Pantheon[22] which rose above the treetops. It was Handel's 200th anniversary, and The Water Music[23] played and the fountains arched and slowly waved over one another like liquid ostrich plumes and the rockets stre[a]ked up and burst and showered down. And they fell on Notre Dame and on that other enduring French monument, Mrs. Bradley.

And now we are in Cornwall.[24] Came here on June 18, and seeing as that was my birthday, and finding, as one does, that I was older than I was only a year ago at the same time, I got down to work. We[']re in a 400 year old mill cottage with a water course, and the jackdaws are nesting in the trees all around and make a weird and wonderful racket on settling to roost at night. Night comes late here. The days are long—long and sunny and hot. The sea is a mile away, and the rocky, gorsy cliffs above, and the wheeling gulls. The wind never stops blowing, and the bushes and the houses, and even the people, all grow to the eastward. A poem I tossed off the other day gives the atmosphere of Cornwall rather well, I believe. It goes:

I think that I shall never see
A tree.[25]

This place grows on you, though. These bare lonely granite farms, rather courageous. These stark cliffs. Great monstrous boulders in heaps running down to the see, like what was left over when they built England.

Well, if you're still with me, I'll close with this: we went back to Wareham for a day or two, and found that the locals of our pub The Pure Drop[26] had all just gone up to London for a day, by private railway coach. First time in his 55 years that our pig-farmer Tom Mears had ever been to London. They were swapping stories of their separate adventures up there. "We was standing in front of a pub," said Tom, "and Joe went in to scout it, and he come back and said he'd seen a woman in there wearing a dress so thin you could see her tits." 'Let's go in and see that," said Bob, "so we did." And Bob looked so hard that the woman come over and said, "Do my breasts interest you then?" she said. "Oh," said Bob, "in our town the girls go about with one of them hanging out." "Do they[?"] said she, "Why only one then?" "Oh, because they be both alike," said Bob.

Yours,
Bill

Still don't have definite passage home. Probably the *Mauretania,* sailing from Southampton on 12 September.

1. In "Swift's Epitaph" (1933).

2. French town near the border with Spain.

3. Rue St. Honoré, one of the most beautiful streets in Paris, in the First Arrondissement.

4. WH would have remembered this as a raffish street on the edge of bohemian Greenwich Village, New York City.

5. WH lists all the major cities of Spain.

6. Region in southwestern France in the department of the Dordogne.

7. Site in southwestern France of the caves with Paleolithic cave paintings.

8. Village in the Eure-et-Loire region, south of Paris. It was renamed Illiers-Combray during the Proust centennial in 1971.

9. Marcel Proust (1871–1922), French novelist, author of *À La recherche du temps perdu (Remembrance of Things Past).*

10. That of the great aunt who ruled her world from her bed by the window in Proust's novel.

11. Lost times.

12. The narrator of *Remembrance of Things Past.*

13. An optical instrument that casts a magnified image from glass slides on a screen.

14. In the comic opera *Genevieve de Brabant* by Jacques Offenbach (1867). Golo is the character who falls in love with Genevieve.

15. The master.

16. The two roads that Marcel remembers from his childhood; the second is spelled "Guermantes."

17. Gothic cathedral, constructed from 1194 to 1260 in the small town of Chartres, southwest of Paris.

18. Blue Guide, a travel book.

19. The oldest bridge in Paris (1606) and the church of La Sainte-Chapelle (1246–48).

20. Named after the hunchback of Notre Dame.

21. The most famous cathedral in Paris (1163–1345).

22. A Corinthian mausoleum for the remains of great Frenchmen, completed in 1789.

23. George Frideric Handel (1685–1759), German composer, was commissioned by George I of England in 1717 to compose "The Water Music" for wind and strings.

24. County in the southwest extremity of England.

25. Alludes to the poem "Trees" by Joyce Kilmer (1886–1918).

26. Pub in Marnhull, Dorset, that Hardy makes the customary drinking establishment of Tess's father in *Tess of the D'Urbervilles* (1891).

TO JEAN LAMBERT

[WH and Dorothy lived in an apartment at 241 West Twelfth Street for about two months after returning from England and before moving to Stockbridge, Massachusetts, at the end of November.]

TLS/LC

New York City,
November 10, 1959

Dear Lambert,

Many thanks for your long and pleasant letter. I congratulate you on being done with the book—and I sympathize with you. I too was glad when at last I could separate myself from the fate of the Hunnicutts.[1] But just imagine: *I* had to live with them for four years!

As to the short stories: the ones you mention are my own favorites, too,[2] and I am very pleased indeed that you liked them. Of course I'd be most flattered if you were to decide to translate one of them for publication in a French magazine. (By the way, if you do, let me know, and I will take care of the arrangements for the permission—the book was printed by a different publisher from Knopf, and I know which person to ask at William Morrow and Company.)

The movie?[3] I have had nothing to do with it from the start, and the only information I have about it is hearsay. Of the actors in it I am familiar with only one, and he is terrible.[4] I have been told that it bears very little resemblance to the book. Ah well, they have ruined better books than mine, so why complain? I still have not heard when it will be released. I believe that the actual filming is now finished.

You had a few final inquiries. No, a confectionery is not a drugstore, at least not in Texas. A confectionery serves ice-cream and "light" meals: breakfast and lunch. I forgot to answer the *kids* question—it's children (page 124, that is). A smoke-house? On farms in the south, a little building, usually of wood, for smoking the meat (pork). The hams and bacon are hung from the roof beams and a fire built on the floor (which is of dirt) and the meats are cured by smoking. And after the meat is cured, it is allowed to hang in the house until eaten (sometimes for a year, or even two or three years). Telegraph template? The machine (a small lever) on which one taps out (in morse code) the telegraph message. When I was a boy one could buy these, and spend hours tic tic ticking. Page 310: no, the man's danger means not the danger to the man, but the danger *to* Theron that the man represents (it's badly expressed; I suppose I should have said his *dangerousness*)[.]

. . . .

I went this morning to the offices of New Directions and got the mss of *Tobiolo.*[5] I shall read it instantly. But alas I must be the bearer of bad news to you. While I was there the young lady who spoke to me said that they had written to you (c/o Justin [illegible word] in 1957, to tell you that they could not publish the book, and asking you what you would like them to do next with the manuscript, and that they had never heard from you. I have promised to return the mss to their offices by next Monday. (I am leaving New York on Wednesday—more about that in a moment). But if you would like me to send the ms to some other publisher, I will be glad to do so. Only, if so, you must write to New Directions authorizing them to give it to me.

But you must not think that I know nothing of you. When I heard that Jean Lambert was doing my book I remembered the name at once from "Les Cashiers du Sud,"[6] which I used to see, and to try to read with my lame wretched French. And when I was in France I saw copies of *Gide Familier*[7] in all the bookstores in Nice and Cannes. (I could not read it, alas). I will write you as soon as I have read *Tobiolo.*

. . . .

I am leaving New York. Our stay here was meant to be temporary. I cannot live long in cities—I am a country man. We have rented a house in Stockbridge, Massachusetts—an old and very beautiful and very small village in the Berkshires in western Massachusetts. We will be there at least until June,1960. After that, I do not know. But if we are in America in September, [19]60 (and probably we will be) we will surely be somewhere in the Northeast, for I would not live anywhere else in the country. And so we will see you, I am sure, and I am sure that we are looking forward to it most eagerly. Yes, I have given up teaching—at least for as long as my money holds out. I was a professor for nine years,[8] and while I liked teaching, I did not like the other aspects of the academic life—administrative work, serving on committees, etc. And so now I am writing. Another novel,[9] which I began on the Liberté going to Europe, and of which I now have about 175 pages.

You say that on the dust wrapper of the book of stories you read that I am a vegetable gardener. That book was published some years ago. In those days I *was* a vegetable gardener, but the reason was hunger. If I ever get back to the soil I too shall devote myself to flowers instead.

I don't yet know my exact address in Stockbridge. But my next letter to you will be from there, and I will tell you the address then. Meanwhile, my heartfelt sympathies to you for the chore that you face of reading proofs. It is a job I hate.

Yours,
Wm Humphrey

1. The fictional aristocratic family in WH's novel *Home from the Hill* (1958).

2. "Quail for Mr. Forester" is one of the stories from *The Last Husband* that Lambert was partial to.

3. *Home from the Hill.*

4. WH refers to Robert Mitchum, who, with his "sleepy, dope-filled eyes," is "just what I had in mind for Deuteronomy the hound-dog" (letter to Annie Laurie Williams, 15 March 1959).

5. Published by Gallimard in 1956, Lambert was unsuccessful in getting his English translation of this book published.

6. An influential literary magazine founded by filmmaker and playwright Marcel Pagnol in 1913.

7. Lambert was André Gide's son-in-law, and this book, a study of Gide in his old age, was published in 1958.

8. Bard College.

9. *The Ordways.*

TO ANNIE LAURIE WILLIAMS

[After living in Stockbridge, Massachusetts, for about a month, WH and Dorothy moved to Glendale for a year before returning to Italy, where they remained until June 1962. Then they alternated residence between Italy and Telscombe,

Sussex, until they left in September 1963 for Virginia, where WH would hold for the fall semester the Visiting Glasgow Professorship at Washington and Lee University in Lexington.]

ALS/CU

Glendale, Mass.
Jan. 10, 19[60][1]

Dear Annie Laurie,

Well, I see we're opening[2]—with choreography by the Rockettes[3]—at the Music Hall. I can see the reviews already: Crowther:[4] Show me the way to go home from this hill! Watts:[5] Hunter's Stew. Journal-American:[6] Most powerful production yet in aromaroma! But if anybody starts running it down to you, Annie Laurie, you just speak right up and tell em you know the author: Robert Louis Stevenson.[7]

Well, I just hope my uncle[8] gets a good write-up. He's got a part in it, you know. He plays a barber. I don't know what kind of an actor he is, but he's a natural-born barber!

So, say hello to your old man,[9] and anytime you need money, why, just write.

Love,
Bill

1. WH misdated this letter 1959.

2. The opening of MGM's film based on WH's *Home from the Hill,* directed by Vincente Minnelli and staring Robert Mitchum and Eleanor Parker.

3. This chorus line performs before the showing of films at Radio City Music Hall in New York City.

4. Bosley Crowther (1905–81) was perhaps the most influential film critic in America from 1940 until 1967, during which time he was critic for the *New York Times.*

5. Richard Watts Jr. was film critic for the *New York Herald Tribune.*

6. This New York newspaper, owned by William Randolph Hearst, was published between 1885–1966.

7. Robert Louis Stevenson (1850–94), Scottish poet, novelist, and essayist, the last line of whose poem titled "Requiem" WH appropriated for the title of his novel: "And the hunter home from the hill."

8. Bernard Varley.

9. Maurice Crane, Williams's husband.

TO ANNIE LAURIE WILLIAMS

ALS/CU

Glendale, Mass.
January 13, 19[60][1]

Dear Annie Laurie,
The MGM check came, for which many thanks. I've endorsed it and sent it right off to the Bureau of Internal Revenue.

That's very nice of them to want to give a showing of the film for me and my friends.[2] But I'm afraid it'll be impossible for me to get down there, no matter how much notice you were to give me. There are no trains out of here and I haven't got a car. That is, I've got one, but it *never* runs. So, I'll just have to wait till the picture gets out to the sticks.[3] Please give the MGM people my thanks and regrets.

Yours,
Bill

1. WH misdated the letter 1959.
2. Scheduled for 21 January.
3. WH avoided ever seeing the film based on *Home from the Hill.*

TO ANNIE LAURIE WILLIAMS

ALS/CU

Glendale, Mass.
Jan. 27, 1960

Dear Annie Laurie,
I sense that I may have hurt your feelings by my jokes about the movie.[1] If so, I am terribly sorry. I'm one of those people who can never resist a wisecrack. If you've taken my jokes to heart I'll be very sorry indeed. I wouldn't for the world have you think that I feel anything but gratitude for your part in selling the book to the movies. If you hadn't, I wouldn't be sitting here writing another book[2]—and making wisecracks. As for the picture itself, whether it's good or bad I don't care. It hasn't anything to do with me. If it's good, no credit to me, if it's bad, none of the blame. It could be the worst ever made and I'd still love em for their dough, and love you for gouging it out of them. OK?

Yours,
Bill

1. *Home from the Hill.*
2. *The Ordways.*

TO JEAN LAMBERT

TLS/LC

Glendale, Massachusetts
January 29, 1960

Dear Lambert,

Bill Koshland[1] has just sent me that copy of your foreword to Home from the Hill. I have just read it—I blush to admit with what pleasure!

I am especially pleased by your praise for the character Theron. Because he has always been my greatest worry. I felt I had done a fair job with the minor characters, but I was always afraid that my hero was not sufficiently convincing. And of course I wanted him to be the important thing. So, to have you single him out for your particular commendation is more gratifying to me than anything else could be.

But I am not pleased only by your praise. One likes to be liked, but it is more rare, and thus more pleasant, to be understood; and I am grateful for your perception. Again, this brings me back to your understanding of my intentions in the character of Theron and to one statement of yours in particular: ["]Chez lui (Mark Twain) le monde merveilleu[x] ou vivent ses jeunes héros n'est pas distinct du monde des adultes; ils en util[i]sent les éléments, les disposent selon leur fantaisie, en sont souvent les victimes, mais dans l'ensemble se tirent avec honneur de leur rôle de petits hommes. C'est qu'en fait ils ne jouent pas: ils vivent avec un grand sérieux, avec plus de sérieux que leurs aînés. Ainsi Théron, pour qui la vie est important[e] et grave."[2] That goes straight to the heart of the book, to my basic intention, and no one else has seen it so clearly, nor expressed it so well.

I am deeply grateful to you for this appreciation, and—of course—for the long and tedious and loving labor you have put in on my book.

. . . .

Koshland says that you are thinking of translating the story, Quail for Mr. Forester, and of suggesting to the editors of the NRF that they publish it,[3] in lieu of an episode from the novel. I entirely agree, and I hope that the editors will like the story. I think it is my best, and it is for me another instance of your sympathy for my work that you have chosen it. [. . .][4]

Thank you again for everything.

Sincerely yours,
William Humphrey

1. One of WH's editors at the Knopf firm; he became president in 1971.

2. "According to Mark Twain, the marvelous world in which these young heroes lived was not distinct from the world of adults. They make use of the elements [of their world],

disposing of them according to their fantasy, and they are often victims of the world, but overall they get by with honor in their role of little men. In fact they do not play: they live with great seriousness, more seriously than their elders. So it is Theron, for whom life is important and serious."

3. The editors of *La nouvelle revue française* did not agree, and so the French translation of the story, "Crailles pour M. Forester," was published in *Le Figaro littéraire* in June 1960.

4. WH then gives Lambert advice on obtaining permission to publish the translation of the story.

TO ALFRED A. KNOPF

[On 16 October 1961, Knopf wrote to WH with concern about progress on The Ordways: *"At a luncheon the other day I met your friend, Dr. Harry Grabstald, and he gave me a long report on his recent visit with you. From what he said I gather that while the novel made very good progress for a long while, we aren't likely to have it in manuscript for another six months at least. [. . .] Do let me have a line when you get a chance. We certainly do miss you from the list." WH's "line" follows.]*

TLS/HR

Corso Vittorio Emanuele, 24
Rome
October 26, 1961

Dear Alfred,

You say you gathered from my friend Harry Grabstald[1] that you are not likely to have my novel in manuscript for another six months, at least. What ever led him to think you might expect it in *that* amount of time I can't imagine!

You have wondered in most of your recent letters just when I was going to finish the book. So I suppose I'd better make this a long letter, and let you in on what I'm doing and what I've done and what I hope to do.

As near as I can guess I'm no more than about two-thirds done with this book. It is a picaresque. Which means that it is improvisational. It is perhaps precisely the sort of book which I, with my Flaubertian fretting[2] over each word and over the carefully cadenced rhythm of sentence and paragraph, and with my dependence on plot (see Home from the Hill) ought never to attempt. Which is precisely why I am determined to do it. But, as it goes against whatever natural gifts I may have, it does not come easy. (No writing comes easy for me: I'm one of those that Hoffmansthal[3] had in mind when he defined the writer as one for whom writing is harder than for other people). Now, a picaresque needs adventures and many characters, and these must be imagined—in a way it is like writing a great collection of short stories, so that you start afresh, with little help from what has gone before, with each new episode. And yet it must all the same not seem episodic. To imagine adventures and characters requires time. Often you have to wait. Often you spend a week or two writing an episode, only to find, once you surface and get your breath and look around, that you have gotten into very shallow water—or to drop the metaphor, that it's no goddamned good, and into the waste basket goes [*sic*] two weeks of your life. Moreover, this book is supposed to be comic—not altogether so, but basically. And there is nothing on earth harder than being humorous, nothing worse when you fail. I don't mean witty and I don't mean smart and diverting—I mean adding something to comic literature.

And that is what I want to do. I am very ambitious. I don't want to write a pretty good book. I want to write a great book. I don't care how long it takes. Unless and until this one seems to me the best I can ever hope to do with the material, I won't publish it. Publication in itself means nothing to me. I don't want to create a season's stir. I want to be remembered after I'm dead.

My work here, except for interruptions for illness, has gone very well, better indeed than ever before in my life. How many pages of the novel I now have I don't know—it must be around 525, maybe only 500—of which say 20 percent (my usual average) will ultimately be discarded. These are in themselves a finished draft. I don't write a "first" draft. Before I proceed, each page is polished and finished. It may come to be thrown away entirely, but it is a finished page. As I say, I believe that what I now have represents no more than about 2/3rds of the final book. When you send a man on a search for his son all over the state of Texas, and on not one but two separate trips,[4] and then bring the book up thirty years later and to a third generation, you are not writing a novella.

Meanwhile, in those times when I'm awaiting inspiration (I am a believer in the old-fashioned notion of inspiration) I work on two other projects. The first is a novel[5] which I think will be about 225 printed pages and of which I now have about 40 percent, or 120 pages (all but 25 written since June). The second is a batch of 10 short stories,[6] all of them begun but none of them finished (though of two of them I have now 30 pages each) and all this too done since coming to Rome in June (most of the spring in Siena[7] I was plagued with kidney stone trouble.) These stories are all on a related theme, the discovery of oil in my part of Texas and Oklahoma in 1935–6, and the changes it made in the lives of the dirt farmers and the Indians on whose land it was found. Of this book of short stories I have about 100 pages, some of it the best writing I have ever done. The short novel concerns the death of a Southern matriarch, the assembling of her large and violent clan (10 children) and the efforts of a couple of these rural Euminides [*sic*][8] to track down and bring home for the burial (while the rest of them keep the old lady's remains in the town ice house) the renegade youngest son in New York City.

Since March, then, I have written a total of about 325 pages—for me a phenomenal amount.

Sometimes it seems to me that the big novel (which has now got a title, incidentally: The Quest of Samuel Ordway) will occupy me for years. I hope not, and all my efforts go towards seeing that it doesn't, but if it does, it does. It (or I, as you choose) will not be hurried, conscious though I am of time's winged chariot at my back.[9]

What will happen more likely is that all three books will finish neck and neck, and this will not be for some time.

I rather suspect, Alfred, that you think me, not exactly lazy, but susceptible to distractions, shall we say? If you do, you are wrong. I suspect also that you think I've become something of a professional tourist these past few years. Again, if so, you're wrong. I am in Europe not to seek but to avoid distractions. I work from 9 to 5:30 six, more usually 7, days a week. I know not one human being in all of Italy, or aside from Ian and Trekkie Parsons in all of Europe, and have called on none of the people to whom friends gave me letters of introduction. My dissipations are confined to ice cream one night a week after dinner on the Piazza Navona.[10] I do not live la dolce vita.[11] I am not and apparently never will be prolific; but while I am not the best writer you ever knew, I am one of the most industrious, one of the least social, and possibly the one least in need of being reminded that time is passing. It is precisely because I have such a strong sense of mortality that I cannot be hurried in my work. This is the only chance I will get to leave a name behind me. To write Home from the Hill took me four and a half years; I now think that with a little more time I might have made a pretty good book out of it. As for the one I'm now on, I think it is already a better book than that one; and to the list of superlatives I've already used about myself let me add, I am one of the most self-critical and least self-infatuated writers you ever struck across.

In sum, I ask you to be patient, to realize that I have set myself a large task and that I judge myself by exacting standards, that I am working hard, and that the results will be worth waiting for.

Yours,
Bill

1. Grabstald and Knopf met at the Lotos Club, a New York City organization that promotes interchange between writers and artists and friends of literature and art.

2. The French novelist Gustave Flaubert achieved style through dedicated discipline and "atrocious labour," as he said in one of his letters in 1853.

3. Hugo von Hoffmannsthal (1874–1929), Austrian playwright and librettist.

4. In a later revision of *The Ordways,* WH reduced the plot to one trip west in search of Ned, the kidnapped son.

5. *Proud Flesh* (1973).

6. Those eventually published in *A Time and a Place* (1968).

7. Ancient Italian city fifty-nine miles south of Florence.

8. The Eumenides were the Erinyes or Furies in Greek myth. WH ended up creating in *Proud Flesh* a modern Texas retelling not of Aeschylus's play *The Eumenides* but of his *Libation Bearers.*

9. From Andrew Marvell's (1621–78) "To His Coy Mistress": "But at my back I always hear / Time's winged chariot hurrying near."

10. This quiet piazza contains Bernini's Fountain of the Four Rivers. In the evenings there were art shows and entertainments.

11. The good life, and a reference to the film *La Dolce Vita* (1960), directed by Federico Fellini (1920–93), innovative Italian filmmaker.

TO ALFRED A. KNOPF

[Knopf responded to WH's 26 October letter by saying that he was "quite touched" by it—"There is very little indeed for me to say in reply to it, except to assure you, if such assurance is in any least degree necessary, that I am with you a thousand percent plus and have nothing but the highest regard for the attitude that you are taking, [. . .]"—and then urges WH to make use of the letters of introduction that he has given him (Knopf to WH, 1 November 1961).]

ALS/HR

Rome
November 12, 1961

Dear Alfred,
Many thanks for your letter. I've never had a moment's doubt that you were with me. Nonetheless your letter did me good. I hope to prove to both of us that your confidence has not been misplaced.

As to your advice that I seek out acquaintances here, well, it's not new friends I miss, it's the old ones. I miss you very much.

Yours,
Bill

TO ALFRED A. KNOPF

TLS/HR

Rome
Jan. 28, [']62

Dear Alfred,

Excuse the silence. Work. Influenza. And income taxes complicated by expenses in three different currencies, dollars, pounds and lire. Hope you had a pleasant holiday. The Italians have a quaint custom. Fireworks are strictly forbidden. Thus this year as every year a bootlegger's stock was accidentally set off by a cigarette butt and blew down the whole building, killing three people. However, at about 11:30 on New Year's Eve you hear something that sounds [like] a squadron of bombers coming over. It begins in the distance, a rumble like bombs falling or the advance troops of a blitz under artillery cover. The Trasteverini,[1] who are a bunch of premature ejaculators by nature, start it. Then it rolls up over the old quarter towards Piazza del Popolo.[2] You have to be careful to close your window shutters because all that you hear is not contraband fireworks; at least half of the bangs is pistol shots, and any lighted window is considered a fair target. The friends with whom we were spending the evening in their apartment just above the steps in the Piazza di Spagna[3] showed us the bullet holes from last year in the ceiling of the room in which we were sitting. Suddenly a new sound complicates the din. This is a mighty rumble and crash and it sounds as if the H bomb has hit. On the stroke of twelve everyone throws out the window and into the street all his old plumbing fixtures: toilets, bidets, lavatories, chamber pots. This year 200 people were hospitalized with head wounds. No dead, fortunately; last year there were three. We picked our way home along the Tiber an hour or so afterwards among the most glorious assortment of fragments of douches and enema bones, dentures, breast pumps, toilet seats, bathtubs and assorted fractured crockery. [. . .][4]

What to do about the Ballad of Jesse Neighbours? Dear, dear, why doesn't anybody like that story? Have you tried it on ESQUIRE?[5] If not, how about it? And if they turn it down, then just keep it, please. I don't have any use for it here.

Work on the novel[6] is going well, I'm pleased with the new things, and see ways to save much of the old stuff, I believe.

Saw the most glorious performance of Verdi's Otello[7] here. Tito Gobbi as Iago[8] was the slinkiest thing you ever saw or heard. Saw a fair Entfuhrung aaus dem Seraglio.[9] Other good things are promised. We're only about two blocks from Santa Cecilia[10] and have heard some good concerts there, including a wonderful one by the Parrenin quartet[11] of the Ravel String Quartet[12] and the last Beethoven quartet[13] and Alban Berg's Lyric Suite.[14] I had not heard of them, but it seems I'm the only one who hadn't.

Will you tell B. Koshland that I do not have copies of the Danish, Dutch, Spanish and/or Hebrew translations of Home from the Hill. I don't want them here, but will he be sure to obtain, and keep for me, copies of them before they should go out of print. And that I'll write soon as I get this tax mess off to my accountant.

Best to Blanche.

Yours,
Bill

1. People from Trastevere, a working-class area on the west bank of the Tiber, the last of Rome's traditional neighborhoods—bohemian, crude, and authentic.

2. The People's Square, a place of much commotion where adolescents congregate.

3. Spanish Steps.

4. A paragraph about WH's not having heard from one of Knopf's friends follows.

5. Knopf did not try *Esquire* magazine immediately, but the story was eventually published in its September 1963 issue.

6. *The Ordways.*

7. *Otello* (1887), based on Shakespeare's *Othello,* is a late opera by Giuseppe Verdi (1813–1901).

8. Gobbi (1915–84), Italian operatic baritone and an actor in films, played the villain in Verdi's opera.

9. *Die Entfuhrung aus dem Serail* (*The Abduction from the Seraglio*) (1782) is a late opera by Wolfgang Amadeus Mozart (1756–91).

10. Accademia Nazionale di Santa Cecilia (The National Academy of Saint Cecilia) in Rome, founded in 1585, had a busy concert hall.

11. The Parrenin Quartet, led by Jacques Parrenin, was formed in 1942 and played throughout Europe and the United States.

12. The String Quartet in F Major by French composer Maurice Ravel (1875–1937).

13. The Quartet in F Major, op. 135, by Ludwig van Beethoven (1770–1827) was completed in 1826.

14. Lyric Suite (1925–26), by Viennese composer Alban Berg (1885–1935), is a string quartet, the first large-scale work to employ the twelve-tone method of composition.

TO ALFRED A. KNOPF

TLS/HR

Corso Vittorio Emanuele, 24
Rome
June 1, 1962

Dear Alfred,

I shall shortly be sending another story to The New Yorker, with instructions, as before, to send the mss. to you if and when they turn it down. I haven't much doubt that they will (and if they do I'll never send them another) so this will explain what it is when you receive it.

Thank you for your offer to act as agents for the story you now have.[1] I have not taken you up on it before now because I felt the story needed some revisions and I wasn't ready to make them. I have now and will send the new version to you in a few days. When you receive it will you please destroy the first one. And as for trying it on any magazine, what do you think of Harper's. A Mr. John Fisher there expressed some interest in having a story from me years ago. The Atlantic Monthly is the only large magazine I know of which never reviewed either of my two books, so I pretend they don't exist the same as they pretend I don't.

In just a short while now (June 14) our lease on this apartment ends and we then leave for England, there to pass the summer and early fall. After that, don't know our plans. We had hoped to find a cottage somewhere in the country but all our efforts to do so by mail have proved futile. We are in bad need of a change of scene so that Dorothy can regain her strength and I my strength of mind. I am just coming out of a kind of crisis arising from a collapse of confidence in my writing the most severe I have ever suffered. Quite suddenly a few months ago I saw that everything I had done on my novel[2] for the past two years was all wrong, worthless. You wouldn't think a grown man could fall into a trance for two whole years, would you, but I did, and the realization has been pretty shattering.

I still have faith in the material and I believe I know where I went wrong and that I can return to that point and (salvaging about 150 pages out of the wreck) still make something out of it. In fact, I have already begun, now that the ends of my mind have begun to knit together again. Only time is short. As you know the movie version of Home from the Hill was a flop[3] and I won't be seeing that other half of the money I thought I would. So my term of grace now has an end in sight (a damn quick end if the stock market takes another and more lasting plunge!). I have accepted an invitation from Washington and Lee Univ. to come there in September 63 and stay one semester [. . .].[4] The pay is good. So I have till then, and Wall St. willing, I've got just about [enough] money to make it till then. So I'm gambling on getting the book done by that time. Meanwhile I have reached page 175 on the short novel[5] and have the short stories all a good [bit] further along. So that's my progress (?) report. Mention me in your prayers sometimes, will you?

We have no address in England. Soon as we have I'll let you know, of course. Meanwhile, it's here till June 14, after that c/o Chatto & Windus, London.

Our best to you and to Blanche.

Yours,
Bill

1. The two stories in question are probably "A Voice from the Woods" and "The Pump."

2. *The Ordways.*

3. In the *New York Times,* Bosley Crowther panned the film: "There must be a point lurking somewhere in Metro-Goldwyn-Mayer's 'Home from the Hill,' a giant film in CinemaScope and color that came to the Music Hall yesterday. But where it is centered precisely in the long, rambling tale that is told, or what thought it is meant to focus, entirely eludes this reviewer."

4. Details about WH's duties at Washington and Lee University, contained in his 9 October 1962 letter to Grabstald, are omitted here.

5. *Proud Flesh.*

TO ALFRED A. KNOPF

TLS/HR

[Old School Cottage
Telscombe
Sussex, England]
July 12, [']62

Dear Alfred,

It was good to hear from you, and delightful news that you are coming here and that we will see you. You will love Bath. It is the one town which is a work of art, the product of a single mind, an architectural entity, really glorious. I rave like this after having spent just one showery afternoon there three years ago. I do think it's the prettiest thing I ever saw.

We are in a pleasant little cottage in a hamlet—too small even to be called a village—down in a wooded vale of the woodless windswept Sussex Downs. Brighton is five miles over the hill but you'd never know it, and Lewes the same distance the other way—both very pleasant towns in their very different ways. The Parsons lend us their car a couple of days a week, when Mrs. P. runs up to London (55 minutes by train) and thus we're able to lay in provisions[;] otherwise we're afoot and take late afternoon rambles on the hills. Aside from the Parsons we know nearby only their good friend Leonard Woolf,[1] a gracious and courtly man who in his time has known everyone and tells amusing anecdotes of Thomas Hardy and Henry James and rather scurrilous ones of Bertie Russell[2] and others. I am working hard, still avoiding the novel[3] and instead turning out more short stories.[4] Speaking of short stories, again many thanks for your efforts with the ones you have. I am pleased to know that you read with pleasure the latest one. I am sure your judgment is sound, as to holding off with it until we know the fate of the other.

Wasn't that shocking news, the death of Faulkner.[5] It doesn't seem possible that he and Hemingway[6] are not still here. I have not seen this new book of Faulkner's[7] but the last previous one, the Mansion,[8] seemed to me a great deal of a comeback. Three fourths of it were poor, but the fourth which was good was miraculous. He was unquestionably the big American writer of the time, and I imagine the big writer of the world. Here in England his death has received the most meaching and stingy sort of notice, a patronizing obituary in the Observer by that ass Philip Toynbee[9] for instance. (Hemingway was even more slightingly treated last year.)

I see by Time magazine's program listings that you've become a TV star.[10] Sorry I'm not where I can [see] you in this new role. What's your Nielsen rating?[11]

Best of everything. Looking forward very much to seeing you.

Yours,
Bill

1. Leonard Woolf (1880–1969), the husband of Virginia Woolf and afterward the lover of Trekkie Parsons. Woolf's most famous book is on political philosophy: *After the Deluge* (1931–53). Woolf and WH became friends immediately upon their meeting.

2. Bertrand Russell (1872–1970), an English author and philosopher at Trinity College, Cambridge.

3. *The Ordways.*

4. Eventually published in *A Time and a Place.*

5. William Faulkner died on 6 July 1962.

6. Ernest Hemingway died on 2 July 1961.

7. *The Reivers* (1962). By 16 November 1962, WH had read the book and wrote to Harding Lemay: "Pretty sentimental stuff. But then Faulkner always was sappy about kids and whores. But doesn't the landscape look wintry without him and Hemingway? They may have been both dead trees, but they still stuck up pretty high in the air."

8. Faulkner's penultimate novel was published in 1960.

9. Philip Toynbee (1916–81), novelist and literary critic, was chief reviewer for the *Observer.*

10. There is no mention of Alfred Knopf in the television "Listings" or in the "Show Business" feature of *Time* magazine during the months of May, June, and July 1962.

11. System by which the viewing habits of selected families are assessed to determine the popularity of television programs.

TO ALFRED A. KNOPF

TLS/HR

Old School Cottage
Telscombe nr. Lewes
Sussex, England
Aug. 13, [']62

Dear Alfred,

That you didn't receive my letter of June 8 until the 3rd of July I can well believe. It was mailed from Rome, and the Italian mails are medieval. The English are supposed to be the best, though, and I have written you twice from here. You ought to have received those. Well, I hope you get this one.

It is really kind of you to go to the trouble you have over these short stories of mine. I appreciate it very much. I too am sorry that Mr. Weeks[1] did not care for The Ballad of J. Neighbours, though I'm not much surprised. As I told you, the Atlantic Monthly just doesn't go for me. Had you (you don't mention) already tried that story on Harper's, and did they also turn it down? You speak of trying the second one on Mr. Weeks. I expect he'll reject that one, too. If so, why don't we try it on Mr. Shawn[2] of The New Yorker. It will recommend itself to him on one count at least—it's in first person, the only narrative voice recognized by the New Yorker. They have spent a quarter century in a determined effort to destroy the division between fiction and reminiscence, and have just about succeeded. Ah, well, this is all an old story to me. Years ago, when really all I wanted to do was write short stories, I gave it up in despair because there was no place to print them. Not that one writes only to get published, but one does not write not to, either. Yet here I am doing it again. I have just finished two more. Even more unpublishable than the two you have. And I have going eight or ten more.

However, I have laid them aside, and gone back to the novel.[3] It goes slowly, but, I believe, rather well. Much altered, and I think for the better. You know when someone breaks his leg and it's badly set and has to be broken again deliberately in order to be set straight, well, that's about what working on this novel is for me. Painful as it is, however, a man can't just leave his leg crooked, he has got to straighten it out. And to continue the metaphor, I haven't really put my weight down on this new version, but I think it will support it.

The weather here has been pretty awful, which is to say typical. We're just about a mile from the sea and the winds howl in with nothing to stop them. These are the South Downs, and when one can get out to see them, extraordinarily moving and beautiful. Rolling, treeless hills, close-spaced, with narrow valleys. The soil is white. Chalk. (And yet unexpectedly fertile.) They tell me that until the second war this was virgin land, never broken. Now the fields are patterned in different kinds of grain, so that purple patches lie next to green, next to gold, next to pink, next to red, and over it all, when the sun does shine, the pastellish English sun. We are just about five miles from Brighton, which far from being only the Coney Island[4] I had always imagined it also extremely gracious, with miles of handsome Regency buildings along the sea front, and old George IV's whimsical pleasure palace[5] in a kind of never-never chinoiserie[6] Hindu Russian Mosque style plumped down in the middle of it like a bed of mushrooms. The Downs are great for walking on and we have a spirited and blustery go at it in the late afternoons. Otherwise there isn't much going on around Telscombe. It's a village of just a dozen houses[,] no store, no post office even, not even a pub. Three days a week we have the loan of our friends the Parson's [*sic*] car, for going in to buy our food, otherwise we'd be stranded. (Ian Parsons, by the way, is looking forward very much to seeing you on your visit here.) The village is stocked with those types without which it wouldn't be an English village, bossy, eccentric old maid, dotty squire, sweet, feeble-minded farmer's boy, etc. I sometimes think that the guidebooks to places instead of listing "Church. Norman interior. Nave. Single Aisle, Tower in late Perpendicular, etc," ought to say, "The visitor is advised not to miss Miss Peabody, typical example of English middle age, fine florid face in Decorated style," and so on to other human treasures and oddities in which this sceptered isle[7] is so teemingly rich.

Meanwhile it's not only Ian but I too who very much look forward to seeing you. Have a gay crossing. Until then,

Yours as always,
Bill

1. Edward Weeks was the editor of *Atlantic Monthly* magazine.

2. William Shawn (d. 1992), editor of the *New Yorker* from 1952 to 1987.

3. *The Ordways.*

4. Amusement park and beach in Brooklyn, New York.

5. The Prince Regent's Royal Pavilion.

6. Chinese.

7. From John of Gaunt's famous speech in Shakespeare's *Richard II:* "This royal throne of kings, this sceptered isle, / This earth of majesty" (2.1.43–4).

TO ALFRED A. KNOPF

[WH defends his short story "A Voice in the Woods" to Knopf, who has passed on to Humphrey the objections made by the editor of the Atlantic Monthly *magazine.]*

TLS/HR

Old School Cottage
Telscombe, near Lewes
Sussex, England
October 7, 1962

Dear Alfred,

Your letter came on Tuesday and I've been trying ever since to read the story without the first 2½ pages which Mr. Weeks objects to, it's now Sunday and I still can't do it. I can see that it might benefit from some compressing, but that's not what he wants. He wants the first 2½ pages "with their endless mourning doves" "Dispensed with" so that "we might begin with the bickering between the wife and the mother-in-law."

Well, from the tone of his letter I gather that Mr. Weeks is none too enthusiastic about the story in any case, so I don't expect to convince him. But you have taken such a lot of trouble for me that I would hate for you to think I had refused his suggestion out of angry pride. The call of the mourning dove is, obviously, what sets the mother's mind off on the reminiscence which forms the body of the story. But it ought to contain a memory for the narrator as well. Though it means something different to the two (a fact in itself of some significance) the more important point is, that it does mean something to both of them, and nothing to the yankee wife.

To the narrator i[t] conjures up an image of his birthplace, a place of heat and languor, loneliness, desolation, and this is contrasted with the spirit of the place of his voluntary exile. Then too it establishes the actual sound of the dove, and this should, for the attentive reader, re-echo as a kind of leitmotiv when towards the end of the story the mother recalls that moment after she had rejected the proposal of her wild lover—something she has always half-regretted, and that mood of half-regret seems to me to be well "caught" by the peculiar sound the mourning dove makes. Further, in terms of the violence in which the story deals, it is calculated that what the narrator should remember is his (unsuccessful) efforts to kill the dove. What's more, he associates it with cemeteries, and it was in a cemetery that his mother, years later, sat listening to the dove after turning down Travis Winfield, an act which needless to say had an incalculable influence on the narrator's life. But enough. It is no doubt true what Mr. Weeks says, that I'm a while getting my narrative in motion. But there's more to a story than its story and this symbol of the dove adds a dimension and a unity which seem to me worth keeping. Without it the narrator's place in the story is even less justifiable, and the story tends towards the condition of mere anecdote. I don't know whether you'll agree, but I hope so. Again, many thanks for your efforts, and I am sorry to have to frustrate them like this.

Yours,
Bill

TO HARRY GRABSTALD

TLS/PH

Old School cottage,
Telscombe near Lewes
Sussex, England
October 9, 1962

Dear Harry,
There hasn't been anything to write. We've been living the quietest life imaginable, in this little cottage in this village, which is too little to have even a store, or even a pub. Dorothy has been feeling pretty well, but has certainly been a long time getting over the last traces of her hepatitis.[1] (Incidentally she had a new liver function test made here. The doctor said her liver is functioning "very nearly perfectly." She may want to send his report (which we've not received) to you for your opinion.[)]

My work, and consequently my state of mind, went completely to hell during the last winter in Rome, which was another reason you've heard so little from me for such a long time. I suddenly saw that my novel[2] was simply awful, after three years work. It plunged me into the deepest depression I have ever known (and I've known some pretty profound ones). So I had to start all over again. That's not easy to do when you're that discouraged, and after three years. It's gone slowly here, but at least the summer has had the effect of making me feel that perhaps life is worth living after all. We've seen much of our good friends, the Parsons, of whom I've told you—he owns Chatto & Windus, my English publishers, and both he and his wife (she's a painter) are fine people, fine company, and very understanding and sympathetic. We've seen as much also of their good friend, Leonard Woolf (Virginia Woolf was his wife). He is eighty years old, in fact eighty-two, I believe, but except for his face (which looks older than the rock of Gibraltar) you'd take him for 16. Full of fun, full of laughter. He has of course known everybody in the English literary world for the last half century and has amusing and interesting anecdotes to tell about them. He is of course a well-known writer in his own right, novelist and historian and writer on politics, from a liberal point of view. He is that rather rare species, an English Jew, which gives him an interesting angle on things. The sort of person you never get enough of.

Well, we're off for Rome again in just three days. Can't stay here any longer—the house just isn't live-in-able for the winter (though these past few days it's begun to seem that summer, not winter, is—at last—on its way). We've no apartment in Rome, but hope to find something. Neither did we have last time we landed there, and found one. This time it may be a little harder because we can't take a year's lease. Have spoken for this same cottage for next summer and are returning to the U.S. in early September. You may remember that in December of 1960 I went down to Lexington, Virginia to give a couple of lectures at Washington & Lee. Well they've invited me to return for a whole semester, and I've accepted for the fall 63 term. No teaching duties, must just give four public lectures on some aspect of fiction during my four months stay. Meanwhile I hope desperately to get this damned book finished. Am also working fitfully on still another novel and a book of more or less related short stories.[3] Am in fact trying to do too many things at once, part of my problem.

After hearing nothing from my mother for months, I got word not long ago that she has re-married. For the fourth time.[4]

Must close and get back to packing. Until we have an address write c/o American Express, Rome. Meanwhile, love to Milly.[5]

Yours,
Bill

1. In December 1961 Dorothy contracted hepatitis in Rome.

2. *The Ordways*.

3. *Proud Flesh* and *A Time and a Place*.

4. Actually, the former Nell Varley Humphrey *married* for the fourth time. After the death of WH's father Clarence in July 1937, she within half a year married Andy Fleming. In 1942 she divorced Fleming and married Butch Troughton, an army recruiting officer stationed in Dallas. His drunkenness prompted her to divorce him and marry a fourth time, this time to Dan Moran in Cleveland, Ohio. WH thought his mother's marital problems stemmed from her original overly hasty remarriage following his father's death, in an effort to support her son. WH had little to do with his mother after his first year in college.

5. Mildred Herr was Grabstald's first wife.

TO IAN AND MARGARET (TREKKIE) PARSONS

TLS/RU

Salita Sant' Onofrio, 23
(presso Valeri)
Rome
November 5, 1962

Dear Folks,

A penny for the guy![1] And I hope you mean to go out tonight and light a bonfire on a down to celebrate what I read in yesterday's Observer. I mean, the court ruling on the book pricing case.[2] Congratulations, Ian! So all that long hard work did pay off! I'm sure it was your testimony that did it. How pleasant to learn that there are still judges in the world—or at least in England—not altogether myopic. And I was particularly pleased to note that this one had been swayed by your best argument: that mute inglorious Miltons, if there be any, would have a better chance of remaining so if the prices of books were to be cut. My cynicism suggests that he himself may have a manuscript in his desk drawer, still . . . bravo, bravissimo!

As from the above address you will have seen, we have got an address. We'd begun to think we wouldn't have, indeed were thinking of packing up and leaving Rome, though with no idea where to go. Since we made our lease on the former apartment 18 months ago, rents have risen by an average of 50%. That's if you can find an apartment at any price. After 10 days of searching door to door, agent to agent (all of whom laughed in our faces), placing ads in the papers ourselves and answering what few were there for places to rent (and learning the price asked over the phone!), we were desperate. And what have we found but the finest apartment in the whole city, I do verily believe! It's on the "other" side of the River,[3] just beyond the river, at the foot of the Janiculum,[4] not far from St. Peter's.[5] We have four big airy rooms plus kitchen and bath and *two* terraces, large, with sweeping views of the Tiber and the domes and rooftops of the city. The "drawing room" is completely glass on two sides. From it one steps out onto the grand terrace, which, like the house, is filled with plants. The weather has permitted us to eat our lunch out there since arriving, and not in overcoats but in shirtsleeves. Salita, as you no doubt remember, means "ascent"—and so it is: a steep cobblestoned street with an overflowing fountain: very much like a street in one of the hill towns of Tuscany or Umbria.[6] Our apartment sits on, or rather above, a corner and the other street is not a street at all but a long long flight of stairs, about 200 steps, with landings here and there with benches to sit down on and catch your breath. The faces one sees of the people resting there and the snatches of conversation to be overheard (when you can understand it: it's in the real Romanaccio)[7] are a joy. There's a school up the way (the school of St. Dorothy, which is convenient) and troops of children come up in the morning and go down in the evening. And occasionally a woman comes up with a huge basket of wash balanced easily on her head. Life on this stairs is intense, and sometimes a little overly so: e.g. the day before we moved in a young man and his estranged wife, coming down from a visit to the children's hospital up the way, began quarreling. He wanted her to come and live with him again and take care of their two year old paralytic child. She refused. So naturally he picked up one of the paving stones and beat her brains out. "Just what she had coming to her," everyone hereabouts says, and the husband will no doubt go scot free. And speaking of crime al[l]'Italiana,[8] there's been this story running on the front pages these past few days, pushing the Cuba thing[9] completely out of the headlines. Two middle-aged English African (Kenya) tourists were murdered while eating a picnic lunch in Sardinia.[10] They'd been in the little town for three weeks, and it was reported that they liked it so well they had said they would like to stay forever. Well, yesterday the bodies of the two most famous bandits of the district (called, by the newspapers, the bandit belt of Sardegna)[11] were found, mutilated in a particularly gruesome way: hearts cut out, mouths slit from ear to ear. This conforms apparently to a symbolic language, legible to every Sardegnan, and was quickly interpreted to mean that the bandits had been killed by their own townsfolks. Apparently the bandits had not been told how much the poor English tourists liked Sardegna. The lesson, in any case, is said to be, that while it's all right to rob overnight touri[s]ts, those who have stayed past ten days or so have become, so to speak, a part of the family, especially if they've shown so much enthusiasm for Sardegna. It's hoped that this will serve as a future warning to bandits to show more care in their choice of victims.

In Rome, meanwhile, as I went up and down the streets looking for To Let signs outside doorways, I had to dodge demonstrations of all sorts. It was a week of demonstrations. Cuba si, yankee no, the young communists shouted. To protest the incarceration of three young Spaniards by Franco's courts, the young socialists marched on the Spanish embassy to the Holy See, in Piazza di Spagna.[12] From one direction they came, from the other came the young fascists, looking for trouble. They met in Piazza di Spagna. The police were photographed cracking heads with billy-clubs, but the heads cracked were all socialists, no injuries reported among the neo-fascists. This has caused a crisis in the chamber of deputies,[13] and investigations, of which, as every one knows, nothing will come, are underway. Then the German-speaking minority in the Alto Adige went on the terrorists trail again. Bombs left in suitcases in Left Luggage depots through north Italy went off, one man was killed, thirty seriously injured. This provoked riots here and all over Italy, with fascists, communists, royalists, and socialists closing ranks and all marching together against the police, shouting, Alto Adige[14] is Ours! They passed a law last week making it a ten thousand lire fine to kiss in the dark in the movie houses, and at the same time passed a law making it a fine of the same amount for raising the hand in salute. I saw hundreds of hands raised in salutes last week and no fines being handed out—how things are going in the dark in the movie houses I don't know. [. . .][15]

I read in the papers that the gov't has just appropriated 4 million dollars for the country's opera houses for the year, this in addition to what they were already receiving. This may not flabbergast and fill with envy you, who though you may complain about the amount received, or not received, are at least not strangers to the entire idea of state support of the arts, but to us it is wonderful and outrageous that a poor country like this can make such a gesture, and America not a penny. Not one red cent.

Millions for defence, to alter a famous American patriotic declaration[16] slightly, but not a cent for tribute to the arts. Well, enough. Truth is, I can no longer see the paper, I've got such a wretched cold in my head, and am just writing from the wrist down. All our love.

Bill

1. English children use this phrase to solicit money for fireworks to celebrate Guy Fawkes Day, 5 November.

2. According to this London newspaper, the Restrictive Practices Court upheld the Net Book Agreement, which gave the Publishers' Association protection against price competition (*Observer,* 4 November 1962, 14).

3. The Tiber.

4. Janiculum Hill, or Gianicolo, is the place in Rome from which one can escape the noise and pollution of the city.

5. The Basilica in the Vatican, the papal seat.

6. Regions of central Italy, Tuscany being just north of Umbria.

7. The dialect spoken in Rome.

8. In the Italian way.

9. See note for the 5 November 1962 letter to Leonard Woolf.

10. Italian island of stunning beauty in the central Mediterranean.

11. Sardinia.

12. Three young Spaniards were sentenced to long prison terms for exploding bombs protesting Francisco Franco's fascist regime in Spain. Spanish foreign minister Fernando Maria Castiella had rejected the archbishop of Milan's plea for clemency (*New York Times,* 14 October 1962).

13. One of Italy's legislative bodies sharing power with the Senate.

14. The region of Italy along the northeastern border with Austria, where German is the common language.

15. An account of musical concerts attended in Rome, contained in the following letter to Woolf, is omitted here.

16. WH appropriates a famous toast given at a congressional dinner in Philadelphia, 18 June 1798, by Robert Goodloe Harper (1765–1825): "Millions for defence but not a cent for tribute."

TO LEONARD WOOLF

TLS/US

Salita Sant-Onofrio, 23
(presso Valeri)
Roma
November 5, 1962

Dear Leonard,

Well, it was touch and go there for a time, but now that the sage of Plas Penrhyn[1] has saved the world, we can all breathe deeply once again. He has also, with his usual fair-mindlessness, apportioned the praise and the blame. Krushchev sets up atomic missile sites in Cuba, entrusting the safety of the world to that political delinquent, Fidel Castro.[2] Kennedy[3] tells him to remove them. Krushchev submits, and Bertie[4] thanks him in the name of us all for keeping his temper in the face of aggressive American militarism and preserving us from nuclear destruction.[5] Well now, I'm as unpatriotic as the next fellow, but one must protest such muddleheaded—or rather biased—nonsense. "Thank you, Mr. Krushchev, for not doing anything rash when those people whom you were trying to bully wouldn't let you." What kind of thinking is that? The attitude Russell seems to recommend that the world adopt towards the Russians reminds me of that young lady in Fielding who was about to be raped, and would have been, had she not prevented it by a timely compliance.[6] But enough for the sainted Bertrand.[7]

The American newspapers and magazines which I've seen here are full of praise for "Who's Afraid of Virginia Woolf."[8] The production is apparently of high quality and the actors superb. The oddness of the title has gone unremarked in the reviews I've read.

The musical life in Rome promises to be fairly intense. We went to a Stravinsky concert conducted by the maestro himself, but didn't much like it. The main piece was "Pulcinella." I'm not very enthusiastic about ballet music presented in concert, anyhow.[9] And Pulcinella reminds me of a poem by T. S. Eliot: the best things in it are by somebody else.[10] In this case Pergolesi[11]—only the paste holding the scraps together is Stravinsky. Then we went to a violin concert, by Nathan Milstein.[12] Superb. Warm tone, deep feeling, altogether satisfying. He played Beethoven—those two old stand[b]ys, the Kreutzer and the Spring Sonata[13]—and a Bach partite.[14] Meanwhile there has been a terrific scandal regarding the great soviet [*sic*] pianist Sviatoslov Richter.[15] Remember when he was supposed to appear at the Edinburgh festival,[16] didn't, and the Russian government gave out laconically that he had suffered a mild stroke? Well, he must have. He gave two concerts, and to describe them the reviewers have had to abandon musical terminology and resort to words usually used in neurological abstracts. We didn't go, as the only seats available were going at about six pounds per. But I have never read such reviews. After the first concert, outrage. After the second, a sort of sickroom whisper.

Literary life seems to be dominated by one Georgio Bassani.[17] His new, second, apparently much-awaited novel, was coming out just as we left

Rome in the spring, now it's the rage. I don't know anything about him, except that he's about 40, an Italian Jew, an editor at Feltrinelli,[18] has written some poetry, and is apparently regarded here as the white hope of Italian literature (in his capacity as an editor, he discovered Lampedusa's *The Leopard*).[19] I don't know whether he's been translated in English.

Hope that life in your menagerie has now settled down at last. Trekkie writes that Zinnie and the one kitten appear to have come through. What a time that was! Change brands of pet food, at least.

Don't feel obliged to answer this chatter. But do drop a note when you've nothing better to do. In the meantime, Dorothy joins me in sending *tante belle cose*.[20]

yours, [*sic*]
Bill

1. Bertrand Russell (see note for letter to Knopf on 12 July 1962) was a friend of Leonard Woolf's. In 1957, he moved to Plas Penrhyn, a modest regency villa in Wales, where those in the antinuclear weapons movement met. In 1960 he had resigned from the Campaign for Nuclear Disarmament in order to form a more militant group called the Committee of 100.

2. Nikita Khrushchev (1894–1971) was first secretary of the Communist Party of the Soviet Union and Soviet premier. In July 1962 he authorized the installation of ballistic missiles in Cuba, creating the most dangerous episode of the Cold War. Fidel Castro (1927–), having led a revolution to overthrow a corrupt Cuban government in 1959, was premier of the new socialist republic.

3. John F. Kennedy (1917–63) was president of the United States from 1961 until his assassination in 1963. He responded to the installation of Soviet missiles in Cuba by initiating a naval blockade against Soviet ships, resulting in the Soviet withdrawal of missiles.

4. Russell's nickname.

5. Russell wrote to Khrushchev that he had never known a statesman to "act with the magnanimity and greatness that you have shown over Cuba." It appears that Russell did play a role in defusing the Cuban missile crisis in October (Caroline Moorehead, *Bertrand Russell: A Life* [New York: Viking, 1992], 514–7).

6. Sophia Western, who at first screamed but then attended to Lord Fellamar without the need of force.

7. Woolf replied to Humphrey's irony on 14 November 1962: "I agree with you entirely about Bertie Russell and his absurd attitude toward Kennedy and Krushchev but his political judgment has been hopelessly bad for the last 70 years."

8. This play by Edward Albee (1928–) opened on Broadway on 13 October 1962.

9. Igor Fedorovich Stravinsky (1882–1971), Russian-born composer, was particularly renowned for his ballet scores. *Pulcinella* is an orchestral suite (originally a ballet) that was first produced in 1920. To the Weisses on 12 November 1962, WH wrote, "Ballet music presented as concert music has never been my favorite way to shoot an evening."

10. WH must have in mind especially *The Waste Land* (1922).

11. Giovanni Battista Pergolesi (1710–36) was an Italian composer whose *La serva padrona* was one of the most celebrated stage works of the eighteenth century.

12. Nathan Milstein (1904–92), born in the Ukraine, was one of the leading violinists of the twentieth century, famous for his interpretations of Bach sonatas.

13. Two sonatas for violin and piano by Beethoven.

14. Johann Sebastian Bach (1685–1750). A "partite" is a baroque term for "suite."

15. Sviatoslov Richter (1915–97), a Ukranian-born pianist, was one of the greatest musicians of the Soviet era.

16. Begun in 1947, the annual Edinburgh International Festival is a venue for classical music, theater, opera, dance, and poetry.

17. Georgio Bassani (1916–2000) published his second novel in 1962: *The Garden of the Finzi-Continis.*

18. An Italian publishing house.

19. Giuseppe Tonasi di Lampedusa, Duke of Palma and Prince of Lampedusa, is the author of *The Leopard,* a novel about his family at the time of the Italian unification movement in the nineteenth century. Bassani's recommendation that Lampedusa's novel be published by Feltrinelli in 1958 was his supreme editorial achievement.

20. So many beautiful things.

TO ALFRED A. KNOPF

[In a letter of 14 November 1962, Knopf told WH that he was "a wonderful letter writer" and that if he did not "in the course of time give me the novels I want, I shall rush into print a volume of your letters."]

TLS/HR

Rome
November 16, 1962

Dear Alfred,

I am delighted to know that my letters give you pleasure. If it's true then you must take a large share of the credit yourself. A letter is always just as good as the person it's addressed to. There are some (not many) to whom it's fun to write.

Yes, we are indeed well and comfortably and happily and spaciously settled, and I am working hard. More importantly (for I always work hard, no matter how badly) I am working well. In fact I think I might permit myself a "very well." I do believe you will get the novels you want from me and not be reduced to publishing my letters, though obviously there's an unintended unhappy signification in your phrase "in time." Nevertheless, following my miscarriage of last spring, I'm once again in an interesting condition.[1] It's too early to send out announcements, but I am definitely beginning to show. I've spent today (it's now evening and I'm listening to Mozart's String Quartet in C Major, no. 19 and relishing my evening Martini) revising the 6 pages with which I've busied myself for the last couple of days, and I must say that though I shouldn't say it, they're pretty first rate. Well, I'm an odd one. Apparently (I hedge simply because I do not really understand myself at all) apparently [*sic*]. I have had to let enough time go by to be sure that everyone has forgotten me—which is to say, forgotten Home from the Hill (assuming that any body remembers it) because I really don't like the idea that strangers are going to read my writing. Obviously I don't dislike it enough to desist altogether from publishing, but I don't like it, and now that I can be sure I'm forgotten once again I'm able to write with greater freedom and greater ease, which is the way I always used to write. But, to paraphrase your friend Misha Elmman [*sic*],[2] enough about me—read any good books of mine lately?

Wonderful item in today's Messag[g]ero,[3] a scene out of Fellini, as a reporter calls it. A young man, badly scratched about the face, reported yesterday afternoon to a station house with this story: he's a door-to-door photographer. He rang a bell, and asked the young lady who came to the door if she had any babies she'd like photographed. Instantly he saw that she was not that kind of young lady and asked her price. "Twenty thousand lire," she said. "Give you five," said he. "O.K.," said she. And then, says the news item, that which had been contracted for was performed. When it came time to pay, though, he had only a 10 thousand lire bill. He handed her that, she thanked him, and proceeded to tuck it away. "Where's my change?" he demanded. "You said five thousand lire." "I haven't got change for a 10," she said, and from there it's easy to see how the young fellow got his face all scratched up.

Yours,
Bill

1. The novel WH was pregnant with is *The Ordways.*
2. Misha Elman (1891–1967), Russian violinist.
3. *Il Messaggero* is a Roman daily newspaper.

TO HARDING LEMAY[1]

TLS/HR

[Salita Sant' Onofrio, 23
Rome]
March 20 [1963]

Dear Pete,

I am delighted at the news of your promotion. Really delighted. Wish I was there to help you celebrate this in proper fashion. Well it's just a celebration postponed. We will indeed do so. I hope you will let this go to your head (there is no not in that sentence.) You deserve it, and you should enjoy it. Congratulations.

I'm very pleased to know that The Ballad of J. Neighbours has been sold. I thought it was pretty good and was disappointed when three or four magazines turned it down. About those montages[2] made of old newspaper clippings: they were cut out of a contemporary newspaper which an aunt of mine found in her attic in Texas. Only ones I had. They're in the copy I gave Alfred as a Xmas present year before last. Ask him to show it to you when he gets back. I think your idea might be very good, and if on second examination of them you too still think so, then show it to Esquire. Speaking of me, did Alfred tell you that I have just been awarded $2500 by the National Institute of Arts and Letters "in recognition of my work in creative literature." This by the way is not for you to make any publicity of as yet. They want it kept confidential until they make their press releases in May.[3]

I write this in a state of semi-exhaustion, for I have just come through the worst shock of my life. My novel[4] has been going extremely well. It is, I should judge, now about 3/4ths finished. 400 mss. pages, closely typed. About 115 thousand words. Some of them, if I do say it who shouldn't, pretty good words. Well, Friday the weather broke and we decided that after this housebound and very industrious winter we would take a little vacation. Three days in Florence. Packed a bag. Decided to take along the mss and read it aloud by night after sightseeing by day. Went to the station and bought 2 second class tickets to Florence on the 8:40 a.m. No seats in second class. Went into first class, prepared to pay the extra tariff. One seat only in first class. To save this one seat Dorothy put down the (new, expensive) briefcase containing the (despite all the warnings I have had) only copy of my novel (no title, no name, no identification) on the seat. I stood meanwhile in the corridor with the suitcase, while Dorothy searched for a second seat. None. "Damned if I'll pay first class to stand up for four hours. Let's get off. There's another train in forty minutes," said I. "Only hurry. This one is about to pull out." We hopped off—leaving the briefcase. Which we realized of course just 15 seconds later—by which time the train was out of sight. We spent the next six hours in the stationmaster's office. He phoned the first stop, Terontola, to tell the police to search the train. Return call: have found no briefcase. Called Florence. Nothing. Bologna, nothing. At three that afternoon we returned home. I sat down to the typewriter to begin rewriting the novel, not really knowing what else to do. It was either that, or throw myself in the Tiber—maybe not either/or. At six that evening the stationmaster[5] called to say my briefcase had been found in Milan. We went to Florence that night. The briefcase was returned to Rome and I went and picked it up just an hour ago. Everything's fine. Except I am still trembling all over, four days later. When my fingers steady down, tomorrow maybe, I shall begin copying, with 11 carbons.

Yours,
Bill

1. WH's editor at Alfred a Knopf, Lemay (1922–) had supervised the publicity department at the firm since 1958. In 1963 he was appointed assistant to the chairman of the board and to the president of the firm. He held this position until 1967, when he quite to write full time. He is the author of a number of plays performed on and off Broadway (*How He Became a Writer, The Little Birds Fly, Look at Any Man, Interior Landscape,* and others). In 1968 he became the head writer for the television soap opera *Another World.*

2. On 28 December 1961, WH had sent a homemade "edition" of "The Ballad of Jesse Neighbours" to Alfred Knopf as a Christmas gift. Its covers were montages of newspaper clippings about Bonnie and Clyde (e.g., one headline read, "Louisiana Town Put On Map for Day When Guns Bark Death to Killer Pair"). Lemay was thinking that these montages might be used as illustrations by *Esquire,* but when the story appeared in the magazine in September 1963 there were no illustrations. Later the story was included in *A Time and a Place* (1968).

3. See Sanka Knox, "Honors Bestowed by Arts Academy," *New York Times,* 23 May 1963, 37.

4. *The Ordways.*

5. Following the novel's dedication, there is an unusual note of appreciation for the Italian National Railways, especially for the stationmaster in Rome, Michaele Fortino.

TO ALFRED A. KNOPF

[In his 4 June 1963 letter on the partial manuscripts of the novels that became The Ordways *and* Proud Flesh, *Knopf began by remarking that "it is an enor-*

mous pleasure to read anyone who writes as well as you do. You are magnificent." Then he offered his reservations—which become clear as WH responds to them.]

TLS/HR

Telscombe,
Lewes, Sussex
June 13, 1963

Dear Alfred,

Well, I'm glad you found the reading of the mss. a pleasure, and thanks for the praise, but I must say I am puzzled and rather disconcerted by your statement, "considering the state they are in, I don't know that I can make a great deal of useful comment." I thought both of them well enough along to give a pretty good idea of what they will be when finished—three fourths of one[1] and half of the other one.[2] The longer novel especially. It needs expansion and elaboration but basically the form is there. Certainly the character is there, and the theme well indicated. At least, so I thought, and if you do not sense these things I can only suppose they have not come across. Which is rather disheartening.

I do think, as I believe I said in one of my notes, that as it now stands the story of Sam Ordway's adventures in search of his son fails to give the impression I want it ultimately to give. That at present it is imbalanced in the direction of humor and satire. This is actually just an accident, resulting from the order (or lack of any) in which the adventures have come to be written. Funny, in part, satirical, in part, I want this section to remain, but I also want the chase after Will Vinson[3] to heat up, and I want Sam Ordway to heat up too. He must, like every picaresque hero, find himself while searching for something else. This means in his case coming to a deeper appreciation of his loss and in doing this he is to undergo a phase of genuine vengefulness towards his enemy, before his final resignation, in a calm spirit. This last alteration of soul I hope to effect through a sense of the discovery of a place (I think of the profound effect of the cliff dwellings on Tom Outland in Cather's The Professor's House)[4] when the search brings him at last to the Big Bend Country on the Rio Grande.

You object to the length of the introductory section. Remember, that the part dealing with Sam's travels will be longer when finished, which will make the preceding section seem shorter. However, this brings up another matter. I do not think of the book as a picaresque. It contains a picaresque, but this is just a part of the larger design. Thus, what you regard as too long an introduction to the hero's adventures is really meant to be something other than that. I see this book as something slightly unusual: not a historical novel, but a novel *about* . . . (a genuine distinction) American history, and more particularly the westward migration. This I try to exemplify in 3 generations of one southern family, and in the ruminations of the narrator, who represents the 4th generation, remembering his cult of the southern and western myths as a boy growing up between the two. Seen in this light, the adventures of Sam Ordway in search of his son, though certainly the largest single episode is just that: an episode. The changing sense of the west is the underlying theme which gives the book its structure and whatever unity it's got.

I agree with Pete[5] in wanting an expressive title[6]—but where's it to come from? I welcome any suggestion.

As to your impatience to see the book finished, I can only say that I know better than anyone how long it's been. And I repeat what I have told you before: I am not lazy. Short on inspiration and hard to please but not lazy. So that however long it takes, that really is how long it took.

As for the other novel, The Renshaws,[7] there too I am rather dejected by your reaction. With it too I thought I had given a pretty fair indication of its final shape. It is a briefer fragment to be sure, but it is to be a briefer book. Your warning not to make the gang of brothers too brutal I shall keep in mind, while pointing out that that *is* the point about them.

I do deeply appreciate your having acted as agents for the sale of the short stories, and the success you have had in doing so. But I am not sure just how I am meant to take your postscript.[8] If by doing this you have jeopardized your relations with the literary agents I am very sorry. If it would regularize the matter I shall be glad to pay you an agent's fee.

Yours,
Bill

1. *The Ordways.*

2. *Proud Flesh.* On 3 June 1963 Knopf had written the following to Ian Parsons: "I don't know that we can exert any influence on that young man, but I say to you in confidence what I wouldn't say to him, that I think it rather scandalous that in five years that have elapsed since we published 'Home from the Hill,' he has only these partial manuscripts to show for his efforts."

3. The character in *The Ordways* who kidnaps Ned Ordway.

4. In Willa Cather's *The Professor's House* (1925), upon discovering beneath the overarching ledge of the Blue Mesa the "little city of stone," Tom Outland says, "Something had hap-

pened in me that made it possible for me to co-ordinate and simplify, and that process, going on in my mind, brought with it a great happiness" ([New York: Vintage, 1973], 250–51).

5. Harding Lemay.

6. Knopf had written to WH on 4 June 1963 that Pete Lemay thought the book should have a title that would "evoke that spread of generations," "the sense of time passing," and "the curious strength of kinship, which you define so effectively in the first section as the peculiar quality of the South."

7. One of the manuscript titles of *Proud Flesh*.

8. The final postscript of Knopf's letter of 4 June 1963 says, "I am enclosing a check to your order from *Esquire* for six hundred and fifty dollars. I hope when I have to appear before saint Peter and give you as one of my references, that you will give me credit then for the sale of these stories without commission. We mustn't let any agents know that we are scabs."

[A SIGNIFICANT YEAR IN VIRGINIA]

1963–64

[In September WH assumed the Visiting Glasgow Professorship at Washington and Lee University in Lexington, Virginia. There he finished The Ordways *and wrote important letters on the themes of his comic novel.]*

TO HARDING LEMAY

TLS/HR

Rose Hill
Lexington, Virginia
October 14, 1963

Dear Pete,

Those terms are acceptable, so I have torn up the two copies of the former agreement and will await the new one.[1]

Nothing to report. Have seen a little of the countryside around here: glorious! Even more beautiful than New York State, I now believe. Went last Sunday to the undiscovered ancient little town of Fincastle,[2] setting for the novels of Ellen Glasgow,[3] and this Sunday down to Appomat[t]ox, where we lost The War. And which reminds me, we came down here via Gettysburg, and that, plus Appomat[t]ox[,] makes me think someone ought to do an essay on the modern (mis)uses of American history. At Appomat[t]ox they have rebuilt the entire village, including the house in which Lee and Grant met to sign surrender terms, not one brick of it is authentic. Some Yankee bought the house in 1893 and dismantled it to take it to the Chicago World's Fair, he didn't, the dismantled house lay there a prey to weather and souvenir hunters for the next 75 years. Now the guide smilingly tells visitors, "That's not the actual chair Grant sat in, but other wise the room is as it was." One feels like saying, "Why, this is better than the More Expensive Spread."

Yrs.
Bill

1. Contract for the publication of *The Ordways;* WH returned the final agreement to Lemay on 30 October 1963.

2. Village twenty-five miles north of Roanoke, Virginia.

3. Ellen Glasgow (1873–1945), the first modern novelist of the South.

TO LEONARD WOOLF

TLS/US

Rose Hill
Lexington, Virginia
November 21, 1963

Dear Leonard,

I can't tell you how pleased I was at your praise of that story.[1] I am proud that you liked it. I am sending you today a copy of Esquire containing another one.[2] And shortly I shall be sending you another copy of Esquire containing still another,[3] both of which have recently appeared.

I certainly ought to have written you sooner and am ashamed of myself for not having done so. But I have signed a contract with Knopf for the novel,[4] with a deadline of the next April 15. There remains a great deal to be done on the book and I have been working eight hours a day ever since we arrived here, what with this and the lectures I must do for the college, and then just collapsing in the evenings. I am desperate to finish the novel; I just can't live with it much longer. I am quite content with the work I have done [on] it since coming here. No doubt I shall be sending it to Chatto[5] fairly soon.

This place and these people would fascinate you (which, of course, is not to say, would please you). Especially on a Saturday when the country people come to town. They are a race apart (my race) as distinct from the rest as the contandini[6] are in Italy. This town calls itself the Shrine of the South. Here are buried the two great confederate heroes: Robert E. Lee and "Stonewall" Jackson. Lee, after the war, was president of what was then called Washington college (now Washington and Lee) and is buried in Lee Chapel.[7] There is in the town the Robert E. Lee Episcopal (Anglican) Church—the only one in the world not named after some saint or other, which will do more than most anything else I can think of to suggest to an Englishman who comes first in the minds of Southern Episcopalians. The house where Lee lived is still the home of the president of the college. In the wall of what is now the garage there is a stone plaque, placed there by the Daughters of the Confederacy,[8] which informs the pilgrim that herein Traveller, Gen'l Lee's trusted horse, spent his postwar years. Traveller's bones, mounted in a glass case, are in the museum in the basement of the Lee Chapel. That War, which ended nominally on April 9, 1865, is still being very keenly fought down here, as you will learn in more detail when you read this novel of mine, which is not about the Civil War, but about all the talk about the Civil War.

I've now given two of my four required lectures.[9] One on the influence of the frontier wilderness on American fiction (more superficially on how the frontier wilderness has made ours a bachelor literature in which are to be found no heroines); the second on the continuing opposition between oral literature and printed literature and how in the works of a few novelists (Hardy, Scott, E. Bronte, W. Faulkner)[10] the oral tradition, specifically the tradition of folk ballads, colors and influences their characters and their manner of narration. Now I must give two more and what they are to be haven't the faintest notion. Now I'm toying with the idea of a lecture on the historical novel—what it is, why there are so many of them, why most of them are bad, and Tolstoy the great exception and why.[11] Has anyone to your knowledge written anything good, a book or an essay, on the historical novel? And by the way, what is a historical novel? What is a historical period? A novel nowadays dealing with World War II is surely dealing with a historical period, yet would not be a historical novel? Is it historical when there is no longer anybody alive who lived through it? My own feeling, being a Southerner, which is to say a natural born Shinto,[12] is that if it could have happened to your grandfather, it could have happened to you—indeed that it *did* happen to you.

Well, I see I am getting down to the end of the page without having said anything. We miss you terribly. Wish we could have seen the oriental potentates in all their inscrutable splendor when they came to the Village Hall ceremonies.[13]

Yours Always
Bill

1. On 13 November 1963 Woolf had written that he was taken with "A Voice from the Woods" and thought it a "perfectly controlled" story with many dimensions.

2. "The Ballad of Jesse Neighbours," which appeared in the September 1963 issue of *Esquire* magazine.

3. "The Pump," published in *Esquire* in December 1963.

4. *The Ordways*.

5. Chatto & Windus, WH's English publisher.

6. Country people.

7. Robert E. Lee (1807–70), general of the Army of Northern Virginia during the Civil War, is buried in the Chapel of Washington and Lee University. Above his tomb is a recumbent white marble statue by Edward Valentine. Lt. Gen. Thomas J. Jackson (1824–63), Lee's most trusted subordinate, is buried in the "Stonewall" Jackson Memorial Cemetery at Virginia Military Institute; a statue of Jackson on a pedestal, sculpted by Valentine, rises above his grave.

8. The United Daughters of the Confederacy, organized in 1894, helped to shape the South's memory of the Civil War.

9. "Ah, Wilderness!" was given on 3 October 1963 and "Novelists and Storytellers" on 14 November 1963.

10. British novelists Hardy, Sir Walter Scott (1771–1832), Emily Brontë (1818–48), and American novelist Faulkner.

11. WH's third lecture, titled "Carthage and Moscow," was delivered on 11 December 1963. Leo Tolstoy (1828–1910) was WH's example of an author who overcame the pitfalls of the historical novel in *War and Peace* (1865–72), an epic of Napoleon's invasion of Russia.

12. The indigenous religion of Japan; WH alludes to the practice of ancestor worship.

13. Woolf had written to WH of a fair to raise money for the Village Hall, which included the high commissioner of Ceylon and his wife in a Sinhalese dress (letter of 13 November 1963).

TO HARDING LEMAY

[After WH had submitted to Knopf all but the final section of The Ordways, *President John F. Kennedy was assassinated on 22 November 1963 in Dallas, Texas, an event that made the author uneasy about his satire on the Texas tradition of lawlessness. WH was immediately on the telephone to Pete Lemay, his editor at Knopf. Jack Ruby shot and killed Lee Harvey Oswald, the accused assassin of President Kennedy, on 24 November. This incident was a further troubling example of "Texas justice."]*

TLS/HR Lexington, Virginia
December 3, 1963

Dear Pete,

It was very good of you to take time, especially over your holiday, to reread that long and fragmentary section of the book, and I am grateful for the comforting things you say in your letter.[1] I hope you are right. I still can't help worrying about it on the two scores I mentioned over the phone: that nothing about Texas justice is now a fit subject for wit, and that a satire on the common Texas expectation that a man revenge his own wrongs outside the law is, after the events of last week, a sort of gallows humor and hardly in decent taste. I can't help feeling that these observations of mine might have seemed illuminating were the book already in print, but that now it is going to look as if they've been made—and made in altogether too jocular a tone—*as a result of* last week's happenings. Satirizing Texas now seems a bit unseemly.

Well, I have had to put the book aside, in any case, in order to write my next lecture for Washington & Lee, to be delivered Dec. 11. I am trying to say something about that deservedly despised genre, the historical novel, using as examples Tolstoy and Flaubert, the Flaubert of Salambo [*sic*].[2] It's not going to be a very good lecture, I'm afraid, as I seem to be in command of only about half of my mind.

Many thanks for reading Pember's book. I am sorry, but not the least surprised, at your decision. He himself will be neither sorry nor surprised. I'll tell you more about him someday—a man with a very tragic story and an interesting man.[3] His brother is married to Harry Ford's wife's sister.[4]

The Penns[5] would be extraordinary even if they were not in showbiz, wouldn't they? Especially Peggy, who keeps right on improving with further acquaintance. (I don't mean to suggest that Arthur doesn't—just that Peggy was the one who kept on astonishing and delighting me.) We have neither seen nor heard from them in 3 years.

I must get back to Tolstoy. Again many thanks.

Yours,
Bill

1. Lemay assured WH that the novel "is an illuminating examination [. . .] of certain attitudes about life, law, and revenge which reveals more about what happened in Dallas last week than anything I have read or probably ever will read" (29 November 1963).

2. *Salammbo* (1862), by Flaubert, failed to resurrect ancient Carthage and Punic civilization, according to WH's lecture.

3. WH tried to persuade Knopf to consider an American edition of Timothy Pember's novel *Not Me, Sir* (1941); Lemay had written on 29 November 1963 that "there have been too many novels and plays about English boys learning life through their public school experiences to give this book much chance [. . .]." Pember lived in Rodmell, near Leonard Woolf and Ian Parsons in Sussex.

4. Harry Ford was married to Kathleen Carey Ford, a psychotherapist.

5. Arthur Penn was the director of several significant films, among them *Bonnie and Clyde* (1967), *Alice's Restaurant* (1969), and *Little Big Man* (1977). His wife Peggy is a noted family therapist and was director of the Ackerman Institute for the Family from 1985 to 1993.

TO HARDING LEMAY

[WH responds to his American editor's response to the completed manuscript of The Ordways, *which the author had posted to Knopf on 2 February 1965.]*

TLS/HR

Rose Hill
Lexington, Va.
March 27, 1964

Dear Pete,

First of all I want to say that your response to the book is most gratifying. I can't myself say that the book is every bit as good as I hoped it would be, but it certainly makes me feel good that *you* can.

I no longer have a copy of the manuscript, and so I can't look into the smaller textual criticisms you offer. Those will have to wait. Instead, I'll go at once to your larger criticisms, pertaining to Part III. These, I think, have to do with the way to see the entire book. I think that perhaps your weariness (which I share) with novels which have for their theme the lack of connections between people may have inclined you to over-welcome, and thus to overemphasize my treatment of the opposite theme. That sense of family feeling which you discern is certainly something I sought to capture in this book, and is one of my major themes, but as it is only one, I wouldn't want to see so much importance attached to it that the others went unnoticed. For although the book is about a family, that family is, or is meant to be, symbolic. Perhaps by explaining what I mean I shall also meet some of your objections to those sections in Part III where the book seems to wander away from this one thread.

This is not a historical novel; but it is a novel *about* history: a valid distinction, I think. When I say about history, I mean of course American history, and I mean more particularly the most important episode in American history, the westward migration, especially that ultimate phase of it, following the Civil War. In the trek of the Ordway clan precisely to Clarksville and no farther, the spot which I speak of as poised on the frontier where two myths met (that of the South and that of the West) and then, in the following generation in the person of the narrator (nourished on western films) I am trying to say something which, while it includes the personal story of Thomas and Ella Ordway, and later on the personal quest of Samuel Ordway in search of his stolen child, is meant to exceed their personal stories and stand for something more. I have wanted to give it a sense of place, and of the importance of place in the formation of one's character, one's code of conduct; thus place is almost a personality in this book. From the start I have conceived the book as one too various, deliberately too loose and open-ended to be exclusively concerned with one theme. I want it to have some of the characteristics of many kinds of books: to be part psychological novel, part picaresque; part family album, part political and social satire, part guide book, travel essay, history, journal of exploration. I felt I had to regard Texas as one of these literary countries not yet heard from, and to take the reader on a journey of discovery to a strange land. For this reason the book had, while keeping always in mind the personal story of its protagonist, to be something of a catalogue of the world through which he is shown to be passing, must reveal something of Texas politics, penology, justice, amusements, etc. To a lesser extent this is true of all picaresques: that the author is as concerned to show a place and a society as to show a character. When such a hero is sent forth into the world on his quest, he finds that much of the world is not interested in him and his quest. The adventures which he is shown to encounter cannot all be made to relate to or reflect upon his personal problem, else the book seems contrived and the experience of life is reflected unfaithfully, for the task of the novelist is always to chart a course between order and variety—the order demanded by art and the variety which is true of the life from which his story is drawn. What is more, too careful a selection of adventures tending always to relate to the hero's personal quest, and the picaresque loses that sense of spaciousness and unexpectedness and freedom which is the peculiar virtue of picaresque. I wanted to make it a portrait of a place as much as a man. To be that, it cannot be so tightly constructed as you would like to see it. Indeed, it is the discovery of a place—Spanish south Texas—which is Sam Ordway's ultimate discovery; there he finds his love for his son, his reconciliation to his loss, a kind of wisdom, even a cure at last for his inherited wound as a son of the Civil War (our family war, if you like). Further, (I am thinking now of your objections to such things as the circus adventure, the arrest and trial, the prairie dog town) you must keep in mind that Sam Ordway's adventures in the west are reaching you through much time, and through the selection of two, if not indeed four, memories. There is the Sam Ordway to whom it happened, and there is the Sam Ordway who thirty-five years later is remembering it and editing it as he tells it to his grandson for entertainment. Then there is that grandson remembering what his grandfather told him as a child, and editing it now as he sets it down on paper thirty years later. Sam Ordway is finding another son (this grandson) as he remembers and relates to him his adventures in search of Little Ned, and this sense is achieved in part by the manner of his telling, and his choice of episodes to relate.[1] It tells us something, something rather pleasant, about the man Sam Ordway that he could have sat all afternoon watching the play of a colony of prairie dogs when he ought (or ought according to romantic fiction and TV and movies)[2] to have been grimly pursuing the man [who] wronged him. It tells us something of the desolation of that country that prairie dogs have a "town" there where the only towns are ghost towns with a shameful and bloody history and a presentday [*sic*] uselessness. And it tells us something about the man that among the many no doubt more significant things which happened to him out there he should remember this comparatively trifling episode, and that he should think this is the sort of thing his grandson would be interested to hear. The same may be said for the circus adventure. I think you overstate the matter when you say, "the reader loses sight very often of the fact that Sam Ordway is looking for his son, and the many adventures you've given him have absolutely nothing to do with it." They do, and on the most simple level of meaning. The circus episode for instance begins with a ruse, a scheme to entice Will to him by using as bait an elephant; that this should backfire on him is proper, that he should find himself pushing that 7 1/2 ton elephant. And that in recounting it to his grandson he should touch up the story a bit and round it off to a humorous finale, that too is indicative of the character of the man. Feeling his debt to society to shoot the man who wronged him, he practices the act, which goes so against his disposition, and is taken to jail for doing so. He is encouraged to proceed in his lawlessness by a jury sworn to uphold the law. These things are not as unrelated to his quest as you say. (I will confess that the trial scene is, to my mind, the weakest thing in the entire book. But I must also confess that I just don't know what more to do with it. I have worked on it endlessly, pruned and cut it, and this seems to be about the best I can do with it.) Finally, I would justify all these seemingly irrelevant episodes on yet another ground: humor (where it works) is its own excuse for being, and in a picaresque, such as Part III is, not only does it not have to be so rigorously controlled as other kinds of novels, it mustn't be, for humor is a holiday from appositeness. In sum, I think you take the *motive* for Sam Ordway's search too seriously; he must have a motive, must have the very motive he does have; but he must remember other things as well as he goes on his way, and he must discover other things as he looks back on it all in the seasoned wisdom of his years, when as a matter of fact, the original reason for the quest is dimmed by time and no longer even painful to him. I have said as much as this in the opening pages of Part III, and

I have set the tone there too, that one is here to encounter adventures seen in the light of ironical detachment and with a satirical slant, a sort of burlesque of vengeance-pattern westerns.

Well, let me know whether you find any of these arguments persuasive.

. . . .

We have pretty well determined to spend the summer in England, back in the same village,[3] the Squire of which has offered us another cottage rent-free. I must give the annual lecture in literature at Bard College on May 19. If we can find passage, I suppose we will sail shortly after that. I suppose we'll stay 3 or 4 months. We cannot keep this house (though we may possibly return to it in the fall) and we've no place else to go, and we've just received an urgent plea that we come from our friend there, Leonard Woolf, a plea hard to resist on account of his age. So, naturally I am eager to settle as many matters pertaining to the book while here as possible. I assume that I can assume that it has been accepted? I'd be grateful to know as soon as possible your intentions as to promotion and publication date. I want it to appear in the calendar year, 1964.[4] I need to know all I can, so as to try to make my own plans. I have not got very much money left now, and if I'm not to have to return to teaching for a living, then this book is going to have to re-stake me to go on writing. As I don't see any hope of a movie sale in it, it must do this on book sales.

Again, many thanks for your close and hospitable reading. Let me hear from you soon.[5]

Yours,
Bill

1. Following this sentence, WH made a handwritten insertion in the margin of his typed letter: "In this connection note that he is called always 'my grandfather.' This is his remembered quest, told long after the event."

2. At this point, WH handwrote in the margin the following: "This travesty on the 'Western' is, as you'll have noticed, something running through the entire section—and is noted in the title 'Sam Ordway's Revenge.'"

3. Telscombe.

4. The publication date was put off until 1 February 1965 for promotional reasons.

5. This last paragraph was added by hand.

TO IAN PARSONS

[On 3 April 1964 Parsons wrote to WH, suggesting that part 1 of The Ordways *"needs cutting quite a bit": "As it stands it's not only [. . .] too long to be in scale*

with the rest of the story, but too slow moving to engage the reader's interest as it should. [. . .] [Y]ou've got to confine the background firmly to essential information so that the reader gets to the opening of the essential action a good deal sooner than he does at present." WH was preoccupied with the sad discovery that Ben Hass had just published a novel with the very title WH had meant to use for the book he eventually resorted to calling The Ordways—Look Away, Look Away!*]*

TLS/UR

[Rose Hill]
Lexington, Va.
April 10, 1964

Dear Ian,
What a blow this is about the title! More than you can realize, because the song it's from[1] isn't charged for you with the rich connotations it is for me. It said just everything I wanted. But apart from my fondness for that title is the fact that it took me three years to find it, and in the search I never found anything else at all. To have to go now back again over that barren ground is really almost more than I can contemplate. I feel licked before I start and have no heart for it. What an incredible coincidence! What unlucky timing!

I don't agree with you about Part I needing cutting but I'm too downhearted to go into my reasons. (Neither does Pete Lemay agree. He would like to see Part III cut. I'm being stubborn about that, too.)

I'll write more when I feel more like it.

Yours,
Bill

1. The song is "Dixie," written in 1859 by Daniel Decatur Emmett.

TO IAN PARSONS

[WH defends The Ordways *somewhat differently to his English publisher, who, in a letter of 3 April 1964, was concerned that part 1 of the novel was "too slow moving": "Obviously you've got to provide a background for the story, and the graveyard working day setting is ideal for the purpose; but I think you've got to confine the background firmly to essential information so that the reader gets to the opening of the essential action a good deal sooner than he does at present."]*

TLS/UR

Rose Hill
Lexington, Va.
April 17, 1964

Dear Ian,

Here (after re-reading it to myself a number of times, and aloud to various literary friends) are my reasons for continuing to think the opening of the book is right as it stands.

It is indeed, as you say, slow moving, but I cannot see that it fails to engage the reader's interest. It establishes a place, a family, the rites and traditions of that place and that family, and begins to differentiate the characters in that family who are to play important roles in the subsequent stories. It establishes an attitude towards the past, and it introduces the two main legends in that family which are to form the substance of the book. I don't see how it could be done with much more succinctness without loss of density and without the adoption of a tone more solemn, because more direct, than I want the book itself to have. But now I come to your more serious objection, and my more serious defence. You say, "You've got to confine the background to essential information so that the reader gets to the opening of the essential action a good deal sooner than he does at present." What is the essential action? As I see it, the essential action begins with the first words of the book. The essential action is Joseph Ordway's (the narrator's)[1] exercise of his memory of his birthplace and the legends in this family which explained why that was his birthplace, and not farther west. I take it that you believe the essential action to begin with the story of Thomas and Ella Ordway's flight from Tennessee. Not for me. To me the most important character in the book is Joseph Ordway, his most important action the recovery of his memories.

This is a novel about the two (related) central experiences of American history: the Civil War and the Westward expansion, and about a place, Clarksville, Texas, a real place and with that very name on the maps (and my birthplace) as well a symbolic place: the frontier where those two experiences of American history met. To Clarksville and no farther, within sight of the new life he sought to find but still within the margin of the shadow of the old life which his courage failed him to quit, could Thomas Ordway bring himself to venture, a man fleeing the South but taking with him the bones of his dead and the weight of his ancestral devotion, and falling victim to the very myth which had betrayed him because, having given his all to it, he had nothing left to cling to. In that statue which itself rises unscathed into the sunlight, and in the twisted shadow i[t] casts on the paving stones of the town square, and by which the narrator as a child on his way to school tells the time, I see an image of the South's own ambiguous attitude towards the war. From this strategic spot Thomas's son Samuel goes farther west in quest of the son who had been stolen from him. Sam as an old man passes on to his grandson the story of Thomas his father, and of his own adventures in the west. In that grandson, born there, heir to these rites and traditions and attitudes, and to these family legends, who lives in the time when the myth of the West has been romanticized in the movies, I am trying to say something about American history which makes of the book something more than the story of Thomas or Ella or Sam or Ned Ordway, and which justifies, indeed demands many episodes, many descriptive and reflective passages which do not contribute directly to their individual stories, but do contribute a great deal to Joseph Ordway's memories and his character, and thus to other equally significant areas of meaning which I hope the book to have. And so these memories of a place and of a clan must be leisurely in pace, must be rich in detail and circumstantiality, must give the sense of being recalled from childhood, the sense of the passage of time. Must give too the sense of having passed through more memories than just one. For remember all this comes to the reader through the memories not only of the narrator, but of Sam Ordway as well. He, Sam, is remembering and passing on the story of his mother and father and how they brought the family to this spot. He is remembering long after the event his search in the West. And Joseph is remembering as a grown man and setting down on paper these stories which he heard as a child. So, as I say, the story for me is not merely the action, in the strict sense, it is the memory. Not merely the narrative, but the place. Not merely the event, but the lingering effect of the event on subsequent generations. Indeed, I am trying in this book to create character in a way in which character is not often created; to show how very much we are the children of historical event and of place, even when these events and these places are remote from us in time and space as we grow up and leave them. To do that space is needed.

But just look how solemn and portentous that all sounds when said that way! How to do it and not have it seem abstract, thematic, portentous and dull? Through humor. Through a tone of irony playing over the surface of it all. And that takes time. Takes the leisurely pace. For while brevity may be the soul of wit, wit is not humor, and the soul of humor is leisureliness.

The assembling of the living and the dead members of the Ordway clan on graveyard working day touches upon another of the central themes of the book, namely that clan spirit which (like that of the Jews in the Exodus—a parallel I frequently draw) held Southerners together after the Civil War on the frontier of the West. That same clan spirit which so shapes the Southerner's character that he retains it forever after, as both a joy and a burden, requiring of him both reverence and irony. So again, all this is not mere background; in its very profuseness it is illustrating a point, elaborating a theme.

It also establishes a tone, and this too is calculated. The establishment of this easy-going and flexible tone in the early pages of the book is what enables me later to go from sentiment to satire, from pathos to farce, without a jarring sense of dischord [*sic*]. And this was from the start one of the biggest problems I had to contend with in this book, a problem solved only by the writing of the opening section.

Whether these are good arguments or not is one thing, but they are not arguments after the fact. I have not just built them up after receiving your criticism. They were the ideas on which I based my strategy as soon as I began to recast the book in Rome two years ago.

Yours,
Bill

P.S. We are now thinking of calling the book But Not Forgotten.[2] What do you think of this?

1. In his original version of the novel, Joseph was the narrator's name; in the revised version, it is Tom. WH has here forgotten that he had made this change.

2. On 1 May Parsons wrote to Harding Lemay, "None of us, alas, feels anything but lukewarm (at the best) about BUT NOT FORGOTTEN. To us, and I think to all British readers, it immediately calls up memories of the old tombstone cliché, 'Not lost, but gone before,' with a slight overtone of a 19th century musical hall song."

TO THEODORE AND RENÉE WEIS

[Following his stint at Washington and Lee, WH was to give the annual John Bard "literature" lecture at Bard College.]

TLS/PU

[Rose Hill]
Lexington, Va.
April 24, 1964

Dear Ted and Renee,

Yes, I had forgotten that ritual pre-lecture dinner for J. Bard speakers. Well, there's nothing to be done about it. I'm afraid though that I'll be a great flop at it (perhaps at the lecture too) because I found down here, where my respect for, and consequent fear of my audience falls much short of what I'll be feeling at Bard, that each and every time was terrible. I get very nervous beginning a couple of hours beforehand, restless, I can't eat a bite, am not much good at chatting. It's afterwards that I want a drink (a?) and a bite to eat. There doesn't seem to be anything I can do to control these feelings, and experience hasn't seemed to diminish them.

After much searching through the mss itself of my novel, and rereading Shakespeare and the Bible, and fending off suggestions from Knopfs, we seem more or less reconciled to this for a title: But Not Forgotten. They like it, Dorothy dislikes it, I find it livewithable, and what's more important, I can't find anything else. The trouble with your suggestion, that I look for something plain and simple, is that such titles have all been taken. I'd of course really like to call it The Works of William Shakespeare, but some dog has already used that one. Incidentally, happy Shakespeare's birthday!

Yours,
Bill

TO RUST HILLS

[A section of The Ordways, *under the title "The Monument and the Shadow," was published in the* Saturday Evening Post[1] *on 7 November 1965, 33–62; this excerpt chronicles the Ordway family's "long and desperate journey West in the aftermath of the Civil War" (33) and includes some of the introductory section. The letter represents a stage in the author's negotiation with the magazine's fiction editor.]*

TLS/HR

Rose Hill
Lexington, Virginia
May 2, 1964

Dear Mr. Hills,

I was pleased to hear from you, although I cannot say I was very pleased at what you had to tell me. I have worked so long, so hard, so painstakingly on that section of my book in which you are interested (as on the entire book) that it is now all but impossible for me to think of it in any other way, any other words. It is so fixed in my mind that I could probably recite it.

As I understand it, the crux of you[r] proposals is contained in three statements. First, you caution me to remember that a person reading a section from a novel in a magazine is suspicious that he has missed something. Well, so he has, and I don't see how you can hope entirely to allay that suspicion. The passage that you have chosen from my book is about as self-contained as an excerpt from a novel can be, I should think; but it is still an excerpt, and the need you feel for what you call a frame is evidence that it is not as self-contained as you would like it to be. You are not going to be able to convince any reader that something hasn't been left out, and I can't help you do it. Secondly, you say, "As it is in the novel, the whole (i.e. the tale of Thomas and Ella Ordway's trek from Tennessee to Texas) is framed by reminiscences growing out of graveyard working day. This works very well in the novel, but I feel it might take too much space to explain and use in this already long novel section." Well, it is very long, but it's as short as I can make it, and to my mind it's essential to the story. It is not merely a frame, it dictates the very tone of the story of that trek. What you are asking me to do is abstract the information contained in what goes before the story of the trek and present it in yet more succinct form. I don't know how to subtract the mere information from the manner in which it is now unfolded. This is as succinct as I can make it, after five years of work. This book, as you say somewhere else in your letter, is all highly intricate—which makes it all the harder to pick out and separate the warp from the woof. Your third indication of what you would like me to do (and this one particularly worries me) is contained in this statement, ". . . whenever a part of the story doesn't seem to fit, just cut, as the section is already a bit too long for us (let me use as an example page 61 where you say, [']my grandfather could recall his sister telling how . . . ['] This is awfully difficult stuff, and if you find that you can simplify and just concentrate on the narrative, moving in close always when there is a choice, and not moving back in distance or in focus or in time, you'll find that things will concentrate on the narrative line nicely. It is the narrative line that we at the Post are especially interested in.)" Well, as must be evident to you from having read the entire book, the narrative line is not what I am especially interested in, and I have no wish to concentrate on it. My method in this book (and not only in this book, but in most everything I have written) is indirect, oblique. I cannot proceed but by interposing between the reader and the plot line a shaping intelligence and an ever-shifting historical perspective, and here, where the tale is presented as a family legend, often told, remembered long afterwards, reaching down through the many memories that have known it, important in shaping the mentality of the later generation represented by my narrator, and this method, if I may say so, is particularly successful. The story of Thomas and Ella Ordway's odyssey is not interesting only in and for itself; it has reverberations far beyond its mere outline. This legendary quality gives it its tone, colors and dictates every word of it, accounts for the many points of view (I am indeed aware how many of these there are: I calculated it. This shifting of stances, of points of view, the reflections and comments along the way of the grandfather and the narrator, are integral; they give this old fable the meaning it has for later times; these are the over (and under) tones which enrich the book and make it something more than a mere story. To go through paring these things away in order to bare the narrative—no, that I cannot do. What would be left would be only an adventure story—possibly a pretty good adventure story, but not my novel. You express the hope that I will want to adapt this piece for the sake of reaching your 23 million readers. My feeling is, the larger the audience the greater the necessity to be, for good or bad, oneself.

Until I hear from you again I shall go on trying to think of some way to do what you want without doing anything which I myself would not want. Meanwhile will you please give some consideration[2] to this suggestion of mine: that you take yet another 20 pages of the book, namely the 15 pages immediately preceding the section in which you are interested, beginning, "Although it was 35 years since any Ordway was buried there, our plot was the most populous in Mabry graveyard, containing as it did every Ordway who ever died in the New World, most of whom never in their lives set eyes on Texas." (Pretty good opening, that strikes me.) And from there going into the rites of graveyard cleaning day, settling down finally (though only momentarily—until interrupted by the essay on Southern character—which, if you wish to save space, you might consider cutting out, though this would be a loss) on old Thomas Ordway, presenting him, first, as he was in his later years, the man with every reason to repudiate the cause which had betrayed him but clinging to it (cutting out possibly the interpolated story of the commissioning and erection of the Confederate monument, though this too would be a loss). (I go into such detail here to remind you of it, as you say you no longer have a copy of the complete mss—neither, incidentally, do I.) Then as for rounding off the story of what finally happened to Thomas, include at the end 5 pages which you have not included in your present excerpt, telling how he went west of Clarksville, only to turn back in fright at the strangeness of the new life he was seeking, and ending up once again in the graveyard, with a final paragraph, beginning, "And there we were still, we Ordways, above ground and below, where that old blind and crippled Moses of our tribe had brought us, and once a year, on graveyard working day, that son whom he never saw but knew only by touch, now grown old, would, like a Jewish patriarch at the Passover *seder,* answering the questions of the youngest male child, recount the story of how we came to be there." This would certainly preserve the integrity of the story and retain its curious, but meaningful, point of view. It would establish the background, provide the essential exposition, it would establish the time perspective and would posit my central intelligence (to use a term of the kind of which I am not fond) namely my narrator, the inheritor of all the legend, whose felt presence in the texture of the story of his ancestors is responsible for so much of the meaning which resides in the piece beyond that of mere plot. I don't much expect you to like this suggestion, as you have said that the passage is already too long for you; but please give it a bit of thought.

Sincerely yours,
William Humphrey

P.S.
I am leaving this address on May 15, going to England for the summer. Please keep this date in mind in replying. I shall be in New York City from May 22 to 29, and could of course see you then if you would like. Finally, my telephone here is unlisted, and if you should want to call me, you wouldn't be able to, so here is my number, if you should need it. HObart 3–4256, Lexington.

1. The *Saturday Evening Post,* a general interest magazine founded in 1821, published the fiction of many significant American writers. Though in 1965 it had twenty three million readers, it ceased publication four years later.

2. Hills did not follow WH's suggestion.

[SUSSEX AND ALASSIO]

1964–65

[WH left Lexington, Virginia, at the end of the spring semester, stopped off at Bard College to give the annual "literature" lecture, and then set sail for England. He and Dorothy went immediately to Telscombe in response to Leonard Woolf's plea: "Without you here the summer dies out of the year for me. I cannot get through it if you do not come" (WH to Weisses, 22 March 1964). At the end of the summer, the Humphreys went directly to Alassio, an Italian town between Capo Crose and Capo Mele on the western Riviera, where they remained until the middle of March 1965. After a week in Rome and two weeks in Sicily, they returned to the United States on 20 April.]

TO ALFRED A. KNOPF

TLS/HR

Oak Cottage
Telscombe
Lewes, Sussex
July 15, 1964

Dear Alfred,

There is a spreading postal workers' strike here, and whether you will ever receive this seems doubtful. Perhaps I ought, instead of putting it into the pillar box, to put it in a bottle.

We had planned, as you know, to return to Lexington in the fall. A house was ready and waiting for us there. Well, now we hear from the owner (last words before postal strike) that we cannot have the house, after all. This leaves us with no place to go, as we had counted entirely on that arrangement and made no alternative plans. So now we are thinking of staying on in Europe for another year. We are enlisting various friends in the search for a house either somewhere in Southern France, or Italy, or a combination of the two, for the winter and spring.

I'm hard at work on the new novel,[1] which is going very well. It's now about 35,000 words. When finished it will be no more than about 65,000, so there is every chance that it won't be too much longer in the doing.

Here is something that I am sure will interest you. In a recent issue of the Sunday Times, one of the many Pope-Hennesseys takes it upon himself in a long and prominent article to suggest a suitable gift from the nation to the Duke of Windsor on his 70th birthday. The gift? That they invite him home, and that his Lady the Duchess be at last presented to her Niece. This is the paragraph which will be of especial interest to you: "Anglo-American relations in the later 1930's could not have been worse, so that the nationality of the Duchess was another thing against her in the eyes of certain people in this country. All this has now radically changed. An American member of the Royal Family would surely be popular in this country and would give untold pleasure to our allies in the United States. In President Roosevelt, Prince Michael (George Charles Franklin) ((author's italics)) of Kent had an American Godfather. Is it not more than high time that the Queen recognized and received her American aunt?"[2] I know that you will welcome this suggestion, Alfred, as I do. I have suffered, in the Duchess, a sense of snub for a great many years, and though you have been brave, and not said anything, I could see that it was painful for you, as well.

Yours,
Bill

1. *Proud Flesh.*

2. "James Pope-Hennessy Suggests a 70th Birthday Present for the Duke of Windsor," *Sunday Times,* 21 June 19664, 29. In 1936 Edward VIII abdicated and went into exile in order to marry Wallis Simpson, a soon-to-be-twice-divorced American.

TO THEODORE AND RENÉE WEISS

[After WH's initial complaints about the dust jacket of The Ordways, *he responds to Theodore Weiss's letter of 24 October 1964 in which Weiss had commented on "the uproarious hullabaloo about (hullabellow?) Bellow's* Herzog." *According to* Time, *writes Weiss, it is "the last word [. . .] in the novel. Renée has read it; I with much struggle am slowly making my way through it. Despite the assurance of Rahv and Co, for us at least this is definitely not it. It*

is certainly jamful of extraordinary things [. . .]. But the general sprawl and mess it is, the extraordinary self-indulgence and self-love it oozes from every chicken-fatted pore, is much too much for us." He declares the novel an example of "art as self-therapy or dirtying your linen in public." Weiss refers to the critic Philip Rahv and his associates William Phillips and Richard Poirier on the Partisan Review. *The rumors of exalted praise for Bellow's novel from this quarter proved unfounded, for* Herzog *was not reviewed in the* Partisan Review *until its spring 1965 issue, and in his review Poirier agrees essentially with Weiss's judgment about the novel.]*

TLS/PU

Villa Felice,
Via Solva, 38
Alassio, Italy
October 30, 1964

Dear Ted and Renee,

I should have written you on Monday of this week to say that your letter addressed to American Express, Paris had at last reached me, and to tell you how delighted we were to know that the book is accepted,[1] and Renee's contract affirmed.[2] But even our delight at this good news was not quite enough to overcome the depression we were plunged into by another piece of mail which arrived by the same post: a copy of the dust jacket of The Ordways.[3] You will judge of my reaction to it when I tell you that I rushed immediately to the Posta Telegrafa and wired Knopf as follows: Jacket unacceptable. Delay printing. Letter follows. Everything about it was wrong. It is the work of one Rudolph Ruszicka, once a distinguished book designer, but now 81 years old, and this jacket is the work of a man whose tastes were formed in the 1920's. Early modern, to use Dorothy Parker's phrase.[4] Semi-abstract, in muddy colors, bad typography, and the photograph on the back looks as if I have a 10 day growth of beard, the reproduction is so bad. You know how eye-catching some of the modern book jackets can be. This one lacks all distinction. I followed my wire with a letter saying all these things. Today's mail brings me the following letter from Alfred: ["]Just as I am about to take off for Oklahoma a copy of The Ordways comes to my desk. I am writing at once to say how perfectly magnificently I feel that this book has come out. I am particularly proud that it bears a jacket designed by my old, old friend Rudolph Ruzicka. He is perhaps the most distinguished man in the field, and though he has been a friend for decades it is only on rare occasions that I can persuade him to do a job for us. You are to be congratulated." I presume he took off for Oklahoma after seeing my wire (which he does not mention) but before seeing my letter. I have been feeling quite disgusted with them for some time, and I expect I'll change publisher after this book. The letter bringing the jacket also brought the news that The Literary Guild[5] has taken the book as an alternate selection for next February. The shame of this is by no means compensated for by the money, which is very little. It also probably means that the book was shown first to the Book of the Month Club[6] (which is shameful enough, but certainly a lot better than the other)[7] and turned down. Meanwhile no answer to three letters of mine to Annie Laurie Williams whether she is having any luck interesting the Hollywood people—not that I ever thought she would, but this seems to mean pretty surely that she is not. Meanwhile the to-do and disturbance about when we were leaving here. So you will see it hasn't been a time when any good news had much of a chance of wading across the moat of miseries.

Thank you more than we can say for the offer of the house for the field period. Comes also today a letter from the owner of this house saying he has no intention of renting the flat below during our tenure. Once again we don't know what to do. It is certain that we are returning to the U.S. no later than early next fall, but as to whether we are returning sooner than that, we're now just as unsettled as we were. If we decide to stay on here through to early spring, we hope and pray that you will do as you have once or twice hinted you might: hop over for a visit. All the room in the world, and as I did say, the house is nice, nice enough that you can even not notice the immediate surrounds, and the sea is really out there, just a touch away.

I disapprove entirely of your wasting time on Pasternak.[8] He is a third-rate writer and why a first rate one like you should make yourself a crutch for him, I don't know. Thanks for passing on the info that Styron[9] spoke warmly of Home from the Hill. Nice to know that someone likes it. I too received a copy of the new Knopf paperback of it. There is also, they tell me, a new drugstore paperback of it, brought out, I believe, by Avon, but I'm not sure, and though Knopf wrote long ago that they were sending me a copy, I have never received it. Probably as well, I can just imagine the cover of that. [. . .][10] So Bellow's book[11] is like that, is it? I'd heard from Pete Lemay something of your same reaction. He wrote that Rahv and Co[.] were declaring it second in importance only to the Bible, but as for him, he found it one more example of the narcissitice [*sic*] intellectual's analysis of his analysis. It is true that I have never known anyone who likes himself so much as Saul. He even dislikes himself with such self-satisfaction. But all I can say is that the piece of it I read was good. And certainly you can't take Henderson[12] away from him. Incidentally, apparently everyone in NYC knows it's a roman a clef. "Friend Ludwig gets a th[o]rough raking over,[13] and I can't say I'm sorry," is the way Pete Lemay sums up that aspect of the thing.

I haven't been able to finish anything in time for the Post,[14] with all these distractions. The fourth story[15] does promise well, but the deadline is here and I'm only just really still at the start of it.

Oh, before I forget: I shall tell Knopf to send you five copies of the Ordways as soon as they're ready, which will be in another week or so. One is of course for you. Would you please give the other four to Andy, Irma, Fred Dupee and Tony Hecht.[16] I'm sorry to ask this of you, but Knopf won't send out individual copies. Accompany each with my apologies for not sending it myself, but can find no other way to get it to them.

Dorothy says, no you haven't persuaded her to like Dutchess County[17] better than Tuscany, but she does want a home, and like a good wife will go with her husband. Meanwhile she urges you again to think of coming for a visit, we miss you very much.

Yours,
Bill

1. *The Medium* (1965).

2. See note for letter of 30 January 1965 to the Weisses.

3. William Koshland had sent Parsons a proof of the jacket in the expectation that it might be used for the Chatto & Windus edition. On 5 November 1964 Parsons wrote to WH, "I tried to pluck up courage to write and tell nice Bill Koshland that I thought it quite hopeless for our edition. [. . .] Now that I know you are as unenthusiastic about it as I am we can get ahead with producing our own jacket [. . .]."

4. Dorothy Parker (1893–1967), an American writer known especially for her incisive wisecracks.

5. A general-interest book club founded in 1927.

6. A book club, founded in 1926, similar to the Literary Guild.

7. On 8 November 1964, Weiss responded, "The Literary Guild does not sound as shameful to us as to you; in fact, in this Sunday's *Times* we see the Guild featuring *Herzog;* after that how could anything be better than the Guild? [. . .] You are a man of subtle distinctions! But I do prefer a louse to a flea."

8. On 8 November 1964, Weiss replied: "As for Pasternak, don't worry: I don't mean to do any more with him. And aside from his improvement of my Russian, he has proved useful;

after all, if Shakespeare could use all kinds of thirdraters for plotsam and jetsome [*sic*, in order to pun], why not me? I got me what may be a handful of pretty good Weissian poems by just taking a quick look at some godawful translations of Pasternak."

9. William Styron (1925–2006), a fiction writer from Virginia, wrote *Lie Down in Darkness* (1951), *Sophie's Choice* (1979), and several other acclaimed books.

10. Two sentences about the death of a Bard colleague are omitted.

11. *Herzog* (1964).

12. *Henderson the Rain King* (1959).

13. Ludwig was, however, pleased with the way his likeness was portrayed in Herzog. "I'm Valentine Gersbach," he boasted to his students (James Atlas, *Bellow* [New York: Random House, 2000], 338).

14. The *Saturday Evening Post.*

15. "Mouth of Brass." Rust Hills had asked WH to contribute a story about childhood for a special children's issue of the *Saturday Evening Post.*

16. Andrews Wanning; Irma Brandeis, a member of the Bard College faculty and one of the first friends WH made upon joining the faculty; Antony Hecht.

17. Dorothy was persuaded to make a home in Columbia County, just north of Dutchess County.

TO THEODORE AND RENÉE WEISS

TLS/PU

Villa Felice,
Via Solva 38
Alassio, Italy
November 23, 1964

Dear Ted and Renee,

I have finished the story[1] for the Saturday Evening Post and am sending it off to them today, with instructions that if they reject it they are to send it to you. They will surely reject it. In the first place they will receive it a month after their deadline. In the second place, they wanted something for a special children's issue at Christmastime, and I have turned them out the grimmest, grisliest little fable you ever saw. Fine professional writer I turn out to be! But I think it may be, of all the fifteen stories I have now written, my best. Well, when you get it will you please send it to The New Yorker, with appropriate return envelope, or if it should come after you're already gone to NYC will you please instruct Betty[2] to do this? After the New Yorker turns it down I'll let you know where else to send it.

It seems I have been working on this one story all my life, that's how hard I've been at it. Actually it's only about three weeks, but those three false starts, on which I wasted another three weeks must be counted too.

So to celebrate we are off tomorrow morning for four or five days in Florence, Pisa, and Lucca,[3] the latter two of which we have never seen. This, we've decided, is the way to live in Alassio, where there is absolutely nothing to do: work hard for a month, then get away for a few days. Meantime enjoy the weather: this morning we ate our breakfast in our pajamas out on the terrace in the blazing sunlight. This of course won't last but it's amazing enough to be able to do it this late in the year.

The Italians are voting today and tomorrow and I am in some anxiety over the results. The inflation I had read about the last few months has really hit this country hard. Prices here on everything are much higher than in the United States, meanwhile wages are still low and with the sudden bust of the great building boom there are many unoccupied people. Italy has got the largest communist party in the world, and this is the sort of situation it thrives on. One would like to see the wretched Christian Democrats ousted, if one could be sure the Socialists and the Social Democratic parties would gain, but they never do. The results will be announced tomorrow. Up till now the law has managed to gerrymander the vote so that although the communists always poll the greatest number, they are excluded from positions in the cabinet, but this time, if they increase their vote as much as may be expected, they will demand, and may get, a change in this situation. Florence is an almost 100 percent communist town; it will be interesting at least to witness it all from there.

Where is this house near you which you keep mentioning? Do we know it? Not that one next to the church in Barrytown[4] which has been on and off the market for years? And what do you mean by a good price?

I wonder if you have yet received the copies of The Ordways which I told Knopf to send you?

Yours,
Bill

1. "Mouth of Brass," which was not published prior to its inclusion in *A Time and a Place*.

2. Apparently a secretary at Bard College.

3. Tuscan cities.

4. Town in Dutchess County, New York, on the Hudson River near Bard College.

TO IAN PARSONS

TLS/UR

Villa Felice
Via Solva, 38
Alassio, Italy
January 13, 1965

Dear Ian,

[. . .][1]

I have been asked by Boston University to donate my manuscripts and correspondence files to their magnificent new library as "the nucleus of a collection of outstanding literary papers." They would be called "The William Humphrey Collection." They would "be housed and curated under optimum archival conditions." I think this is absolutely killing. I've written the dear delightful and demented man who wrote me, that my manuscripts along with my collection of rejection slips repose in one small cardboard carton in the hayloft of a friend's barn in New York State, and that that is the place for them.

And meanwhile, also from Boston University, comes an as yet indefinite feeler, would I come and be their Writer in Residence next year? These writers-in-residency have become a racket in America, a very nice racket, for usually they pay you a mint of money and you work 3 hours per week. We'll see.

A letter from D. to Juggs[2] will be coming along soon. Meanwhile all our love.

Yours,
Bill

1. This letter begins with a paragraph touching briefly on some business matters, most of which are included in other letters: the author's photograph for the English edition of *The Ordways,* reviews of the American edition of the novel, and the excerpt of *The Ordways* published in the *Saturday Evening Post.* There also is a brief comment on a possible visit.

2. From Dorothy Humphrey to Juggs Corner, the Parsons' Sussex house.

TO THEODORE AND RENÉE WEISS

[WH answers Ted Weiss's letter of 26 January 1965, in which he made generous comments about the just-published The Ordways: *"[I]t contains some of the sweetest, most tender, most poetic, most ambitious writing ever to come from your—even your—pen. That you have epas an epic here is obvious; cer-*

tainly this is the first book, novel that is, I know that tries to come to grips with America, its origins, its genuine myth and myths, its fundamental meaning."]

TLS/PU

Villa Felice, Via Solva 38
Alassio, Italy
January 30, 1965

Dear Ted and Renee,

First of all, we are terribly sorry to hear about the bout with sciatica. I know it is one of the most painful and most inescapable of pains. And that winter weather aggravates it. It is good to know at least that the worst of it now seems passing off. But keep away from osteopaths! They're a passel of quacks, and the momentary relief you get from having them maul you is no compensation for the risk you run that they may do you serious damage. In desperation with my aching back I too went to one years ago: a mistake. Stick with the m.d.'s. and what they tell you to do, you do. Take care of yourself. We don't like to hear of you in anything but a rosy state of health.

Received the following letter the other day from a lady in California: "Dear Mr. Humphrey, I paid $5.95 for your book,[1] thinking it would be interesting to me because I grew up near Texarkana, Texas and the fact that I had a heritage there. I wrote an article about the graveyards where I had my great-grandfather etc. buried. But I never paid [$]5.95 for such a dull, boring book as yours—I cannot imagine anyone in or out of Texas, who would want to read your book—Too bad your manuscript was ever returned to you in Italy—I hope that you and Knopf share my [$]5.95—there will be few more to donate the same. As I am 73 years old I feel free to write as I think. Yours Truly." Well, bless [her] hard little old heart! I hope there will be many more like her. Nothing sends people (or Texans at any rate) to the bookstores in greater numbers than the prospect of being outraged.

Still, I did enjoy getting another kind of response (and yours, aside from that little lady is the only response I've had; no one else to whom I sent copies of the book has uttered a peep) and I was more gratified by yours. You have seen what I had hoped you would see (and what I hoped you wouldn't!) I am deeply touched by your feeling that I have measured for you something of your own family sense, that particular complex fate[2] of sensing or not sensing what place and parentage mean to one in America.

(I had you in mind, by the way Ted, in having little Ned called at one point Ted.) As for your regrets about the book, they are, of course, and alas, the same as mine. I should have liked Sam Ordway to attain more inner stature than he does; he could only acquire as much as his maker could give him, and his maker is not Cervantes, or even Mark Twain. I do think he comes to some self-knowledge and some knowledge of the world in the end, however; meanwhile, if the adventures he undergoes do not deepen him as much as we all would like, they do, it's hoped, at least deepen the reader's awareness of a place, and perhaps tell him a little something, through Sam Ordway, of the nature of justice and the law, revenge, and reconciliation. As for the audacity of the invention; that I think really needs no apology. Nothing risked, nothing gained. Well, what the reviewers have said I don't know (you will, by the time you have received this). Reports reaching here are encouraging. A cable came from Pete Lemay the other day which said, RAVE FRONT PAGE REVIEW NYTIMES JAN THIRTYONE ALSO RAVE PAGE FIVE BOOK WEEK SAME DAY. And a letter from him that Newsweek has knocked itself out over the book.[3] Styron, incidentally, decided, according to Pete, not to review the book for LIFE, after all. His reasons I do not know.

Meantime, amongst other people from whom I do not hear is Joe.[4] No further word, despite the fact that I told him I would have to know at once, as many other plans would attend upon any such decision, such as reservations on boats, renting or not renting the cottage in Telscombe again for another, last, summer etc. Naturally, I would be greatly more interested in any possible offer if there were any likelihood that you were to be there,[5] as you so tantalizingly hint at in your letter. In the complete absence of any word from America, which might or might not influence our plans, we have written the Squire of Telscombe to ask if we might not have the cottage again, for the period from May 1, to August 1, on or before which latter date to sail for home. It is possible that we cannot have the cottage for that long—he may have already rented it for some portion of that period—in which case we'll have to begin all over again to decide what we are to do. In any case, we will be returning home *no later than* that date, August 1.

It is too bad, all the trouble Renee has had with Macmillan's.[6] Although if she were to get a somewhat more stable sounding editor out of it, I don't know but what it will have been worth it. In the midst of all this literary activity, how fares the fiddle?[7]

Thanks for your invitation to stay with you on our return. But I know of no surer way to wear our welcome out with you permanently than to be underfoot for an extended stay.

Sorry, we're not there to hear your Y lectures. I'm sure they're fine. Having just finished reading, for the first time, all of T. Hardy's The Dynasts[8] (an amazing book!) I'm beginning, this evening, to read Shakespeare aloud to D.[9] Starting on Macbeth, then Anthony & Cleo, then Othello, which are all we have in the house. We drove through the site of Birnham wood[10] this summer on our Scottish trip, and all around that country so it will have a new feature of interest this time, making it all the wilder for memories of that wild landscape.

Thanks again for the friendly care with which you read the book.

All our love,
Bill + Dorothy

1. *The Ordways.*

2. WH is recalling a phrase used by Henry James, who wrote in a 4 February 1872 letter to Charles Eliot Norton, "It is a complex fate, being an American [. . .]" (*Henry James Letters,* ed. Leon Edel, vol. 1 [Cambridge: Harvard University Press, 1974]). Marius Bewley used the phrase in his 1952 book *The Complex Fate: Hawthorne, Henry James and Some Other American Writers.*

3. "It is [. . .] a celebration of character, of goodness, and of honor as they are defined by, and as they define, a place in the American landscape. One is not only pleased but proud to read 'The Ordways.' It is that rarest of volumes, a novel to keep for the children to read—as soon as they can" (*Newsweek,* 1 February 1965, 77, 78).

4. Probably Joe Summers, who apparently had corresponded with WH about the possibility of his teaching again at Bard.

5. Weiss was contemplating his move to Princeton University, which eventuated in 1966.

6. Although Renée's children's book had been accepted in April 1964, her editor at Macmillan was fired in January 1965, leaving her book in midstream with no illustrator.

7. Renée played viola in several musical groups, including the Dutchess County Symphony.

8. Hardy's epic drama of the war with Napoleon, published in 1904–8.

9. Dorothy.

10. Compare *Macbeth* 5.3.2.

TO LEONARD WOOLF

TLS/US

Villa Felice
Via Solva, 38
Alassio, Italy
February 8, 1965

Dear Leonard,

We were very pleased to get your letter. The first thing I want to tell you is this, that your autobiography[1] was reviewed on the weekly literary program of the Italian television the other night. I did not see it, for although this house has a telly, it brings in only the First Channel, and the program was on the Second Channel. But an Englishwoman here who knows of my friendship with you did see it, and reported. It was a careful, perceptive, and appreciative review, concentrating on the most recent volume, but with glances backwards at the other two, and at the milieu of which they treat. It pleased me much to know of this.

Meanwhile, oh dear, what weather you seem to be having! Why is it that the interesting portion of mankind elected to pitch their tent in the most inhospitable climes, while in comfortable places such as Alassio bright vacuity reigns? Not that our weather here through January has been all that tropical. One day will be sunny and warm enough to sit out in the garden in shirtsleeves and eat your lunch while around you bloom roses, irises, mimosa (glorious stuff!), narcissi, bougainvillea, geraniums, even the first lone daffodil. Then down from the mountains behind will come a knifelike north wind. Not cold enough to frost the flowers, but cold enough. You wish we were there in a perfect spring and summer—well, we'll be there in spring and summer, whether perfect time must tell. But after much uncertainty we have written Squire and it's agreed that we're to have Oak Cottage again earlier this time, the last week of April. We won't be able to stay quite so late this year. Must go around the first of August, in order to get to America and find a house and get settled into it before winter shuts down. But by arriving earlier, we'll have a good long stay.

My book[2] is off to a good start. Knowing your interest in literary economics, I pass on these statistics. Knopfs did a first printing of 12 1/2 thousand copies. On publication day, Feb. 1, they had in the bookstores around the country 10,904 (and had sold to the U.S. Army 526 copies). On that day they ordered a second printing of 5000.

I left instructions with both my publishers and friends that I did not want to see any reviews—no matter how good they might be.[3] No one believed me, of course, thought I was being coy. So they've been sending them in batches, and the 5000 miles I though I had put between me and all that has done me no good. They are indeed what is called in the trade, "rave notices"—and they make me boil. Mainly because each of them plays the game of adding up my literary debts. William Faulkner they have hung around my neck like an albatross,[4] but beyond him the count, ranging from Angus Wilson[5] to Anton Checkov,[6] and including seven writers I have never read, 7 more to whom I am indifferent, and another 7 I can't abide—never mentioning the writers to whom I am, and should be proud to acknowledge that I am, most indebted. I am beginning to feel like a walking anthology. And is there anything on earth more heartsickening than imperceptive praise? Oh, well, these are the well-known joys of authorship. Meanwhile, one pleasant bit of news. From my mother comes word that my hometown, Clarksville, Texas, has set aside a "William Humphrey Day." Exactly how this is to be observed she doesn't say. I envisage a barbecue, a moment of silent prayer, and the singing of the state anthem, "The Eyes of Texas Are Upon You" to the tune of "I've Been Working on the Railroad All the Livelong Day."

I never did tell you how much I sympathized with your estimate of Bertolt Brecht.[7] Isn't he the most all-round nothing? And what I particularly resent about Brecht is that present-day directors think that Shakespeare was the Brecht of his day, and produce him accordingly. And the saddest part of all is that Brecht is probably the best modern playwright. The theatre has been moribund since Shakespeare.

Glad you've got a gardener. Your description of him as "revolutionary" is tantalizing. Tell him, says Dorothy, to plant a pot of sweet basil for her summer salads.

Don't be so long writing again. Meanwhile, all our love.

Bill

P.S. Did you ever give any further consideration to taking on my friend Theo. Weiss as a Hogarth poet?[8] You really should. Word just reached me that his new book,[9] his fourth, has been accepted by Macmillan's (Macmillan's of New York, that is) for publication in October, and is said to be his best yet. He is getting more and more of the recognition he deserves in the States. I am sure he is going to be seen as a poet of importance.

1. Three volumes of Woolf's five-volume autobiography had been published by 1965, the most recent being for the years 1911–18, *Beginning Again* (1963).

2. *The Ordways.*

3. On 8 September 1964, WH wrote to Harding Lemay: "Please, do not send me any reviews of the book, pre- or post-publication. One of the reasons I'm glad to be out of the country for the coming months is to be out of the range of reviews and can feel no temptation to look at them."

4. For example: "Perhaps most threatening of all for a chronicler of the American South is the shadow of masters like Warren, Lytle, Styron, and—above all—Faulkner. [. . .] A lot of readers will be forcibly reminded of such works as *The Unvanquished* and *Sartoris* [. . .]" (James R. Frakes in *Book Week*, 31 January 1965, 5).

5. Angus Wilson (1913–91), English writer whose only similarity to WH is that he was a great humorist. I have found no references to Wilson among the reviews of *The Ordways.*

6. Anton Chekhov (1860–1904), Russian dramatist and short-story writer, is an unlikely influence on WH's novel.

7. Bertolt Brecht (1898–1956), German dramatist and poet who discarded the idea that plays should create an illusion of reality.

8. Virginia and Leonard Woolf established Hogarth Press in 1917.

9. *The Medium.*

[HOME IN THE HUDSON VALLEY]

1965–73

TO LEONARD WOOLF

ALS/US

Poughkeepsie, New York[1]
May 22, 1965

Dear Leonard,

I have been running down to New York City (a hundred miles South of here) on business connected with the book,[2] rather, the secondary rights in the book, so often that I've had no time to write. Did I tell you, or did I say in a note to Ian,[3] that the book has been bought by Hollywood?[4] Columbia Pictures. No fortune, as such sales are reckoned in this madly monied country, but to us a large sum. Now I must work out how best to save on the income taxes.

Mean while [*sic*] we have been house-hunting with no success and with growing distaste for the quest. What dreary places most houses are! I sometimes wonder that more crimes of violence are not committed out of sheer exasperation from the drabness which surrounds us. And which our generation, with what H. L. Mencken called the American libido for the ugly,[5] seems bent on extending. But I keep hoping that somewhere there is the nest I seek. Maybe we ought to buy the site and build our own. That's what we're beginning to think.

Well, now comes an offer from M.I.T. (Massachusetts Institute of Technology) in Boston to teach one course—my choice of the subject—at fabulous pay. I don't really need the money but I do rather like Boston. So I'm considering it seriously. We're going up there this coming week for a closer look at things. Our weird crossing of the Atlantic now seems blessedly well behind us, and my knee, after three weeks of careful neglect, is all right.

In the current issue of one of the prestigious literary quarterlies here,

"The Kenyon Review," there is a biographical-critical article on Virginia. I saw it a[t] Ted Weiss's house but did not have time to do more than glance at it. It seems to be an account of the process of composition of *Mrs. Dalloway,* following her revisions from the original manuscript to the finished book.[6] Perhaps you've already been sent a copy. (I can't now recall the author's name, don't know whether he's English or American). If not, shall I send a copy?

My bedside reading these nights is the new novel entitled *Dog's Years,* by that crazy German Gunter Grass who wrote *The Tin Drum.*[7] Don't know yet what I think of it. I may never know. Still don't know whether I think The Tin Drum is nonsense or a masterpiece.

What should I offer to teach if I do go to M.I.T? What do you think our atomic scientists and our moon-explorers of tomorrow ought to hear from the side of disorder and anti-progress? Shall I do what I can to stop the dialogue between the Two Cultures?[8]

Don't be so long to write. We miss you terribly and a letter helps.

All our love,
Bill

1. The Humphreys lived temporarily in a Cape Cod cottage owned by the painter Norman Rockwell.

2. *The Ordways.*

3. Ian Parsons.

4. Though the novel was sold to Columbia Pictures and the production schedule set, a motion picture based on *The Ordways* was never made.

5. Henry Louis Mencken (1880–1956), a scholar, literary critic, editor, and newspaperman, was a pungent critic of American life.

6. Wallace Hildick, "In That Solitary Room," *Kenyon Review* 27, no.2 (1965): 302–17.

7. Günter Grass (b.1927), German poet, novelist, playwright, sculptor, and printmaker. *The Tin Drum* was published in 1959; *Dog Years* was published in 1963.

8. WH alludes to *The Two Cultures and the Scientific Revolution* (1961) by C. P. Snow (1905–80).

TO HARDING LEMAY

TLS/HR

[8 Francis Avenue]
Cambridge, Mass.
October 20, 1965

Dear Pete,

Many thanks for the NY Times book on gardening. *Art and Anarchy* has not arrived yet; thanks for sending it, too.[1] A young painter friend of mine here, who is also chairman of the fine arts department at Boston University, says this is the best work of art criticism of modern times.

I'm glad you like the Indian story in the Sat. Eve. Post.[2] Astonishing, isn't it, that the Post should print that? Well, they may not be doing much more of the same—Rust Hills has left there. He just wrote me so, Why—whether forced to or what—he doesn't say. But I am very sorry he has gone. He made that discredited magazine a very fine one indeed, in fact the finest literary magazine in the country, and I can't imagine any successor being as good as he was. Well, the Post had tentatively accepted another story[3] of mine while Rust was still with them. I say "tentatively" because they saw the story while still unfinished and paid me a retainer to finish it, which I have yet to get around to doing but am starting on now. It's longish, also more or less in the same series as the others you've been reading. And it would bring the number up to six. I have another couple more about half done. That's eight. Not enough for a book, only about 175 pages. So if you're serious about wanting to bring out a collection of stories next year I'll have to put my mind to turning out two or three more. The trouble is, so far they are all more or less related, if not about the oil boom, then about those same years and that same place. I'm attracted to the idea of a book of stories with that kind of unity, but the unity must not become monotony.

Incidentally, I've just heard from Stuart Millar[4] and he and Arthur Penn, who've now got a production company, are interested possibly in making a film out of one or more of my recent stories, and I've written them to come up to the house in Hudson, as they want to do, to talk things over.

I don't think the Renshaws will be ready for 66, and the reason is not only that I've not done anything on it lately, but also because I've got some ideas for making it a bigger book than I'd originally planned, ideas which need more thought.

These are the stories that have appeared:

The Ballad of Jesse Neighbours, Esquire, Sept. 1963
(Reprinted as 3rd prize winner in O. Henry Stories, 1965)
A Voice from the Woods, Atlantic, October 1963.
The Pump, Esquire, January 1964
(Reprinted in Martha Foley's Best Stories, 1964)
A Good Indian (my title), Sat. Eve. Post, Aug, 65
A Job of the Plains, Quarterly Review of Literature, Fall, 1965

The unfinished one that the Post has bought is still untitled.

All the best to you all.

Yours,
Bill

1. The gardening book is probably *New York Times Garden Book* by Joan Lee Faust (New York: Alfred A. Knopf, 1962); Edgar Wind's book *Art and Anarchy* (London: Faber, 1963), based on his influential Reith lectures in the 1960s, examines the forces that formed the modern view of art.

2. "The Gaudiest Thing on Wheels," *Saturday Evening Post*, 28 August 1965. The story's title in *A Time and a Place* is "A Good Indian."

3. WH was to title this story "The Rainmaker." It appeared in the *Saturday Evening Post* on 2 December 1967.

4. Stuart Millar was a film producer, his most recent film having been *Bird Man of Alcatraz* (1962).

TO LEONARD WOOLF

[In his Christmas Day letter to WH, Woolf had complained about the bells ringing in the church next door to Monk's House and the "gloomy herds of the gloomy congregation [passing] above the garden wall."]

TLS/UR

8 Francis Avenue
Cambridge, Mass.
January 7, 1966

Dear Leonard,

Yes, it must be a nuisance to have a branch of God & Son, Ltd. right next door, and I don't blame you and Coco for being Scroogy and barking at the communicants on Christmas Day.

Here's how we spent Christmas. A week or so prior we had a visit from a friend. While here she went out [to] McLeans' Sanitarium, which is Boston's big mental hospital, to visit Robert Lowell there. You know his name? He is universally considered our best poet. Poor fellow spends much time in the mental hospital. Our friend returned to report that they had him in a ward with a lot of juvenille [*sic*] drug addicts. And that he had been promised that he could go out for Christmas dinner here in Cambridge with friends, but that he could not go home to New York and his wife[1] and children, and that the friend had suddenly been called away to Washington so he was going to have to spend Christmas there. How awful, we thought, and we called the hospital and said that although we were not friends of his, we had met Mr. Lowell once at dinner may years ago, and that if he would like, and the officials were willing, we'd like to have him for Christmas dinner. Well, he said he would like, and they said they were agreeable. I was to come fetch him at 12 noon [on Christmas Day]. This I did, leaving Dorothy at home making oyster soup and a big roast, etc. When I got there I found Lowell lying on his bed in anything but his going-out-to-dinner clothes. Poor fellow, I said to myself, he's forgotten all about it. So I said, get dressed, dinner's ready. He very docilely did this, and only when he was finished, said, "Are you sure it isn't for tomorrow?" I said I was sure, and he rather pathetically agreed that time had not much reality there. As we were going out of his room, he said, "Have I been given permission to go?" I assured him that it had all been arranged. "Let's just check," he said. I went to the office, he stayed outside. "Mr. Lowell has been given permission to go to my house for dinner," I said. "Good," said the young man. "I'll just check it, if you'll wait a moment." He returned with a notebook in his hand and in his eye a very queer look for me. "It's tomorrow," he said. My heart sank "Isn't this Christmas?" I said weakly. "No, it isn't. Tomorrow is Christmas." "Oh, dear," I said. "My wife has got Christmas dinner ready today." "Well, it's been approved in principle that Mr. Lowell may go out with you, I don't see that it matters a lot which day, so go ahead, and have a good time." I returned to Lowell, out in the hall, and tried to hustle him out. Two doors had to be unlocked for us. "Is it all right?" he asked. "Am I allowed out?" "Yes, you're allowed out," I said. "The question now is, whether they're going to let me out, or not." At last I got him outside. "Tomorrow is Christmas, isn't it?" he said. I admitted that it was. He roared. "And they've let me out in *your* care?" he said. And then, "Well, this is a treat. To be let out of there to go to Christmas Dinner with the one man alive who doesn't know when Christmas comes." We all had a marvelous time, and vowed to Celebrate [*sic*] Christmas a day early every year from now on.

I think that's an extremely good idea of yours to come visit us here. Not that we are never going to get back to Sussex, you musn't think that. One of the main reasons for buying the house in the country[2] here is to make it easier, not more difficult, to go abroad. But you ought, as Dorothy recently suggested, to spend that Smith's loot[3] on something practical like a trip to America instead of blowing it off on bread and cheese. I won't be so long to write again, because some of the pressures are off now that the house *is* bought, and at least beginning to look partially furnished. Meanwhile we both send all our love.

Yours,
Bill

1. Elizabeth Hardwick (1916–), literary critic, short-story writer, and author of the novels *The Ghostly Lover* (1945) and *The Simple Truth* (1955).

2. High Meadow, the house about five miles from Hudson, New York, on Gahbauer Road, which WH purchased in June 1965. Built in 1795, the house sits on a 165-acre tract with an apple orchard, a stream, and about 50 acres of swamp. WH lived there with Dorothy until his death.

3. Woolf had just won the W. H. Smith and Son Literary Award for one thousand pounds.

TO KATHERINE ANNE PORTER

TLS/HL

8 Francis Avenue
Cambridge, Mass.
April 28, 1966

Dear Katherine Anne,

I hope there has been no reason why I haven't heard from you in such a long while.

I've been busy dashing in a triangle from here down to our farm in upstate New York and from there down to New York City for conferences with publishers. Seymour Lawrence and his group have been trying to induce me to leave Knopf, and Knopf to induce me to stay. I've given myself until today noon to reach a decision. I don't like making big decisions and put it off as long as I can. All these offers for a book as yet only half written have made it impossible for me to write a line and the higher the offers have climbed the more uncertain I am of the worth of the book.

Guest[s] from England coming tomorrow, two of our favorite people, Leonard Woolf, at age 86 making his first trip to the U.S. and with him the wife of my English publisher, Mrs. Ian Parsons, herself a fine painter. If this awful weather will only break we plan outings to Salem and Ipswich and maybe New Bedford.[1]

And you? You're still planning your May visit to us, we hope?

Must get to my problem of which publisher.[2] Let us hear something from you. Meanwhile much love from us both.

Yours,
Bill

1. Three of the oldest towns in Massachusetts.

2. WH decided to stay with Knopf, which had offered him an advance of eighty-five thousand dollars on *Proud Flesh.*

TO KATHERINE ANNE PORTER

[WH hired a carpenter to make renovations on High Meadow, his Hudson, New York, house.]

TLS/HL

Hudson, N.Y.
Sept. 24, 1966

Dear Katherine Anne,

This carpenter whose assistant I've become being Jewish, and today Yom Kippur,[1] I've got the day off. The things one has to do these days to get workmen to work for you! Broken toe and all, I've been climbing ladders carrying my end of a ten foot sheet of sheet rock to make a ceiling. We start in at 8 a.m., knock off at 6 p.m. with half an hour for lunch. It has its compensations, though. Mr. Levitt is a treasure. He was pianist on board cruise ships until his wife made him take up a less dangerous line of work after having three ships either burn up or break in half under him—one of them was the *Moro Castle.*[2] So he became a carpenter. On the job he utters an unbroken stream of obscenities and a litany of weh iz mir's.[3] He approaches each new problem with the declaration that it's impossible and curses God for getting him into this mess, then proceeds to do whatever has to be done with dispatch. He brings his lunch and mine to the job: knishes,[4] kugle,[5] gehochte liver sandwiches on onion pletzels.[6] The house is an incredible mess, for we are running three or four wood-working machines in what used to be a living room in Empire style.[7] Now the hall is piled up with furniture and the furniture piled up with chips and sawdust and plaster. I shall miss Mr. Levitt but I'll be glad to see the last of him. "How did you learn to work like this?" he asks me. "That was easy," I reply. "The hard thing was to learn not to work like this." I recall that I was writing a novel, but the memory is vague.

It sounds jolly having a baby in the house.[8] You were getting rather a plenitude of solitude. I'm so pleased with the way Abe[9] has stepped in and relieved you of annoyances. He is a fine person and I depend on him entirely, don't know how I'd have gotten along without him these last 6 years. Will report more shortly, meanwhile, stay well and happy.

Love,
Bill

1. Day of Atonement, the most solemn Jewish fast day.
2. This U.S. ocean liner caught fire off the New Jersey coast in 1934.
3. "Woe is me's" in Yiddish.
4. Meat- or cheese-filled dough, baked or fried.
5. Casserole of noodles or potatoes.
6. Boiled liver, usually spelled *gekochte,* on fried or baked onion pancakes.
7. Furniture with classic and oriental motifs, long curving lines, and some carving.
8. Probably Robert Penn Warren's daughter, Rosanna, Porter's godchild.
9. Abraham Badian, C.P.A., handled WH's financial affairs, as he did Katherine Anne Porter's.

TO JEAN LAMBERT

TLS/LC

Hudson, N.Y.
January 13, 1967

Dear Jean,

I'm pleased to hear that you are enjoying Bellow's *Henderson.*[1] Of all his books it is the one that has had the least notice, and yet it is his best. You may find, as I did, that it does not end as well as it begins; that doesn't mean, however, that it is not an excellent novel. The episode in which H. blows up the frog pond I remember with especial pleasure. And also the one in which he and the chief have a wrestling match. Perhaps even Bellow does not succeed in getting all there is to Chandler Chapman[2] down on paper—but then who could? As you say, he is a storm of a man.[3]

It's good to know that you are doing some writing of your own again.[4] You've chosen an important subject and I look forward to reading what you have to say on it. A pity I can't reciprocate and translate you into English!

As for the "division of the spoils" why don't we do as we did before in the case of Quail for Mr. Forester?[5] 50–50. If that's agreeable with you?

We're off to NYC for a few days. Just can't stand the banging of the plumbers and the hammering of carpenters any longer without some rest from it.

Yours,
Bill

1. Saul Bellow's *Henderson the Rain King* (1959).

2. WH introduced Bellow to his friend Chandler Chapman when Bellow first arrived to teach at Bard College in 1953, and Chapman was the basis for the character of Henderson. Chapman was an eccentric Dutchess County aristocrat, publisher and editor of the *Barrytown Explorer.* WH captured a bit more of Chapman in the character of Tony Thayer in *Hostages to Fortune.*

3. WH used Lambert's appellation in his published remembrance of his friend: "Storm of a Man," *Barrytown Explorer* 24, no. 2 (April 1982): 2.

4. Lambert would publish *Le plaisir de voir* in 1969.

5. In 1960 Lambert translated "Quail for Mr. Forester," which was published in *Le Figaro littéraire.*

TO JAMES W. LEE

[Lee, a professor at what was then called North Texas State University (now the University of North Texas), Denton, Texas, wrote to WH on 29 January 1967 asking for biographical information to include in his pamphlet William Humphrey, *to be published by Steck-Vaughn Publishing Company in Austin, Texas. Lee laments the lack of published information about WH's life, remarking that he is not even listed in* Who's Who in America.*]*

ALU/HR

[Hudson, New York
February 1967]

Dear Mr. Lee,

I was brought up to believe it's bad manners to talk about yourself, and the more I see of this age of self-advertisement the truer that teaching seems to me. I try not to raise the noise level. Besides, even if I wanted to I could never provide you with enough biographical information for you to make 8 or 10 pages out of it. Writing and earning a living have not left me time enough to do all that much. My career has been pretty much creating what's inside those books and if the personal information on the dust jackets seems to you meager, there is a reason. As for Who's Who, I don't approve of it and don't answer their letters.

I had a great-grandfather who was blinded and crippled at the battle of Shiloh, but that is everything I know about him. I never saw the man, and how he got to Texas I've no idea. Probably in some less difficult way than Thomas Ordway. Unlike the narrator of The Ordways I've never been much interested in genealogy. No. The Ballad of Jesse Neighbours is not based on any real event; I made it all up. About A Voice from the Woods, I remember being told that the bank in my home town was robbed when I was a child, but I no longer know whether I was told the details or whether I invented them. Which is true of so much of what one writes.

Best wishes with your pamphlet.[1]

Yours—
[unsigned]

1. *William Humphrey,* Southwest Writers series, no. 7 (Austin: Steck-Vaughn, 1967).

TO THEODORE AND RENÉE WEISS

[WH and Dorothy escaped the demands of renovating and keeping up High Meadow by sailing to England on 14 November 1967. They took up residence in London, first just outside the Dean's yard at Westminster Abbey, then in a more salubrious flat in St. John's Wood. WH finished the remaining of the ten stories for A Time and a Place *there and returned to the United States on 19 April 1968.]*

TLS/PU

[39 Tufton Court
Westminster]
London
December 29, 1967

Dear Ted and Renee,

Don't groan, "Oh, here's another depressing letter from Bill," because things are looking up. We've found another place to live, one just as nice as this is not. It's a house in its own little garden behind a wall off the street, with bedrooms and a great hall downstairs, kitchen halfway up the stairs, and then a grand studio about as big as our entire house in Hudson. And beautifully furnished. It belongs to a man named Jeremy Hutchinson, who was the lawyer who defended Penguin Books in the *Lady Chatterley's Lover*[1] case, and who was Peggy Ashcroft's[2] husband, which was how we met him some years ago. We move in a week from tomorrow and have the place till April 17. We sail back on the *France* on April 19. The address is 2A Nugent Terrace, St. John's Wood, N.W. 8. In order to make the change we must pay for a certain time double rent, but it's worth it.

We've just come back from Christmas in the country with the Parsons. We had a good time, as we always do with them, but there was felt a certain strain[3] which all this has put on our friendship.

Last week at the Aldwych[4] we saw something we'll never see again: a perfect production of a play. It was *As You Like It,* and how we did like it! Everything and everybody faultless.

I am reading Motley's *The Rise of the Dutch Republic,*[5] and enjoying it very much. He's a fine old fire-eating 19th century American democrat who can work himself into a passion of indignation and his reader too over the machinations of Philip II,[6] and he can write. I'm sorry it's only 1600 pages of close type long.

About Caliban:[7] there's nothing to say except that it's just wonderful. You have caught the ebb and flow of Caliban's mind and what has happened to that mind through its exposure to Prospero and Miranda,[8] and you have made him very very touching. Shakespeare's Caliban says, "You taught me language, and my profit on it is, I know how to curse." But your Caliban has learned to do a good deal more with his tongue than curse. It is, in fact, about the power of words, isn't it? Which is the theme you have made your own. Have no misgivings about it, it's very likely the best thing you've written, and it's sure to be the outstanding thing in the book.

Rather hung up on my new story at the moment. The title has been changed. It's to be called The Last of the Caddoes.[9] The Caddoes were the local tribe of Indians where I grew up. Long extinct. Not about oil, this one. Hope it gets unjammed soon.

Stay home and cultivate your garden[10] instead of going off on any more midwestern lecture tours. I know those parts and those so-called seats of higher learning set amid the cornfields. I attended not one but two of them, and lectured at another (Washington and Lee.) Abandon all hope, ye who enter here,[11] is what ought to be carved on the campus entrance gates.

You get the feeling here that the country is slipping into the sea and that not only is no one trying to prop it up but nobody is even concerned. The only worse leader it might have than Wilson[12] is the leader of the opposition, Heath.[13] He makes Geo. Romney[14] look like a leader of men. This is the way England ends, not with a bang nor even a whimper,[15] but a snigger.

Yours,
Bill

1. On 2 November 1960, Penguin Books was found not guilty of obscenity for publishing D. H. Lawrence's novel.

2. Dame Peggy Ashcroft (1907–91), a renowned English actress for more than half a century who played roles in the plays of Shakespeare, Shaw, Chekhov, and Ibsen, was a friend of the Humphreys.

3. Owing to the Humphreys leaving the unsatisfactory flat that Trekkie had found for them outside the Dean's yard at Westminster Abbey.

4. Shakespeare's *As You Like It* was performed at the Old Vic in December 1967, not at the Aldwych Theatre. Apparently WH liked the authenticity of this all-male production.

5. John Lothrop Motley published his three-volume *The Rise of the Dutch Republic: A History* in 1898.

6. King of Spain, 1592–97.

7. Weiss's poem "Caliban Remembers," based on the monstrous son of Sycorax in Shakespeare's *The Tempest,* was published in *The Last Day and the First* (1968).

8. Prospero is the exiled Duke of Milan who takes up residence on a remote island and practices magic. Miranda is his daughter.

9. The last story in WH's *A Time and a Place.*

10. An allusion to chapter 23 of *Candide* by Voltaire (1694–1778): "cultiver notre jardin."

11. The inscription at the entrance to Hell in Dante's *Inferno* (1.3). H. F. Cary's blank verse translation (1805–6) is the origin of the phrase in English.

12. Harold Wilson (1916–95), Labor Party prime minister of the United Kingdom, 1964–70, the first of his two terms.

13. Edward Heath (1916–2005) became Conservative Party prime minister in 1970.

14. George Romney, a three-term governor of Michigan, was a contender for the Republican Party nomination for president of the United States in 1968.

15. An allusion to the final stanza of T. S. Eliot's "The Hollow Men" (1925).

TO THEODORE AND RENÉE WEISS

TLS/PU

[2a Nugent Terrace
St. John's Wood
London]
The Great Emancipator's Birthday,[1] 1968

Dear Ted and Renee,

[. . .][2]

Yes, I've now heard from the New Yorker re the story.[3] They sent it back with a form rejection slip via slow mail (six weeks a-coming) and so packaged that the mss was [a] wreck and had to be retyped. Why I let my self in for this sort of discourtesy from those sonsofbitches I don't know. I've sworn before never again. So do I again and this time I mean it. Well, retyping it convinced me it is good work. More's the pity then that it's been turned down by the Post, Esquire, and them. Now I've sent it to the Atlantic, telling them if they don't want it to return it to Knopf, telling them then to try it on Harper's. And that's the end of the line as far as the commercial periodical world goes. Oh, well, you may say, you've placed six out of seven. Yes, but this one is the best of the lot, and what's more it cost me as much effort as all the rest put together: I can't afford not to sell it. Interesting you should say I ought to consider a title for the volume which is the name of the place where the stories are set: I'd just been thinking of calling it "Red River Valley." I'm thinking of course of the old song.[4] Please tell me what you think of this. I rather like it. If you like it then keep it to yourselves: I'm rather superstitious about naming a baby until one is sure it's got the proper allotment of limbs and organs, etc.

I do feel for you, Ted, in your hour of revisions. Is anything so maddening and disheartening as when a piece of writing just refuses to be a masterpiece. Yes, terrible to be smarter than one's gifts. There is just one thing worse, and that would be to be Richard Eberhart: gifted and with no brains at all, so that he thinks everything he does is just pie.

Speaking of poets, we had dinner the other evening with the new Laureate.[5] It was at Peggy Ashcroft's house, a party of six. He wears the robes of his new office with suitable jauntiness. There was some discussion in the papers before his appointment as to who ought to get it, he was asked, and said, "The best English poet alive, namely Robert Graves."[6] The talk our evening together was pleasant and inconsequential. He did surprise me, the only moment things got serious, by differing with one man present on Eliot. He, Day Lewis, maintaining that Eliot was really an artist of practically no significance whatever. "He'll make a footnote in the history of Eng. Literature, nothing more," he said. He of course adores Thomas Hardy,[7] but I didn't think even that would carry him so far as to blaspheme. I believe I am the first person he's found who agrees with him about Eliot, so we enjoyed one another's company right well. We'd already found out each other's joy in Hardy when we met before some years ago.

That's my one contact with the literary scene. As for my reading, I'm now in volume three of Motley's *Rise of the Dutch Republic,* probably the only person alive under 130 who has read this once-important classic. It is a very good book, the kind of history I like, passionate and angry. Old Motley hated Philip Second as he might have hated his own neighbor, and for all the good reasons. He was one of those Washington-Jefferson democrats before the sap headed Whitmanism set in,[8] hater of bigotry and oppression and Spaniards. Me too, so with some 900 pages behind me and only a couple of hundred to go I'm sorry to have no more of the pleasure of his company.

Have been to no more plays since writing last. Paul Scofield[9] is doing *Macbeth* and I'm sure I won't like it but am going to go anyway. The Season at Stratford opens in early April with *King Lear.* God, what I wouldn't give to see that play once in my life.[10] Maybe I will go. I'd like to tell you about last night only I can't, because I don't know how to describe it. We went to hear Menuhin[11] at the Royal Albert Hall, sat in the second row. He played the Brahms concerto[12] and the Mozart one in G, K216.[13] It was enthralling. The composer, the player, and the musical instrument were one. I never knew the violin could be that sweet. That frail little man, that frail little wooden box, and in that great barn full of four thousand people a breathless hush.

I'm sorry to report that the pretty picture book of Chardin you wanted, Ted, is no longer in print, nor does Zwemmers[14] have a secondhand copy. At the Royal Academy currently is a show called *France in the Eighteenth Century,* which the critics here have praised till they're all hoarse. We went, mainly to see the Chardins.[15] Worst exhibition I ever saw in my life. Poorly chosen and poorly hung and the Chardins all by that fellow who did all the fake Vermeers.[16]

Delighted to hear that the house continues to delight you. Be a pity to let anything interfere with it, really, so maybe you ought to say to the University that you find you won't have time for them.

Love,
Bill

1. Abraham Lincoln's birthday, 12 February.

2. The opening paragraph, which concerns illness in the Weiss extended family, is omitted.

3. "Mouth of Brass," the only story in *A Time and a Place* that was not published in a magazine prior to the publication of the collection in 1968.

4. The song "Red River Valley" is widely thought to be a Texas reworking of an American folk song of 1896, "In the Bright Mohawk Valley." WH's editor at Knopf, Robert Gottlieb, strongly objected to the song title for the collection because it reminded him of television cowboys.

5. Cecil Day-Lewis (1904–72), poet and detective novelist, became poet laureate in 1968.

6. Robert Graves (1895–1985), a prolific writer in all genres but mainly a poet.

7. Lewis was such an admirer of Thomas Hardy that he would arrange to be buried as close as possible to the grave of Hardy's heart in St. Michael's churchyard, Stinsford, Dorset.

8. WH appears to be politically confused; Washington was a Federalist. WH would seem to refer to Walt Whitman's influence on American politics and to him as one easily taken in in his all-embracing acceptance of all that he beheld.

9. Paul Scofield (1922–), English stage and film actor.

10. *King Lear* is the bleakest of Shakespeare's tragedies.

11. Yehudi Menuhin (1916–99), American violinist.

12. The Violin Concerto in D Major, op. 77, by Johannes Brahms (1833–97).

13. The Violin Concerto in G Major by Wolfgang Amadeus Mozart (1756–91) is identified according to its Kochel number in the cataloging system.

14. Charing Cross Road Bookshop in London, founded in 1922 by Anton Zwemmer.

15. Jean-Baptiste Siméon Chardin (1699–1779), French painter known for his meticulous renderings of daily life.

16. Hans van Meegeren (1889–1947), Dutch painter and notorious forger.

TO THEODORE AND RENÉE WEISS

TLS/PU

[2a Nugent Terrace
St. John's Wood]
London,
March 23, 1968

Dear Ted and Renee,

I'm almost well at last, now that the doctor has put me on a new drug, one of the -cylcine family. Out of doors yesterday for the first time in almost two weeks. Went to the theater last night. Saw at the Royal Court D. H. Lawrence's "The Widowing of Mrs. Holroyd."[1] This dates from 1914, the period of Sons and Lovers,[2] Nottingham coalmining background. I'd read it years ago, rather liked it, forgotten it. It was superb. There's a scene—the last one—when the dead miner is brought home in his "pit dirt" and this unloving wife and his long suffering mother wash his body (the pieta was surely Lawrence's most persistent image—one of his paintings[3] is himself with Mabel Dodge Luhan[4] and Frieda[5] doing the honors) that is one of the best things I ever saw. What's so fine about the play is its quietness. It was magnificently acted, down to the children, everybody just perfect. A reviewer here contrasted it to Synge's Riders to the Sea[6] (the sea which claims the women's men: the pits which do) and said that Synge is stagey and Lawrence real. That's a very good comparison, and just the right conclusion. Of course, it's also that Synge is Irish and the Irish will wail, the English lower cases will mumble, at catastrophe. How much more heart-rending that mumble is. And there was absolutely nothing of what there would have been in some naturalist: none of the Industrial-managerial-capitalism grinding down the worker baloney. They're also doing others of the same period, and I shall try to see one of them at least, called "The Daughter-in-law."[7]

The Atlantic has rejected my story "Mouth of Brass" with this comment, "an effective evocation of its time and place, but the problem of Negro/white relations has moved so far, and become so complic[a]ted since the time of your story that it is something of an antique." To which my reply is: "an effective etc. but parent/children relations have moved so far, and become so complicated since the time of that story, that King Lear is something of an antique." Or, "Penicillin destroyed Ibsen's Ghosts."[8]

Whatever you say, Ted, about when I'm to come for that reading at Princeton.[9] If Knopf does print the book[10] about the same time as Macmillan does yours[11] it would be nice to celebrate together. November: suppose it's election time and either Nixon or Johnson[12] is in—we'll have a lot to celebrate all right, won't we?

Although I've turned in the mss of the book of stories[13] as completed, truth is, it's not. I don't like the last chapter of the long story I've mentioned, called "The Last of the Caddoes." And I just can't seem to get it to come right. [. . .][14]

Yours,
Bill

1. D. H. Lawrence's first play, published in 1914.

2. Lawrence's third novel, published in 1913.

3. Lawrence's painting is titled *Resurrection,* plate 6 in *Paintings of D. H. Lawrence* by Mervyn Levy, Harry Thorton Moore, and D. H. Lawrence (London: Cory, Adams and Mackay, 1964).

4. Mabel Dodge Sterne Luhan was a wealthy American who invited the Lawrences to Taos, New Mexico, in 1922. She lent "us this new and very charming adobe house which she built for us: because she wants me to *write* this country up" (Lawrence to S. S. Koteliansky, 18 September 1922, in Harry T. Moore, ed., *The Collected Letters of D. H. Lawrence,* 2 vols. [London: Heinemann, 1962], 2:715).

5. Lawrence's wife.

6. *Riders to the Sea* (1904), by John Millington Synge (1871–1909), caused a riot when it was first performed at the Abbey Theatre in Dublin.

7. Play by Lawrence probably written in 1913, first performed in 1967 at the Royal Court Theatre in London.

8. In the play *Ghosts* (1881), by Henrik Ibsen (1828–1906), Oswald Alving is doomed by syphilis.

9. WH read "The Last of the Caddoes" on 13 November 1968.

10. *A Time and a Place.*

11. *The Last Day and the First* (1968).

12. Nixon was the Republican candidate for president in the 1968 election. Lyndon Johnson (1908–73), thirty-sixth president of the United States, announced, a few days after WH wrote this letter, that he would not seek the Democratic Party's presidential nomination.

13. *A Time and a Place.*

14. A brief paragraph with comment on a lost newspaper clipping follows.

TO KATHERINE ANNE PORTER

[Illness prevented Porter from gathering and arranging the items for her Collected Essays *(1970), and so she asked Humphrey to do the task for her.]*

TLS/HL

Hudson, N.Y.
November 5, 1968

Dear Katherine Anne,

When you called we'd just returned from going out to vote. Our polling place, about eight miles away, is the West Ghent, N.Y. Volunteer Fire House. I could see just two kinds of looks on the faces of the other voters waiting in line with me: knee-jerk-Republican-Nixon and Wallace-surly.[1] I got inside the booth and drew the lever that draws the curtain and stared at the bank of switches in front of me, and I thought this is one thing wrong with the way this country is governed right here, this machine. It ought not to be made this easy and automatic. You ought at least to have to sit down with a piece of paper and a pencil and mark your choices with x's. That way you'd have to say the candidates['] names to yourself at least. Well, around here the little levers on the Democratic or other party rows are so rusty from disuse they hardly work. Or maybe it was that I didn't pull very hard because my heart was only half in it. When I pulled the Humphrey-Muskie[2] lever I expected to hear a loud buzz, the way a pinball machine cries foul and gives you away when you tilt it. So I was feeling pretty much like today's weather, gray and chilly and barometer falling, when you called. It was awfully good of you to do it. I'm delighted that you liked the stories.[3] You know, the ultimate compliment I ever pay myself when I'm feeling really pleased with something I've written is to say to myself, "There, I think Katherine Anne is going to like that." Wish I felt like that more often than I do.

I've been working evenings on your book of essays, and it won't be much longer now before I'll have it finished. That is, if you approve of the way I'm going about it, which is simply to use the basic form of *The Days Before*[4] and expand on that. I mean, keeping your divisions:[5] Critical, Personal and Particular, and Mexican, inserting the hitherto uncollected pieces in what seem to me appropriate slots therein, and adding two new categories[—]I've given them working titles of Biographical (the three Cotton Mather pieces)[6] and Poems. I've got just one question: do you wish to retain the piece on Mrs. Onassis?[7]

I have not yet received from Prettyman[8] the final three things, including the opening address to the writers' congress in Paris. I suppose they'll be coming along presently. If you think you don't approve of the sort of arrangement of the essays I've suggested let me know so I can think of some other.

Robert MacAlmon [*sic*].[9] Oddly enough I too had a sort of a connection with him. Back in 1946 I used to read letters from him. He was then running an automobile tire business in El Paso, I was clerking for that old harpy Frances Steloff at the Gotham Book Mart. (I was about the three-thousandth clerk she had had up to that time; I stayed with her three months, breaking a record, not because I got along with her but because I, along with my wife and step-child, were starving, before I threw three 100 watt lightbulbs to the floor at her feet one day in a final fit of exasperation). Well, MacAlmon was a tire dealer then but still a tireless reader of books, used to send us an order just about weekly, accompanied by an always-interesting letter to La Steloff. Poor man, he didn't know she was illiterate but for Yiddish and *that* she had to spell with her finger. She never read any of those avant-garde poets and novelists she sold; she read nothing but smudgy pamphlets on theosophy. While on this topic I remember the time Cyril Connolly[10] came on his postwar literary safari to America. She heard he was on his way and planned a party in his honor for the occasion. He was to arrive around seven in the evening but about four that afternoon he came in. He didn't announce himself, he just appeared and started brow[s]ing. Have you ever seen Cyril Connolly? He looks just like an ape. Ugliest man, as we used to say in East Texas, that God ever wattled a gut in. Well, Miss Steloff didn't know him from Adam and she didn't like what she saw and I saw a chance for a little mischief and didn't tell her. I recognized him from a photograph I'd seen. There was no mistaking him. Pretty soon he'd worked his way with his big shabby briefcase back to the back room where she kept all those signed Shakespeare and Co[11] first editions of Ulysses that she had bought from starving writers for a dollar and a half per copy and now was asking five hundred for, and she began to get very nervous. "Go back there and pretend to be doing something and keep an eye on that man, I just know he's going to steal something," she said to me. I went, she stayed out front wetting her pants with anxiety and calling to me to come out every five minutes and give her a report. "What's he doing now?" she'd say, and I'd say, "Going through that file of Little Reviews[12] last time I looked." Finally she could stand it no longer. "He has stolen something and put it in that briefcase. I just know it," she said, "Go out and get the policeman on the corner." I went. When we returned she was chatting with Mr. Cyril Connolly who had obviously introduced himself to her in my short absence, trying to be affable with him and keep an eye out to forestall me. "Here's that policeman you sent me for, Miss Steloff," I announced as loud as I could, and looking very puzzled at her frowns and wavings. She could have killed me. I used to see Connolly on the streets of Lewes, the little town in Sussex where he lives and where we spent three long summers, and I used [to] feel tempted to go up to him and tell him how he very nearly got pinched on suspicion of book theft at the old Gotham Mart.

Well, if I don't shut up I never will. Take good care of yourself. Again, bless you for calling and saying those sweet things to me. I'll be in touch.

Love,
Bill

1. George Wallace (1919–98), the governor of Alabama who led a fight against federally ordered racial integration in the 1960s and was a third-party candidate for president of the United States in 1968, was endowed with a constant sneer.

2. Hubert Humphrey (1911–78) of Minnesota was the Democratic candidate for president of the United States in 1968, and Edmund Muskie (1914–96) of Maine was his running mate.

3. Those in the just-published *A Time and a Place.*

4. Porter's essays and occasional writings published in 1952.

5. WH did keep to the organization he here describes, though he included one additional category: On writing.

6. Cotton Mather (1663–1728), one of the most prominent New England Puritan ministers, played a significant part in the Salem witchcraft trials of 1692. Porter had been working on a book about him since 1928, *The Devil and Cotton Mather,* but she never finished it. These "pieces" are what she had completed of the project.

7. Jacqueline Bouvier Kennedy Onassis (1929–94), widow of President John F. Kennedy, afterward married to Greek businessman Aristotle Onassis. Porter did wish to retain the essay on her.

8. E. Barrett Prettyman (1925–71), Porter's lawyer and close friend from the mid-1960s until her death. He served on the U.S. Circuit Court of Appeals for the Washington, D.C., circuit for twenty-six years.

9. Robert McAlmon (1896–1956) was an American poet of the Lost Generation. Most of his books were published in Paris, and he helped edit some of the little magazines of the 1920s, including *Contact.*

10. Cyril Connolly (1903–74) was a contributor to the *New Statesman* and literary editor of the *Observer* (London); his novel *The Rock Pool* was published in 1935.

11. This English-language bookstore in Paris was opened in 1921 by Sylvia Beach; it first published Joyce's *Ulysses* and Lawrence's *Lady Chatterley's Lover,* both banned in England and the United States.

12. The *Little Review,* founded by Margaret Anderson with Ezra Pound as foreign editor, was one of the most influential literary magazines in the early twentieth century.

TO WILLIE MORRIS

[Southern writer Willie Morris (1934–99), just before publication of his North Toward Home *(1967), became editor-in-chief at* Harper's Magazine, *a post he held from 1967 to 1971. In a letter of 21 November 1968, Morris had invited WH to contribute to a special issue of* Harper's Magazine *to be called "Going Home"—about ten writers who are living "a long way from the places where they grew up." "Could you be persuaded to go back to Texas?" Morris asked. WH's response is on the back of the invitation.]*

ALU/HR

[Hudson, New York
21 November 1968]

Dear Mr. Morris,
Thank you for asking me to contribute to your special issue "Going Home" but for me that would mean a longer trip both in miles and in memories than I've got the time to take just now.

Sincerely,
[unsigned]

TO IAN PARSONS

[In the winter of 1968, depressed by the dreary cold of New York and his failure to make progress on Proud Flesh, *WH and Dorothy embarked on their first transatlantic flight—to Paris—for a more agreeable climate in which to write. They remained there until 9 May, returning on the* Île de France.*]*

TLS/UR

42 bis Rue Boursault
Paris, 17
March 4, 1969

Dear Ian,
Thanks for your good letter, which just came. I did get your cable sent c/o American Express, in which you said call you at the Davids,[1] but was coming down then with the flu and just wasn't well enough to make the call. As for the typescripts,[2] destroy both. I've got the one Knopf used to set their edition, and one is enough. I doubt it'll ever be worth tuppence ha'penny,[3] but if so, then the fewer copies the better. Or if you'd like, I make you personally a gift of either or both copies which you have got.

OK? And with no conditions; or in other words, dear boy, if you can get tuppence ha'penny for them, my advice is cash in on the market quickly. And speaking of money, if it's difficult for you on account of travel restrictions,[4] to think of a hop over here, borrow from me. I've got a good bit of money on me in the form of traveller's checks, and I could easily let you have whatever you need. You'll pay me back someday when I'm in Britain.

Many thanks for sending on the review from The Observer. I am grateful to that reviewer for noting two things. First, that I have dared to take figures which in mere outline are stock figures and have (tried) to bring them to life by giving them what he so well calls complex untidy emotions.[5] And second, that I write dangerously: i.e., on a tightrope.[6] Because a writer must take risks. The writers I admire are not those who succeed in doing what they know they can do, but those who fail trying to do what they know they can't do. It's a killing way to write, but it's the only way worth doing. Besides, something has got to kill you—it might as well be something you enjoy.

I'm pretty well recovered from my bout of flu but poor Dorothy keeps a wracking cough and the worst of it is it keeps her awake all night so she can't get rested and well. . . .

Well, don't lose too much of yourselves in thinning down because we will miss anything that's missing.

Love,
a bientot,
Bill

1. Richard (a Shakespearean scholar) and Norah David, 41 Barton Road, Cambridge, England.

2. Of *A Time and a Place*, published in the United Kingdom on 27 February 1969.

3. Two and a half old pence.

4. Harold Wilson's Labour government, to discourage British people from spending money abroad, allowed them to take only fifty pounds per year out of the country.

5. The reviewer in the *Observer*, 2 March 1969, wrote (with "A Job of the Plains" especially in mind) that the "ancient illiterates," the "plain girls taking extensive beauty treatment in order to make better 'catches,'" and others "become objects of pity, with complex, untidy feelings and enormous unsatisfied ambitions—Mr. Humphrey, in a word, makes them real."

6. According to the *Observer*, WH "walks an unnervingly thin tightrope between tragedy and farce, coming perilously close at times to the routine humour of that appalling television series, 'The Beverly Hill Billies' [. . .]. That he doesn't topple over is an indication of the quality of his writing."

TO LEONARD WOOLF

TLS/US

42 bis rue Boursault
Paris 17
March 9, 1969

Dear Leonard,

I'd better get this off to you while I can. A one-day general strike has been called for Tuesday with all services to be interrupted, but the papers are all saying here that it won't end with one day. The government is saying that if the workers get a raise in wages it will mean inflation and the workers are saying they don't care if [it] does. So spring has come again to Paris and everybody is just praying it won't be a re-run of last year,[1] except the students and the communists who are hoping it will. The other news, la scandale Marcovich, [*sic*][2] I seem to be the only person in town who does not have some of the feelthy photographs for which Mme. Pompidou[3] is said to have posed at orgies with Francoise Sagan[4] and Alain Delon.[5]

So here we are, and par avion for the first time and the last, I hope. I was never so happy in my life as when I got off that damned airplane, and as soon as she was well enough from her bout of flu I sent D. off to exchange our return tickets for a cabin on the S.S. France. Not that I like boats. In fact, I loathe boats and usually spend most of my time in my berth seasick. But I still do not believe in airplanes. There those men are out there in space going 28,000 miles per hour and crawling in and out of each other's space ships[6] and my attitude is I still don't believe Lindbergh[7] will ever make it [to] Orly Field.[8] Trouble is, ship travel is disappearing. Nowadays it's impossible to get across the Atlantic any other way except by plane, unless, as I told Trekkie and Ian, you can walk on water, and Dorothy can't.

You'd have laughed to hear me in my execrable French being interviewed on a literary program over National radio here. I have never studied French, you know. I can conjugate just about two verbs in the present indicative, after that my way is, I take an English verb which I suspect of having a French parentage and I just add an ait sound to the end of it, and hope it's French. You'd be surprised how often it is. Anyhow, I have not let the fact that I don't speak this language keep me from doing it. The best way, I find, is to avoid verbs whenever possible and speak mainly in nouns. Lots of cognates there. Also I prefer plurals of nouns because then there isn't that annoying problem of gender. So with me most things come in pairs or more. It further simplifies things I find just to stick to the second person plural and not be bothered with the rest. As for the pronunciation, this is such a problem for most foreigners because they have not asked one basic question, namely, *why* do the French not speak more understandably than they do? Did you know that more Frenchmen than anybody else suffer from cirrhosis of the liver due to drink? In that statistic lies the secret to pronouncing French. *The French talk the way they do because they're drunk all the time.* Since discovering this I have had no further difficulty, and I find that after say two liters of Beaujolais I'm talking French with the best of them. Beaujolais, of course, gives me a certain accent; by drinking the vin du pays[9] one can converse with the natives of any region.

If we don't get caught here in a new French Revolution we hope to see you in May. Our boat sails back on May 9, and present plans are to take it from Southampton, spending the last few days before among you.[10]

Hope all goes well with you. Let us hear from you. Dorothy joins me in sending all best wishes.

Yours,
Bill

1. Widespread student rioting in Paris threatened to topple the government in 1968.

2. Stefan Markovic, a Yugoslav employed as a secretary-bodyguard of Alain Delon (see below), was found beaten and shot to death, his body wrapped in a mattress cover. Various Paris publications suggested that his death had to do with his organizing of sex parties for prominent guests, at which he would take photographs of participants and later use them in blackmail (*New York Times,* 8 November 1968, p. 2, sec. 4).

3. Claude Cahour Pompidou was married to Georges Pompidou, president of France. The couple were in March 1969 called on to testify in the trial of the man charged in Markovic's murder (*New York Times,* 15 February 1969, p. 4, sec. 3).

4. Françoise Sagan (1935–2004) is a French novelist, author of *Bonjour tristesse* (1954), and *Un certain sourire* (1956).

5. Alain Delon became a French cinema star in 1960 in the film *Plein soleil.* He and his wife were questioned extensively in the murder of Stefan Markovic (*New York Times,* 15 February 1969, p. 21, sec. 1).

6. On 3 March 1969 three *Apollo* 9 astronauts began a complex ten-day flight involving linkups between the lunar module and the command ship, in preparation for a moon landing in July.

7. Charles A. Lindbergh (1902–74) was the American aviator who was the first to make a nonstop solo flight across the Atlantic in May 1927.

8. Airport in Paris, France.

9. Local wines.

10. Besides Woolf, Ian and Trekkie Parsons.

TO THEODORE AND RENÉE WEISS

TLS/PU

[42 bis rue Boursault]
Paris
March 21, 1969

Dea[r] Weisses,
Nice young man we just met named Michel Gresset, prof. of American literature at the Sorbonne, (and editor of the forthcoming Pleiade edition of the complete works of Faulkner) spent 1965–66 in Charlottesville, Virginia doing research on Faulkner, with his wife and small children. The other day, he tells me, the smallest one asked, "Papa, l'Amerique, y'a-t-elle encore?"[1] I'm curious too. Tell me, is it still there?

He, Gresset, is taking it upon himself to try to get some of the stories from the book[2] translated and published in magazines here. This is part of a campaign to overcome French publishers. Gallimard, damn them, who did both the novels,[3] the last one (just recently out) to rave reviews everywhere,[4] has turned it down,[5] saying, as publishers everywhere do, books of stories don't sell. So has the next house it was sent to. We prefer to wait for M. Humphrey's next novel. (Like my mother, who telephoned shortly before we left, and said, "When is your new book coming out?" Me: it is out. Been out three months. Didn't you get the copy I sent you? Mother: Oh, that. That's just stories. I mean your new *book*.) It's now with a third and no doubt they'll say the same. Meanwhile Ian's edition[6] is out in England and the two reviews I've seen, *The Observer*[7] and the *New Statesman*,[8] have been more than kind.

What else is new? My old alamo mater SMU[9] came through with the offer of an LLD (you're not supposed to tell anybody) and I've accepted though Lord God A'Mighty how I dread the thought of going back down there! And I don't know how I'll get there. Be damned if I'll risk my life on an airplane for a degree from SMU. Oxford, Cambridge, Muhlenburg[10] maybe. The train trip, as I remember (it's 25 years since I took it) takes three days and two nights. I am seriously considering hitch-hiking.

Been exploring our local quarter[11] on foot in the afternoons after work and what do you know, just around the first corner and over the railroad tracks lived Stephane Mallarme.[12] For 23 years he lived at No. 89 rue de Rome. You remember reading about his famous weekly soirees[13] to which came Verlaine[14] and Valery[15] and Proust and James[16] and Turgenev[17] and Flaubert and Degas[18] and Whistler[19] and tout le monde artistique.[20] Well I mentioned en passant[21] (I hope you've been admiring my French all along) the railroad tracks. These do more to explain Mallarme's poetry than a book of close explication. No ordinary railroad tracks, these. These are the Grand Canyon of railroad tracks, or chemins de fer, to keep up the atmosphere. There are about 24 sets of tracks with accompanying cinderbeds, signals, wires, noise and everything else un-poetic you can conjure up to your mind, in a chasm some hundred and fifty feet deep and about two hundred yards wide. They terminate about two blocks further down in the Gare St. Lazare. These tracks were for 23 years Mallarme's view. What it is to be a poet in the age of steel. So no wonder he dreamed of pure poetry. Of words divorced from things, becoming things themselves.

Write. Meanwhile all our love,
Bill

1. Father, America, is it there any more?

2. WH's *A Time and a Place.*

3. *L'Adieu du chasseur (Home from the Hill)* and *Les Pionniers du Texas (The Ordways).*

4. See, for example, *Bulletin critique du livre français,* February 1969, and *Beaux-Arts,* 25 January 1969.

5. Gallimard reversed its decision and published *D'un temps et d'un lieu* in 1972.

6. Ian Parsons was president of Chatto & Windus, who published *A Time and a Place* in London.

7. Paul Bailey reviewed the book in this London newspaper on 2 March 1969.

8. Janice Eliott reviewed the book in this magazine on 28 February 1969.

9. Southern Methodist University, Dallas. WH matriculated in the middle of the 1941 academic year; after transferring to the University of Texas in Austin for his sophomore year, he returned to SMU but then left without a degree.

10. Ted Weiss was graduated from this liberal arts college in Allentown, Pennsylvania.

11. The apartment was on rue Boursalt, just west of the Montmartre area.

12. Stephane Mallarmé (1842–98), French poet considered head of the Symbolist school.

13. These evening gatherings, attended by famous poets and artists, both French and foreign, were held regularly in Mallarmé's home on Tuesdays.

14. Paul Verlaine (1844–96), French poet.

15. Paul Valéry (1871–1945), perhaps the most important French poet of the twentieth century. See note for letter of 17 July 1959 to Alfred and Blanche Knopf.

16. Henry James (1843–1916), American novelist.

17. Ivan Turgenev (1818–83), Russian novelist.

18. Edgar Degas (1834–1917), a painter and sculptor who lived in Paris, organizing with Monet and Manet the first impressionist exhibition in 1874.

19. James McNeill Whistler (1834–1903), American painter famous for nocturnal scenes of London.

20. All the artistic people.

21. In passing.

TO RUST HILLS

[Hills, then fiction editor at Esquire *magazine, wrote to WH on 24 June 1969, asking him to "outline" his writing plans for the 1970s. WH's answer was to become part of a feature involving a number of other writers, together with "excerpts from several works in progress." Apparently the feature on the several writers did not appear in the magazine, but "Mrs. Shumlin's Cow Trixie: An encounter that makes a broken leg seem hardly funny at all," chapter 10 of* Proud Flesh, *a work in progress, appeared in the December 1969 issue (246–7, 277–82).]*

TLS/HR

R.D. 1, Hudson, New York
June 27, 1969

Dear Rust,

It's been a long time since anything bucked me up like your letter asking my personal plans for the coming ten years. That you and presumably your bosses H. Hayes and A. Gingrich[1] believe I will be here ten years from now, that you will, that Esquire will, that people will and that they will still be reading: that has given me courage to face another day. Me: on the other side of the coming ten minutes all I see is bog and fog. I bought myself a cemetery plot three weeks ago in Texas, meanwhile I'm working on a novel. Could you extract something from it? Well, there's one chapter about a poor fellow trying to get fifteen miles to the gin with all his cotton crop in a borrowed truck meant to be broken-leg funny. [D]oes that sound like something you'd be interested in? Talk to Harold about his plan for getting us all together up here or at his place near New Paltz[2] or both. Do it soon—don't count on doing it sometimes in the next ten years. For, to update the poet, at my back from time to time I hear the sound of fuses burning near . . .[3]

Yours,
Bill
(Humphrey)

P.S. Tell Harold that the movies have now bought the second of the two stories of mine he published last year: The Human Fly.[4] (You don't participate in these glad tidings: you were off in retirement at the time.)
P.P.S. Thanks a lot for the self-addressed stamped envelope.

1. Harold Hayes was editor of *Esquire,* and Arnold Gingrich was its publisher.
2. Village in the central Hudson Valley, New York.

3. An allusion to T. S. Eliot in *The Waste Land* (ll. 196–7)—"But at my back from time to time I hear / The sound of horns and motors . . ."—alluding to Andrew Marvell's "To His Coy Mistress."

4. Published in *Esquire* in September 1968; the other story is "The Pump," published in January 1964.

TO KATHERINE ANNE PORTER

TLS/HL

Hudson, New York
July 14, 1969

Dear Katherine Anne,
Forgive me for not writing in such a long time—life has been hectic for us here lately. We returned from Paris in mid May and almost at once flew off to Texas. My old school S.M.U. gave me an honorary degree—1st college degree of any kind for me, though I was a college prof. for ten years—and I took the occasion to pay a week's visit to my home town Clarksville. First time Dorothy had ever seen the place and the first time I've been back in 32 years although I write about the place all the time. I read in the newspaper the other day some fellow who said you didn't really have the happy childhood you think you did in some small midwestern town in the thirties with memories of porch swings and locusts in the trees etc. He's wrong, I did. Until my father was killed in a car crash in 1937 (he was 38, I was 13) my childhood had been pretty unhappy inside the house but very happy out on the streets. But I was always afraid to go back, I didn't want anything to have changed. It was changed. In that part of Texas everything is changed. When I was a boy it was cotton country, share-cropping, tenant-farming, a hard life whether you were white or black, but as nobody was much better off than anyone else, we didn't complain too much. Now the people, black and white, have left, and the land is used to graze beef cattle and the town has shrunk in size and grown tired and sleepy. I went back out to the old country graveyards where my mother's and father's people are buried, and saw the crumbling old tenant farm houses that my people came from (I knew we were poor, but I was really moved to learn how poor we had been) and roasted in that unbelievable heat. The town gave me a very warm welcome.[1] We returned here to find that on that very day Dorothy's grandchild, Laura, two years old, had been taken unconscious to the hospital with spinal meningitis. She was in [a] coma and not expected to live for over a week, then in [an] isolation ward

for another two weeks after that, but is all right, no after effects.[2] During this period I smoked so much I forgot what air tasted like, so I decided to quit smoking. So as not to climb right up the walls from tobacco withdrawal anxiety I drink myself into a stupor every night and come out of my hangover about noon—another reason I haven't written. How are you liking your new place? Let us have some news of you. Until then Dorothy joins me in sending much love.

Yours always,
Bill

1. A reception held in WH's honor was attended by about eleven hundred.
2. Laura Lord now lives in California.

TO KATHERINE ANNE PORTER

TLS/HL

Hudson, New York,
Jan. 15, 1970

Dear Katherine Anne,

Dorothy's is the only face I've seen in six weeks and I seldom see hers any more as she has rented a vacant artist's studio in a village 15 miles away and, when the roads are passable, hies her off over there to paint every morning Sunday included with her lunch in a basket and gets back home at sundown. I went to the door this morning to answer a rare not to say unique knock and looked out and saw what I thought was a pair of human faces but I was mistaken, they weren't human they were angels. It was nine a.m. and the mercury stood at ten degrees below zero and the snow banks at six feet above ground when I received this visitation. At my door were two females one of whom, the short fat one, told me while the other one, the long lean one, nodded, that they had been sent by the Lord Jehovah to set me on the path to heaven. I said thank Him for me next time they saw Him but that I was too busy right then cleaning up the mess caused by what my Homeowner's Insurance Policy in the fine print calls one of His Acts to go anywhere. Yes, I am still emptying pails and wringing towels from the drip in the roof following the Big Snowstorm, and Phoenix Mutual of Hartford, Conn[.] has passed the buck to the One where the buck stops. The fat angel spoke in an accent which seemed vaguely familiar to me, and Lord knows until I was nineteen years old I'd never been above

Hugo, Oklahoma.[1] I was pretty soon able to place it. The flaming red Ford from which they had descended bore a license plate which was not from the District of Redemption but from some county in West Virginia. A kind of middle-age spread has extended the Bible Belt and just as we now see in these New England skies turkey buzzards driven north by tractors and the consequent dearth of dead mules and plow horses in their native climes so we also have these soul-scavengers at our doors.

So here I sit in this vast empty house with the only sound the drip of drops into pails and the clatter of this machine. If the Lord is really serious about wanting to do me a favor why doesn't He send somebody to finish this novel for me? Or at least to wring out those towels while I do it?

That roof. I found a lean wiry tough little guy in the neighboring village with so many children to feed and clothe that he was willing to risk his neck and climb up there with a sledge hammer and bust up and throw down the accumulated ice which was melting underneath from the heat of the house but not on top and running down inside the walls. He broke up and threw down about three tons, I reckon. Some of these chunks of ice would weigh two hundred pounds. Luckily the one I was standing under steadying his ladder so as not to have the orphaning of his five kids on my already overladen conscience was smallish—about fifteen cents worth it would have been in Clarksville, Tex. when I used to go to the ice house with my coaster wagon to fetch it home. But falling from forty feet it hit hard enough to raise a knot on my head the size of a horse apple and to open a gash about two inches long and half an inch wide and to give me a mild concussion. This was ten days ago and I'm ok now. I still can't part my hair but I begin to think I'm not a great deal crazier than I was before it happened.

Sold my 50[-]page essay on the sex life of salmon and salmon fishermen to *Esquire* who will run it in their next May issue.[2]

Hope all had a good time at the party we missed and that you are well and enjoying your constitutional right to happiness, or at least the pursuit thereof. Love from us both.

Yours always,
Bill

1. Town due north of Clarksville, Texas, just over the state line.

2. *The Spawning Run* appeared in the June 1970 issue of *Esquire* and in book form, published by Knopf, later in the year.

TO SEYMOUR LAWRENCE

TLS/UM

Hudson, New York
June 20, 1970

Dear Sam,

I must write Ugne Karvelis of Gallimard soon about a piece of business and I just can't do it without being able to say something about her man Rudnicki. Please come to a decision about him so that if you don't want him I can try him on another house.[1]

Saw Katherine Anne[2] in the hospital about a month ago. I was on my way back from Alabama where I had gone to do an article on an aspect of conservation for LIFE. We had a great couple of hours together. I smuggled in a pint of Virginia Gentleman in the pocket of my raincoat (the sun was shining bright) and she and I and Stan Weyman, the Life photographer I had been down south with, just about did that bottle in. She then revealed that she had a whole case more of the same medicine under her bed.

Hope you saw my long essay on the sex life of salmon and salmon fishermen in the June Esquire.[3] It's to be brought out as a book here and in England in the fall, and I'm getting inquiries about the film rights. Had more fun writing it than I ever had doing anything in my life. Hope it amuses you.

All best wishes, in which Dorothy joins.

Yours,
Bill
(Humphrey)

1. At the request of Ugné Karvelis, an editor at Éditions Gallimard, WH had two years earlier sent Lawrence French translations of works by the Polish Jewish writer Adolph Rudnicki and had been pestering Lawrence since then. Lawrence declined to publish Rudnicki, whereupon WH turned to Knopf.

2. Porter.

3. See note number 2 for the previous letter.

TO NICK LYONS

[Nick Lyons was WH's student at Bard College in 1957, a teacher of English for twenty-six years at Hunter College, and afterward president of Lyons Press, a publisher of outdoor literature. He has written eighteen books, among them A Flyfisher's World, *which was illustrated by his wife Mari, a well-known painter*

of "some of the most acute witty impressions of (New York) streets [. . .] ever seen" (Jed Pere, New Republic*).]*

TLS/SMU

[Hudson, New York]
October 28, 1970

Dear Nick,

Herewith my check and with it my thanks for sending the books.

The Wannings are coming here to dinner (my French translator[1] is our weekend guest) on Saturday night and I do believe it will do them good to get out of the house and not just sit there alone together in that same silence, but they are obviously both crushed. How does one ever get over such a thing?[2]

About Ted:[3] I don't understand what has come over him. He used to have what I can only call a gusto for gloom but now the gloom is there without the gusto. Every breath he fetches is a deep sigh. He's got a sister who is driving him out of his mind by going out of her's, but even this, drag though it is, seems hardly enough to account for his constant sense of being finished and done and depressed. The ebullience you remember: that's gone. I haven't seen any of that in a long time. Well, God knows, none of us has much of that precious quality any more.

Many thanks for sending me the book on grouse shooting. So far my prediction to you has proved entirely accurate: I shall have to imitate Tartarin[4] and lay in a stock of inexpensive hats to have something to shoot at. I've owned my cute little L. C. Smith 20 gauge for two weeks, *and haven't fired it yet.* Oh, for the days when my father and I used to bring home fifty ducks from a day's hunt. Honest to God. The day's limit is those times was 25. I used to get one and he got 49, making the bag for the two of us.

Yours,
Bill

P.S. Thanks for the cutout from The Bookseller.[5] I hadn't seen it, and obviously wouldn't have if you hadn't. Chatto had not sent it.

1. Jean Lambert.

2. On 16 October 1970, Margaret Sommer, the daughter of Andy and Pat Wanning, committed suicide in Philadelphia.

3. Weiss.

4. Tartarian of Tarascon, a brave hunter of caps, is a character created in 1872 by Alphonse Daudet.

5. Very likely a review of *The Spawning Run* in the 29 August 1970 issue of the *Bookseller.*

TO KATHERINE ANNE PORTER

TLS/HL [Hudson, New York early August 1971]

Dear Katherine Anne,

I am so terribly sorry to hear about your attack of angina. I have been told how very painful that is and I wish I could come down there and be of some comfort to you. But I can't go anywhere nor be of any comfort to anybody. I am still on crutches,[1] beginning the eighth week of it. My doctor here finally got back from his long vacation this week, took new x-rays, and these show that in addition to a toe I broke a large bone in the foot, and broke it real good: its whole length. The pieces have aligned themselves right and are healing together but the foot just won't respond to any of my commands, it just want[s] to be left alone. On crutches I'm helpless. Can't fetch anything for myself that I can't carry between my teeth, and have to get up steps on all-fours. My disposition, never exactly sweet, is sour and I growl at people and everybody is glad not to see me. My one pleasure is knocking little children and other cripples out of the way with my crutches. Can't get any work done because I must keep the foot elevated and can't sit for any time at this machine. Well, you see: all I do is gripe and whine and complain, and now I'm doing it to you. Conduct unbecoming . . . Best thing for me to do is just shut up, after saying I do hope you are feeling better and that we both send you all our love.

Yours,
Bill

1. WH injured his foot on 18 June at Cape Cod while playing baseball.

TO KATHERINE ANNE PORTER

TLS/HL Hudson, New York August 21, 1971

Dear Katherine Anne,

I am sorry to have missed your telephone call. We are out of the house quite a lot these days. Dorothy takes me for drives because I have been getting so stir-crazy. I am walking now without a cane. If it can be called walking. Shuffling. About minus twenty miles an hour is my speed and it hurts like old billy hell. But I am self-propelled and I'm not complaining.

I was so pleased to get your sweet letter. We went down to the town immediately after it arrived and looked in the stores for a copy of the August Ladies Home Journal.[1] No luck. That issue is off the stands already. Do you suppose it would do any good if you were to ask the editors to send me a copy? Would you mind trying? Otherwise I shall miss it.

I was delighted to learn that you have been writing. Esquire? They're all right. I've published a lot there—more than in any other magazine, and have always gotten along well with their people. The editor, Harold Hayes, is a pal of mine. The magazine is a mess typographically and if you grow inattentive and let your eye wander into the advertising columns you could upchuck but of what magazine isn't that true, and they do leave what you write alone. I'll see whatever you write for them: I have a lifelong complimentary subscription.

Having your brain photographed? Whose nutty idea was that? Nothing wrong with your brain.

Would you like to visit us here in early October? If you could take a plane from Washington to New York City I could meet you and drive you up. It's pretty here at that time of year. We would love you to come. There is just one question: how are you at getting up and down stairs? Your room would be up one flight. Could you cope with that?

We are going to visit friends on Long island next week. If you should try to call and get no answer that's why. But drop me a line and say what you think of the idea of coming here for a visit.

Love,
Bill

1. "The Spivvleton Mystery, or the Importance of Being Deadly Ernest," *Ladies' Home Journal,* August 1971, 74–5, 101. Porter had told WH on 17 August that this was "a memento from my misspent past."

TO F. W. AND BARBARA DUPEE

TLS/CU

Hudson, N.Y.
October 5, 1971

Dear Fred and Andy,

Your letter was forwarded to Wellfleet,[1] but in care of the friend[2] whose house we had, who had left instructions that his mail was to be forwarded to NYC. So I finally got it from him.

Wellfleet was good for body and soul. When I got there I could walk about one city block down the beach below the house; I was up to three mile walks before we left. We lived on oysters, yours for the picking just outside the door, and the weather shone on us. Helped a lot to make up for the lost summer. I still limp[3]—it begins to seem to me I always will—and it still hurts, but the improvement has been very great.

Have you read Edmund Wilson's *Upstate*?[4] I picked it off a shelf in a store on the Cape and put it back thinking from my glimpse that it looked dull. A couple of days later we were in the parking lot of one of the Wellfleet beaches when a car drove up and parked beside us. Wilson, whom I recognized from photos, was the passenger. He looked so unhappy. Why should the fact that he looked unhappy make me think I had better read Upstate after all? Well, of course it wasn't only that. It was also the thought, who do you think you are not to read a book by Edmund Wilson? It isn't dull. The man who emerges is wonderfully attractive and sympathetic and I regret that I [do] not know him, have him for a friend. He is so alive to everything, so open to people of sorts whom you would not expect to interest him at all.

Pleased to hear that you go on enjoying yourselves there so much. D. joins me in sending love.

Yours,
Bill

1. Town on the outer tip of Cape Cod.

2. Edmond G. "Ted" Thomas, a longtime fishing companion of WH's.

3. During the previous June at Cape Cod, WH had broken his foot playing baseball with the Thomases' children.

4. Edmund Wilson (1895–1972), one of the most eminent twentieth-century American men of letters, published *Upstate: Records and Recollections of Northern New York* in 1971.

TO DOROTHY HUMPHREY

[WH and Dorothy decided not to try to endure another bleak winter in Hudson with Proud Flesh *to be finished; therefore, Dorothy went ahead to London to find a flat—one of the rare times when the couple were separated.]*

TLS/HR

[Hudson, New York]
New Years Day [1972]

Dear Dorothy,

You made me promise to write you every day only I didn't promise to and certainly won't if I have no more to say than I have to say now. It's about

4 in the afternoon and I feel like resting from my work for a while before thinking of having a shower preparatory to going up the hill to supper at the Stearns.[1]

I went to dinner with the Stones[2] at Elaine's[3] where even in Peter's company I was greeted with a snarl by the fat and evil-natured proprietress who took my coat from where I had hung it on entering and put [it] on what I suppose must have been a less desirable hook. We ordered dinner. It arrived. We took about three bites whereupon Mary, who really did look very pale, said she was very sick and would Peter please take her home at once and then come back and rejoin the party. As the only thing to do, and because it wasn't all that gay a party, I said we would all go immediately home. Which we did. Next morning I awoke early but being afraid to disturb them lay abed. Not a sound. The morning passed away and I missed the 10:30 train I had meant to take. Well, never mind. There was one at 12:30. Then I discovered that the one at 12:30 does not stop at Hudson. So I said goodbye to Pete at half past eleven so he could go about his business—Mary, though he said she was better, never appeared—and went and sat in Grand Central Station reading The House of the Seven Gables until 2:30 and got home at 5 o'clock. One of many days in my life that I should not much care to be given back again.

You left just in time. Yesterday was arctic cold and wintry and today is too. Clear and less windy today but cold cold[.] I have spent the day writing but haven't got much to show for it. Never mind. I expected it to take a while for me to get in stride again. Went to bed last night at nine o'clock and got up this morning at half past six which is a pretty good schedule for a hermit trying to get some work done.

I hope your flight was smooth and easy and that you were taken in by one or another of Sussex friends.[4]

I forgot to add that another of the pleasures during my short stay at Elaine's was that of seeing Tony Tuttle who promised without my enquiring to send me a copy of his new book.[5] I don't know why, because I don't like to think of myself as hard-hearted, indeed I like to think of myself as responsive[,] particularly to people who obviously need a little sympathy, and he does if anybody ever did (he looked like a mad ghost) but that fellow just makes me want to hide myself so he won't see me.

Well enough and too much of this empty gabble. Enjoy yourself and keep well and don't be a silly fool and bury yourself in some third rate hotel in order to save a few pennies if to be comfortable is possible for a little more money. With much love and with many wishes for a happy new year.

Yours,
Bill

1. Physician Kendall Stearns and his wife Kate were the Humphreys' friends and neighbors. They lived in the house nearest the Humphreys on Gahbauer Road.

2. Peter Stone (1930–2003), a former student of WH's at Bard College, was a librettist for Broadway musicals; his wife is Mary.

3. A restaurant on Second Avenue frequented by the literati of New York City.

4. The Parsons or Peggy Ashcroft.

5. Anthony Tuttle's *Songs from the Night Before* (New York: Doubleday, 1972).

TO DOROTHY HUMPHREY

TLU/HR

[Hudson, New York]
9 o'clock Tuesday night
[4 January 1972]

[No salutation]
Weren't you the one who said you were going to write every day? Well unless you sent me the Pennysaver I didn't get any word from you this day. A long day for me it has been. Up at 7 (I go to bed these days about half past 9) and at this machine ever since except for a trip into Philmont[1] to the pharmacy to pick up a prescription. Have had a pretty bad case of the trots for the past three days—maybe something I picked up in NYC—so bad I finally got scared this morning and took my temperature and found I had a fever of all of about 1 degree and while not scared of that was scared of it getting worse and being here with nobody to take care of me so called Stan Bardwell[2] who called in the prescription. Feeling better now but living on nothing but cheese and milk.

Went to the Stearns last Sat. night for dinner. Their friends the fishing Fenns. For cocktails our unknown neighbors down the road the Freidus'es [*sic*], in what used to be Mr. Olson's house. They came bringing nine friends, among them a young couple fans of my writing. Said they were doing a two week motor trip through Brittany[3] this spring. I said if I had two weeks to do a motor trip in [F]rance instead of Brittany I'd choose the Dordogne.[4] Never heard of it. So I invited them to drop in next day and look at our old picture book guide. They did. Nice-ish people. I was glad to get a look at these Freiduses (he looks like that man who reviews the movies on the local TV, she is [a] rather handsome woman of about say 33, they have just enough pretensions to culture and smartness to be pleasant and not enough to not be able to live up to it) and to think that we might have much worse people down the road.

Just called your brother Seymour[5] and have had a pleasant talk with him. He says he is very well and he did sound as if he were, says he will resume full days work in his office next week.

Am to go to the Stearns for dinner again this Sat. Kate obviously feels she must look after me in my solitude. Actually I don't feel solitary at all. Don't feel bad. I miss you in the evening but I wouldn't know it if you were here during the daytime, I am so engrossed in what I am doing. Really in a sort of hypnotic trance. I make myself go for a walk of about half an hour each afternoon but it's an effort to tear myself away.

You would hardly believe it to see what is happening on NBC television. They in a way much more subtle and much more effective than CBS[6] are going after Nixon, calling him a liar—have used that very word, not only at every chance *he* gives them to do it, but finding occasions for it on their own. It is simply incredible. On David Brinkley's already skeptical face there appears every evening now a look of final disgust as he simply demolishes whatever pi[e]ce of diurnal bullshit has issued from the White House. Even bland John Chancellor[7] in his sweet bland way now tells you what, first, Mr. Nixon said yesterday, and then what the facts are. The two never jibe. There is a tremendous hue and cry here over the renewed bombing of North Vietnam. I heard a POW's very ordinary-looking but very intelligent and very disillusioned wife (he in prison for *six years* and she still just a girl) say yes I am saying that Mr. Nixon is a liar, he is not telling the truth when he says all that is keeping us there is the prisoners, on the contrary, he is using the prisoners (Geo. McGovern[8] said the same thing this morning on the front page of the NY Times) as a way to keep bombing the north in order to support the corrupt regime in So Vietnam. Something big is building up—something really big, you feel it in the papers and in everything on TV.[9]

I am so tired. I really must stop. Good things, some really that surprise me, keep coming out of this machine on the book. Hope you are having a pleasant time. Snow here and cold and more of the same promised for tonight but I hear cars whizzing by outside so it hasn't come yet and maybe they'll be wrong as they so often are. I go up daily to check on the studio. Everything fine.

Am going on with my reading of Hawthorne and for the first time ever have read The Blithesdale Romance,[10] his little screed on Brook Farm,[11] and by extension on utopian socialistic colonies in general. It is in too many ways a period piece, with lots of Gothicism of plot—long lost children and Svengali types[12] influencing young maidens against their will into mesmeric nonsense, and yet with all that really quite wonderful. I finished and really loved The House of the Seven Gables.[13] Last time I read it was by requirement as a junior in high school. The last book on earth to give to anybody male o[r] female black or white southerner or northerner under 25 years of age because, again despite a lurid tacked-on plot with sliding panels behind ancestral portraits activated by now-long-rusty springs containing rotting parchment wills to the long-disputed family claim to lands in the Indian territories nonsense, it is a quite domestic and really sweet book. I find him really congenial in temper and spirit. Now reading the Scarlet Letter[14] again, and that's the best of them all.

Must close and go to bed. Fagged out. Wonder what you did with yourself today? Amusing and sweet to me to think of you doing whatever you do with yourself all by yourself in a distant and foreign place. Love you.

Bill

What did you do with the rest of these letter forms you bought in Ghent, I can't find them.

1. Small town about four miles east of WH's residence.

2. A local physician who was a friend of the Humphreys.

3. The peninsula in northwest France, bordering the English Channel.

4. The Dordogne River Valley, in the center of France.

5. Seymour Feinman was an attorney in New York.

6. Columbia Broadcasting System, the television network.

7. David Brinkley (1920–2003) and John Chancellor (1927–1996) hosted the National Broadcasting Corporation's *Nightly News* from 1970 to 1982.

8. George McGovern (1922–) was the Democratic Party's nominee for president of the United States in 1972.

9. Investigations would soon expose rampant corruption in the Nixon administration. Nixon would resign in 1974 in the face of imminent impeachment for crimes related to the coverup of the Watergate break-in at Democratic Party headquarters.

10. Novel by Nathaniel Hawthorne published in 1852.

11. George Ripley's Brook Farm Institute (1841–47) was a utopian community whose members shared in manual work and intellectual pursuits.

12. Common name for those who hypnotize others to do their bidding, from George

Du Maurier's novel *Trilby* (1894), in which a model is hypnotized by Svengali and made to sing wonderfully under his spell.

13. Novel published by Hawthorne in 1851.

14. Novel published by Hawthorne in 1850.

TO NORAH SMALLWOOD

[Norah Smallwood became president of Chatto & Windus on 1 January 1974, after the retirement of Ian Parsons, and served until 1982, when she retired. WH considered her "one of the very dearest friends" (WH to John Charlton on 19 October 1984).]

TLS/RU

Hudson, New York
June 7, 1972

Dear Norah,

Many thanks for your good letter and for all the trouble you have taken to compile your suggestions about the book.[1] About those suggestions: I can do nothing about them at the moment, for I have no copy of the book. You have the one and Bob Gottlieb[2] has the other. But I am expecting him to mail me the one he has from Europe and shortly. There will still be some trouble, for that copy and yours are not paged the same. But they are not so different that I ought not to be able to figure out your references.

You say you are confused sometimes about what is happening, when, and whether the incident actually took place or is imaginary in the mind of the character. I may have overdone this in places, but I do want the reader to undergo a certain amount of such confusion as you have experienced. A certain hallucination is what I am after. This is a book that cannot be read once and understood but must be read twice. Not every reader is going to do that, I realize, but the ones I am after will. Still I shall consider carefully all such passages as you have marked out for query.

The only salmon I caught in Ireland[3] was one already smoked—consolation prize from one of the hotels where we put up. Sorry to have missed Bryan Moyne.[4] La Bussola[5] was fun, wasn't it—but for lunch only. After you and I had been there for lunch I took Ugne Karvelis of Gallimard there for dinner one evening. Disastrous. Same food but the place has a band and the noise level is not to be believed and every Angl[o]-Italian in London comes there to dance on the dance floor. I screamed my displeasure in my lowest Italian at them, swore I'd call the police if the amplifier on the band's loud speaker wasn't dialed down, left no tip, and parted with curses. So remember go there a mezzogiorno[6] only.

Yours,
Bill

1. *Proud Flesh.*

2. Robert Gottlieb became WH's editor at Knopf in 1968 and subsequently president of Knopf.

3. Upon completion of *Proud Flesh* in April 1972, WH headed for County Kerry, Ireland, under the sponsorship of *True* magazine to salmon fish for two weeks.

4. Bryan Walter Guinness, second baron Moyne (1905–92), poet, novelist, and playwright.

5. Italian restaurant in London.

6. At midday.

TO KATHERINE ANNE PORTER

TLS/HL [Hudson, New York]
June 16, 1972

Dear Katherine Anne,

Now that the roof has been ripped off the house and a new one hammered on and the roofers have gone and you can hear yourself think again in this house, I can write you a note.

We're home again after a most needed and most successful stay abroad. Needed because of my last summer of broken foot and bad temper—happy because Dorothy found us that wonderful London apartment where I finished the novel I began in 1957[1] and laid aside time and again and despaired of ever finishing. Last October, when I got off the crutches, I looked at the mound of tattered unnumbered pages of manuscript which nobley [*sic*] and least of all I could make any sense out of and said to myself well, you have this choice: throw it away now, or give yourself one more year—it will take that at least—and then throw it away. I worked eight, ten, twelve hours a day on it from then until April 8. You know, few people who don't write know how much physical labor goes into it. I say nothing of the more important sort of labor, just the sheer physical stamina that is needed!

At the end of our London stay TRUE magazine, the one that sent me to the Bahamas last year,[2] sent me to Ireland for two weeks of salmon fishing. We were in the far southwest part. Near the Lakes of Killarney, in Country Kerry. We started off in Dublin, a dreary, depressed and depressing place, and drove down to Tipperary, then on. Barren, rocky country with sudden mountains, not majestic as in Scotland but impressive enough in scale. A watery part of the world, with the sea never far away and with enough rivers and streams to satisfy even an angler like me. But I caught my usual: nothing. No, I caught one salmon, on my last day. One already smoked. Consolation pr[i]ze from the hotel where we stayed. We followed this up with a week of riotous living in Paris.

You would think that after the long agony of the one just finished I would swear off writing books, but no, I've already started another one.[3] How's old Cotton Mather these days? How's old woman river?

Love,
Bill

1. *Proud Flesh.*

2. Where WH bonefished and wrote "The Rigors of Bonefishing," for *True,* reprinted in *Open Season* (1986).

3. Before the depression that accompanied the critical reception of *Proud Flesh,* WH had plunged into writing "The Last Refuge" (later titled "The Horse Latitudes"). It was never published.

TO HAROLD HAYES

[Hayes, editor at Esquire *magazine, had offended WH by failing to include him in a list of writers, as Hayes explained in the answering letter of 17 October, "devised [not] to compare writing talents or to suggest a pecking order" but one "made to suggest the character of this magazine over the years [. . .]." Hayes made a distinction between his role as editor and his relationship with WH based on friendship.]*

TLU/HR[1]

Hudson, New York
October 13, 1972

Dear Harold,
If, as Pascal[2] said, the style is the man,[3] then it is even more true that the writer is the man, and the man the writer. I should have thought you would have learned this in your experience as an editor. When have you deeply offended a writer and remained friends with the man? I am flabbergasted at your saying, let's stay friends because the author-editor relationship is mainly horseshit anyhow. Not to me it isn't. If you can think,

for instance, that Norah Ephron's article on the size of her tits is more worthy of inclusion in the issue of your magazine containing the 50 best things you've ever published than any of the six things I have sent you, then you're no friend of mine, nor are you the editor I thought you were. The meaning of my asking you to return the mss. of my novel[4] is that you have seen the last of my writing and of me. We'll both survive this, I expect, but it saddens me—a poor reward for my loyalty to Esquire and for what I thought was Esquire's loyalty to me.

1.Unsigned original retained by WH.

2. Blaise Pascal (1623–62), French writer who said something close to what WH attributes to him: "When we encounter a natural style we are always astonished and delighted, for we expected to see an author, and found a man" *(Pensées).*

3. The phrase "le style est l'homme" is from George-Louis Leclerc de Buffon (1707–88), *Discours sur le style.*

4. Hayes responded immediately: "I'm sorry I caused you hurt by leaving you out of that ad. I will of course return your manuscript to Knopf though it seems from my end the fine you impose is out of proportion to the offence."

TO KATHERINE ANNE PORTER

[This, WH's last letter to Porter, shows no sign that their relationship of twenty-three years was about to end. Between the writing of this letter and the proposed March visit, WH apparently heard about Porter's expressions of outrage that WH and others had been credited by Seymour Lawrence for their role in the preparation of the Collected Essays and Occasional Writings of Katherine Anne Porter *(1970). Porter had solicited WH's help in selecting and organizing the essays (which she was unable to do on account of illness). Perhaps Porter's behavior was an early sign of the memory failure that became prominent in 1976. Whatever the case, WH must have reacted to her ingratitude by cutting off the relationship altogether.]*

TLS/HL [Hudson, New York]

Jan. 4, [']73

Dear Katherine Anne,

We were running a resort hotel all fall. Guests followed one another so quickly the beds never got a chance to cool off. After two months of this we both just wore out. Then came galley and page proofs of the novel—a chore I hate. I read them—Dorothy read them—I read them again—she read them again. And still I'm sure we didn't catch all the errors. Well, that's out of the way now, the holidays are out of the way now—so, how are you? Somebody told me—well, what was it I heard? That you had been sent to the moon? That you are to be Playboy's girl of the month?[1] But seriously, I was delighted to hear about that junket—delighted to know that you were getting out and around and having some fun.

We're here, as you see, rather than off in England or some such place. I felt I had to be here to answer the phone in case it was Hollywood or some other source o[f] money. For although I am about to publish a book[2] I have already eaten (and drunk) most of the money the sale of the book will ever bring. So in an effort to learn to stop hating winter and learn to like it, we have bought ourselves sets of cross-country skis. Not the alpine variety—that scares me to death—but the flat-country kind. And wouldn't you know: no snow. It amuses me to find that I have joined the ranks of those whom I previously despised: people who in the winter here were unhappy when the sun shone and were rattling their gourds for a blizzard. I grew up as I need not tell you where when it did snow (I saw it just twice in my first thirteen years: a quarter of an inch each time) we went out with teacups and scooped it up and poured vanilla extract and sugar on it and ate it. No winter-sportsman I. But I am determined to become one and stop spending the winter like the groundhog.

But March is something else. Mudtime. So we are thinking maybe of going to Florida (never been there) for the month of March. More specifically to Key West, which somebody tells me isn't the Disneyland that the rest of the state has become (I plan to drive through the state lengthwise with my eyes closed). If we do then perhaps we can pay you a visit,[3] either on the way down there or the way back. Want also to see Charleston and Savannah. Never have.

Found a title for the novel. Proud Flesh. It fits somehow. Now have begun another one.[4]

Much love and happy new year,
Bill

Ever read a forgotten (1899) novel entitled The Awakening by Kate Chopin? It's interesting.

1. *Playboy,* a men's entertainment, issue, and interview magazine, features a monthly nude female "playmate."

2. *Proud Flesh.*

3. WH and Dorothy never made the visit.

4. "The Last Refuge" (later "The Horse Latitudes").

[AFTER *PROUD FLESH*]

1973–79

TO JAMES ELLIOTT LINDSLEY

[Christopher Lehmann-Haupt wrote a vicious review of Proud Flesh *for the 4 April* New York Times, *calling the "dreadful" novel a "tricked up [. . .] parody of William Faulkner" and "hands down the worst piece of fiction I've read so far this year"—"even the title stinks a little." When the Reverend Lindsley, an Episcopal priest who had been a friend of WH's for many years, read the review, he immediately went to his friend, because he knew he would be devastated by the critic's attack.]*

TLS/PH

[Hudson, New York]
April 18, 1973

Dear Elliott,

I am deeply touched to know that you made that trip up here early that morning because you were concerned over me and wanted to comfort and support me. I shall never forget it.

Gratefully and affectionately,
Yours always,
Bill

TO PAT BLACK

[Pat Black, from a prominent Clarksville, Texas, family, was offended by WH's Proud Flesh. *He wrote to WH on 27 March 1973 to complain that in writing the novel he had confused 1940s Clarksville with the town in 1969. Black flatly told WH that if he wanted to write about the contemporary South, he really ought to spend some time there.]*

TLS/PH [Hudson, New York
April 1973]

Dear Mr. Black,

Too bad that you were disappointed by my new book but not surprising, for it seems to have hurt your sense of local pride and because you were looking for something you didn't find: uplift.

I can't compete with you in your knowledge of the outward look of present-day Clarksville. I was there, however, for a short visit in 1969, and I saw unpaved roads, for instance (we have them where I live, too; no invidious comparison meant.) I saw stray livestock wandering on them (we have those too). It may be that there were no migrant workers picking cotton in Red River County, but I saw work gangs in east Texas (we have those here, too). You do credit me with saying that they had all but disappeared. And it was still possible to discuss whether or not to pick cotton with a machine. I did not say that the schools had not been integrated. I said there had been incidents of racial trouble on the schoolbus [*sic*]—without suggesting that east Texas was the only place that could happen, either. As for the age of strong families being over, in Clarksville or anywhere else, in 1969 or ever, that has not been my experience. In the case of my fictional family I tried in every way I could to say that they represented a way of life whose day was ended, that they knew this though they denied it to themselves and fought to disprove it to the world.

But this does not go to the heart of your dissatisfaction with my book, as you point out. What you think I misrepresent is today's black Texan, his position, and the attitude of his white neighbors towards him.

I did not say that by being "melodious" a work chant was a happy sound . . . contented darkies working in the fields for ol' marster. I do not need you to tell me that it is the sound of oppression. I called it a "melodious moan." A moan is a lament, a cry of pain. It is still melodious, in a mindless way, as my more extended description of it should have conveyed to you.

You feel that I did not give my black characters sufficient humanity. I am not sure exactly what you mean by that, whether it is that they lack the complexity you find in some of Faulkner's early books, or that you think I condescend to them. If the first, I can only say that I gave them the complexity which the demands of my story laid upon them. I was writing a novel, not a guidebook, and the black characters in my novel are not the major characters. If the second, I can only deny your implied charge that

I, like the later Faulkner, held the view that no black man would trade his chance to be a buck in niggertown for a decent job and acceptance as a full and equal man. I put such notions into the mind of Clyde Renshaw, but I depicted Clyde Renshaw in such a light that I did not believe it necessary to give him a placard saying that he spoke for himself, not the sponsor.

You feel that I have been anachronistic, that I have misrepresented the progress in equal rights made in the new South, and that I have thereby betrayed my duty to make Northerners feel a pang of self-recognition for their racism. I am aware of the progress in equal rights made in the South. I am also aware that there is much racism in the North. But when you say that by 1969 things had improved to the point that a real-life Clyde Renshaw would have gotten his ass kicked all over Red River County by Shug's brother, and with the approval of the local whites—what brand do you drink? The New South is a lot better place for both races. But there has been a New South every decade since the first one was proclaimed in the eighteen-eighties. While accusing me of sentimental nonsense about the darkies chanting softly in the cottonfield [*sic*] you should caution yourself against becoming a local booster and sounding like that old southern cry, our niggers are happy, come on down and see. If way to the better there be, it exacts a full look at the worst.[1]

I have not suggested that racism is confined to the rural South, as you say I have, nor even that it is worse there. What period are you living in, to think that the world needs me or anybody else to tell it that racism has no geographical boundaries? You can read that in the newspapers, you don't need a novel. That was neither my duty nor my theme. Which brings me to another of your points. "It's not worse down here, only different, and the nation should be taught that fact by its best fiction," you say. You are right in your first point, and nothing in my book disputes it, and dead wrong in your second point. Fiction does not "teach" anything. Edification—up-lift—political, social, moral—is not the aim of art.

In all these things I differ with you. This I resent: your snide remark that, as I depict it in my book, racism is not something that could disturb "the civilized folks who inhabit Upstate New York." There is nothing in my book to suggest that I think the people where I live are any more "civilized" than the people of the place where I was born and raised. When will Southerners get over their hypersensitivity to anything said about them by anybody living anywhere to the north of them? Maybe when they, along with everybody everywhere else, have purged themselves of their guilt instead of congratulating themselves on having done so.

Sincerely,
William Humphrey

1. A quotation from Thomas Hardy's "In Tenebris."

TO BERNARD VARLEY

[WH's uncle operated a barbershop in Clarksville, Texas; in 1979 he was elected mayor.]

TLS/PH [Hudson, New York]
May 1, 1973

Dear Bernard,
It was good of you to call. Here is my correspondence with your neighbor, Pat Black. Needless to say, I was drunk when you called, and it was the liquor talking when I said I didn't want you to cut the man's hair. Forget that nonsense. Send back the letters when you have read them. Wish I could give you herewith some better news about the book but I can't. It looks pretty bleak.[1]

Love to you both,
Bill

1. WH alludes to the critical reviews of *Proud Flesh,* which were not favorable (for example, "Ten-Gallon Gothic," *Time,* 30 April 1973, 94).

TO NORAH SMALLWOOD

TLS/UR Hudson, N.Y.
December 21, 1973

Dear Norah,
[. . .][1]

I have tried for months to get around to writing you but just have not been able. I haven't had any good news for anybody, and I still don't. The disastrous reception of Proud Flesh both here and in England has simply left me stunned, bewildered about what has happened, uncertain about the future, and unable to make any plans, unable to work.[2] This could not go on, so in early autumn I forced myself to sit down to the typewriter and work on a new book. The world having so decisively rejected one on which I had done my best, it is not easy to work on another one, but what else could I do? So I have 125 pages of a novel written.[3] Whether that is good news or not I don't know, but at least I am able to put aside my bewilderment and my bitterness while working. If these blows have hit me hard, they have hit Dorothy much harder. I am now counting the days remaining of this hateful year. Auguries of the one ahead do not look very good, but at least it will be good to be done with this one. I need not tell you, I'm sure, how bitterly disappointed we were at the cancellation of Ian and Trekkie's visit.

I hope that you are well. Things are bad here now,[4] but I shudder when I read the news of what's happening in Britain.[5] Dorothy joins me in sending love. Do let us hear from you.

Yours,
Bill

1. This letter begins with a paragraph (here omitted) on a legal question about "British commonwealth rights" in connection with the reprinting of "The Pump," a story in *A Time and a Place.*

2. After Christopher Lehmann-Haupt's initial attack on *Proud Flesh* (New York Times, 4 April 1973), there was an avalanche of devastating reviews. See Alfred Reeves, "Portrait in Failure," *Times Literary Supplement,* 3 August 1973, and the *Observer,* 2 September 1973, p. 34. WH's dejection went on for months.

3. "The Last Refuge" (later titled "The Horse Latitudes"), never published.

4. The Watergate scandal was unfolding, and many gas stations in the United States were closed on account of the fuel shortage.

5. By the end of 1973, unemployment was up, growth down, and there was a deal of bickering between unions and the Tory government. The OPEC oil embargo had caused the price of petroleum products to soar, resulting in general economic uncertainty. The country was headed toward the great coal strike of 1974.

TO HARRY GRABSTALD

TLS/PH

Hudson, New York
January 16, 1974

Dear Harry,

Every time I think of writing you life deals me another blow. The latest—yesterday: Toni, with no husband, with a child, after working hard and finally getting her masters degree in teaching, got the only job she could find last September, teaching in a school for mentally retarded and delinquent boys, big, difficult boys of 18 and 19. Her pay has been next to nothing and she is living in a one-room house with no water. Yesterday she was fired, with two week's notice. I can't give her any more than the $75 a month I have been giving her right along, in fact, I don't know how much longer I can go on giving her that much. Dorothy lives in a state of permanent deep depression, with frequent total breakdowns. I too live in a state of permanent deep depression and yet I must sit at this machine[1] and try to be entertaining. Except for exactly five, every friend I thought I had has dropped me following the failure of my last book. All the world loves a winner, but nobody knows you when you're down and out. For ten months I have sat in this big silent house where the telephone never rings and the postman stops only to leave bills and circulars. It's no fun for anybody to get a letter like this, and that's why I don't write any more of them than I do. Don't bother answering this one. I just wanted you to know that there is a reason—lots of reasons—for my silence.

Yours,
Bill

1. WH kept pounding away at the never-to-be published novel "The Horse Latitudes," whose main character holds "that the world has gone completely to hell."

TO HARRY GRABSTALD

TLS/PH [Hudson, New York]
Feb. 25, [']75

Dear Harry,
Every time my conscience begins to prick me and to say that I have owed you—and others, too, for that matter—a letter for a long time, some new something happens to depress me and I say, who wants bad news? Well, I haven't got any good news now, but here at least is word that we're still alive.

I am making an effort to get back into teaching. Not because I yearn to, but because I can't—and don't want to—go on with this killing life of writing for a living. It's a bad time just now to look for a teaching job. Colleges are hurting more than anybody else, what with government cutbacks in aid to education, endowment monies shrinking in the shrinking economy, higher tuition costs and consequent drop in enrollments, and all this complicated by a kind of club-membership etiquette of a sort which I suppose must exist in your profession,[1] too: namely, that you don't really apply for a job, you just stand there looking pretty and smelling sweet like a flower, waiting for the bee to sip your nectar. I have alerted the few friends I still have in the academic world to my need of a job—so far nothing.

Meanwhile we are making the first tentative efforts to sell this house[2] and furnishings. I need the money it represents, what's more I want a house I can rent without worry if a job offer does come along that would take me away for a year or so.

Bodily, we're well enough.

That's what news I've got. How are you? Dorothy joins me in sending love. Drop us a line.

Yours,
Bill

1. Medicine.

2. High Meadow.

TO BERNARD VARLEY

[WH decided to set aside the novel about Cecil Smoot, "The Horse Latitudes," which had been unequivocally rejected by Robert Gottlieb on 18 January, and give his attention to a memoir of his first thirteen years, which was published in 1977 under the title Farther Off from Heaven.*]*

TLS/PH

[Hudson, New York]
Feb[.] 25, [']75

Dear Bernard,

I am once again writing something set in Clarksville—this time in more real-life detail than ever before. It would be good if I could make a visit there and walk all over town in o[r]der to get it all laid out right in my head again and not have to depend entirely on my memory, but I just can't afford the time or the money. Is there available a street map of the town? Up here in even the smallest towns a local newspaper will sometimes have for sale a map of the place—is there such a one for Clarksville? If so, please make an effort to get a copy to me. It would be absolutely invaluable to me.[1] And, incidentally, it would be just as well to keep it to yourself that I am writing about Clarksville.

Things haven't gone so well for us lately. Oh, we are well, but I mean financially. I am making tries at getting a job teaching again. This killing business of writing for a living has gotten to be too much for me. Not a very good time for jobs teaching, but I must try.

And how are you two?[2] I hope you are in less pain, Bernard.[3]

Dorothy joins me in sending love.

Yours,
Bill

1. On 17 March 1975, WH acknowledged receipt: "It must have been a great deal assembling all the m[a]terial that you sent me. I am truly grateful. They are all helpful to me, especially the street map. Good as my memory of the layout of the town is after half [. . .] a century, I had forgotten the names of some of the streets. It's good to have it spread out before me."

2. The other is Bernard's wife Rebecca.

3. Varley had severe pain in one of his hands, a condition that was mystifying his doctors.

TO NICK LYONS

[In April WH was asked by Gerald Walker of the New York Times *to write an article on the lore and attractions of Catskill fly fishing.]*

TLS/SMU [Hudson, New York]
May 29 [1975]

Dear Nick,

We had owned this house about a week when, 10 years ago, I had Walt Frick out to give me an estimate on putting a dormer in the guest room. He looked it over, said he would figure out an estimate, and see me in a few days. I have never seen him since. I understand that he does good work—when he works.

Finish what article? The order from G. Walker was, "Go over to that shrine of fly fishing, the Beaverkill River.[1] Write us about its history, legend and lore. Stay in that hallowed temple of angling, Antrim Lodge.[2] Get to know the regulars and gather a trove of amusing, interesting anecdotes from them." I am putting the words in his mouth, but that was the drift. So early one morning we set off headed west for the angling experience of a lifetime. Stopped in for a moment to see Frick—who is on the way. "You don't want to go over there now—the water is so high you can't get into a single stream," said the sage of Westkill.[3] But it was a pretty day, it was our 30th anniversary,[4] it was a break from garbage dumps, and so we did not heed the oracle but went on. Never mind that we could not fish today, or even tomorrow—there would be people in Roscoe to interview, a lot of research to do on the Lodge, fishing could come later.

Why did nobody ever tell me about Highway 17? Right along side the river it runs and over it run buses, milktrucks, double tractor trailers and a million traveling salesmen in a rush to get to Binghamton. That is to say, it runs alongside the river when it is not crossing over it. I drove up and down old highway 17 past pools each one of which is a book in itself: Junction Pool,[5] Cairns' Pool,[6] Cook's Pool.[7] Underneath these bridges stood some specimens of a bree[d] of fishermen who are very different from me—people who would fish in Times Square oblivious of where they were so long as they had some hope of hooking a fish. Not this one. I like to hear birds sing, not motors roar, when I go fishing—this means more to me than hooking a trout—especially in a section of a stream where you have got to throw it back anyway. So, I remembered me that there is another storied stream there, the Willowemoc, and I went off down along it. Such squalor I have never seen, not having been in Appalachia. Raising my eyes to mountaintops, I could say to myself, how beautiful this must once have been, but lowering them I said to myself, what's the nearest way out of here. The Antrim Lodge turned out to be a saloon, its patrons the night I spent there—(with Highway 17, raised on its bed, my view, and the traffic roaring all night long even through wax ear stoppers) all people on their way to a stock car race. Had there been any fishermen, there was no place to sit down and fraternize with them, unless strung out along the eight stools at the bar. I ordered for my dinner a steak: rare. What came would have done to resole my waders. I sent it back. Next morning from Margaretsville [*sic*],[8] on my way back home (fully intending to chop my rods up into kindling) I phoned Walker and told him the story he was after was no longer there—another victim of progress and the highway lobby.

Yours,
Bill

1. In south-central New York state, this river flows through the Catskill Mountains.

2. Established in 1890, once the traditional stopping place for fly-fishing heavyweights, in Roscoe, New York.

3. Westkill Mountain Wilderness in the Catskills.

4. Not of WH and Dorothy's marriage but of their meeting in 1945.

5. Where the Beaverkill River and the Willowemoc River join.

6. A long, deep, clear pool believed to hold a tremendous number of fish.
7. Cook's Falls Pool is a popular fishing spot in the last ten miles of the Beaverkill.
8. Margaretville is a village on the northwestern edge of the Catskill Park.

TO NORAH SMALLWOOD

[In October 1975 Jean Lambert offered WH the use of his country house in Souvigny-en-Sologne, a village in Loir-et-cher department in central France. This setting provided the seclusion that WH needed to make progress in writing Farther Off from Heaven: *between October and January he produced one hundred pages.]*

TLS/UR

c/o Lambert
Souvigny-en-Sologne
41600 Lamotte-Beuvron
France
January 16, 1976

Dear Norah,

It is such a long time since I wrote you! But then it is such a long time since I had any very good news to write anyone! Things are looking a little better now. We are here in the home of Jean Lambert, my French translator. He is a professor of French at Smith College, in Massachusetts. Until this year, this house was lived in by his very old mother. She died last year, and he offered the house to us. It's been a mixed blessing. Charming little village but in ten minutes you've seen it all, and everybody in it; No [*sic*] one to talk to, no shops even to keep house out of; and without a car, no way out of it. One bus once a week to Lamotte, 13 kilometers away. I've had Jean's spacious and well-stocked library to work in, but poor Dorothy has been pretty miserable.

One good thing has come of it. You may remember that in Home from the Hill there is a very long episode of a hunt for a wild boar. Well, I never saw one of the creatures in my life, and I doubt that they even exist in Texas. Here they have them in such numbers, they are a nuisance to farmers' crops. I got taken on a wild boar hunt—had the time of my life, and from it have gotten a 20 page essay[1] with which I am quite pleased. And while I am on the subject of my current writing: I now have 200 pages done on a work of non-fiction: a memoir,[2] treating of the three days between the time my father was found dying in a road accident until his burial 3 days later, with memories of that time with him and my mother and my little home town. Those who have seen it say that it is the best thing I have done. If you ever see the American magazine called "Sports Illustrated" (it is published by TIME-LIFE[3] and is very widely circulated in the US) they are running a long episode (one which interests them because it deals with hunting) in their Jan[.] 29 issue. A second episode will appear sometime in February)[.][4]

We got here in October, just in time for the publication of Gallimard's edition of *Proud Flesh;* called in French *Les Liens du Sang.* I know it will please and vindicate your faith in that book to learn that it is getting here the reception we had hoped it would get in America and in England. Wonderful reviews[5] in all the major journals, interviews, long essays planned in the learned journals. I am sure, Norah, that you will know this is not boasting but rather sharing with you, who shared my hopes and my disappointments for that book, the fact that it is not dead but still alive. (Time, I see, for me to apologize for this typing: it is being done on a borrowed machine of vague East European origin: it's got at least a dozen keys where my fingers don't expect to find them; it wants to write Czechopolackian).

You will have read of the death at Christmas of Gaston Gallimard. They have published my books here. I had lunch with Claude, now head of the firm, in Paris last week. He said[:] "Ugné Karvelis (an editor at Gallimard, an old friend of mine) tells me that when she visited you for the weekend in the Sologne to do the interview for 'Le Figaro'[6] that you read aloud to her fifty-odd pages of this memoir that you are writing, and that it is a masterpiece." We were standing on a corner of the rue Jacob when he said that, and there being some dirt available, I modestly dug my toe in it. He continued, "She tells me also that you are beginning to weary of your life confined to the village down there. Well, my father's apartment is standing empty. Come and live in it as my guest for the next two or three months. It's got a bonne.[7] I was born in that house; my father was born in it, my grandfather was born in it. It would give me great pleasure to know that you finished, or had written some part of this book, in my ancestral home." You may believe that I accepted. So, unless some hitch develops we will leave here in the next ten days or so and after that the address will be c/o Gallimard, 39 rue Saint Lazaare, Paris 9[.]

And we have decided that on our way back to America in April or May we will go by way of England to see 4 friends; you being one of them. I hope that suits your plans.

In the meantime, Dorothy joins me in sending love, and all best wishes for a happy new year.

Yours,
Bill

1. "Royal Game," which appeared in *Sports Illustrated* and later in *Open Season* (1986).
2. *Farther Off from Heaven.*
3. An entertainment corporate conglomerate.
4. "The Guns of Boyhood" (*Farther Off from Heaven* [1977], 97–113) appeared in the 26 January 1976 issue of *Sports Illustrated,* 56–60, 62, 64, and is identified as an excerpt "from a work in progress, 'Farther Off from Heaven.'" An additional excerpt from WH's memoir did not appear in February.
5. Examples are Alain Bosquet, *Magazine littéraire,* November 1975, and François Wagner, *Le Monde,* 30 October 1975.
6. Karvelis's interview appears in connection with her review of *Les Liens du Sang,* in *Le Figaro,* 24 January 1976, 14.
7. A maid.

TO NICK AND MARI LYONS

TLS/SMU [Hudson, New York]
June 12 [1976]

Dear Nick and Mari,

Must tell you what happened after you put me in that taxi. The driver, even more inquisitive than taxi drivers generally, wanted to know what I did for a living. College professor, I said. Where? Here and there. Smith this fall.[1] "My first wife was a Smith grad," he said. "Wish I had her still. What you doing down here? You don't belong here. Tell that from your Texas accent." I complimented him on his ear. Said, in fact, it was a [big?] day in my life: I'd just finished a book and was in NYC to discuss terms with my publisher. Get a good advance? Not settled yet. We are now nearing my destination. When'll you[r] new book be out? Spring sometime. Good. I look forward to it. I've read everything you ever wrote, beginning with *The Last Husband.* You're (not William) Humphrey. I knew it when I picked you up. I said nothing like this had ever happened to me before and asked what I owed him. Nothing. So if you ever ride with a balding fellow with a little turned up moustache and twinkly eyes named Lowry, that's my tax[i] driver-fan.

Phyllis called yesterday: very enthusiastic about the mss.[2]

Drove over to Sherburne, N.Y. last week to visit old college chum in his country place.[3] Lovely country. Rather poverty-striken. What a pretty old town Cooperstown[4] is: Touristy, of course, but pleasant.

It was nice to see you, if only for a minute.

Yours,
Bill

1. WH was Elizabeth Drew Professor of English for the fall semester at Smith College, Northampton, Massachusetts.

2. A Knopf editor's response to the manuscript of *Farther Off from Heaven.*

3. Harry Grabstald, whose farm in central New York is midway between Sherburne and Earlville.

4. Site of the National Baseball Hall of Fame and Museum, between Hudson and Grabstald's farm.

TO IAN AND MARGARET PARSONS

TLS/UR

Northampton, Mass.
November 24, 1976

Dear Ian and Trekkie,

Well, you're too good to the book,[1] but I shall be grateful to you always. I am so glad you liked it. It's a funny feeling: I feel I know you better now that you know me—at least my childhood—better. But it was painful, too, getting the letter and wishing we were with you. We miss you so.

Your letter was brought by the postman who took away mine to you about Jean Lambert's Gide-bussy [*sic*] book.[2]

Ian, as to your editorial suggestions. Let me begin by saying I am much impressed and deeply grateful to you for the closeness of your reading. I must explain that you were reading a Zerox copy of a typescript which I made in great haste, under time pressure from Knopf. Thus a good many of your notations are (1) typographical errors and absentmindednesses of mine which do not appear in Knopf's compositor's copy; (2) errors of graver sort which Knopf's extremely punctilious copy-editor will have caught and corrected. But beyond that, real problems arise. I don't see how setting two editions can be avoided if you insist on many of your suggestions meant to make the book more easily available to English readers. I can certainly see the desirability of setting only one edition, but an Anglo-American edition of this book is impossible. (A small instance: you say that none of the three of you, Trekki[e], yourself nor your secretary could make any sense out of, "one chance on the punchboard in the diner on the Paris Road." I'll wager you couldn't! For I am talking there about something very American, and, indeed, something which has largely disappeared from America. But as recently as twenty years ago one often found in diners (which are cafés made out of old railroad dining cars, or, nowadays, made to look as if they were out of old dining cars) lying on the counter at which one was served his meal, a block of cardboard about a foot square and about an inch thick in which were rows of perforations very much like a comb of honey, and like a comb of honey, with each of these perforations sealed up, as though it had a grub inside. These perforations were waiting to be punched out (thus the name punch-board) with a little stick attached to the board by a cord. You paid, say, five cents (that's a nickel) for each punch (each "chance"). You poked the little stick in the hole and out the other side emerged a little piece of paper all folded in pleats so that it could be squeezed into that tiny hole. On unfolding and reading the paper, you learned whether or not you had won one of the prizes: a sum of money, a doll, or in my father's case, a shotgun.[)]

Now, an American does not need this explanation—does the English reader *want* an explanation this long? If he does, how in God's name am I to supply it without boring hell out of him? This is just one of the many problems which our being divided by a common language and quite dissimilar popular cultures brings about. There is yet another problem, even more serious. Knopf is already well along in the production of their edition. I have already agreed to at least as many changes suggested by them as you have suggested, they think they have got the text exactly as they want it. I am quite sure they would think some of the things you want done to it to make the book more accessible to English readers would kill it for American ones.

I don't know how you are going to work this out, but it seems to me that if you want an Anglicized edition you are going to have to print it. Finally, although I shall consider carefully and as much from your point of view as I can, each and every one of your suggestions, it must be remembered that I am after all American (to complicate matters further, a Southerner). Thus there will have to be retained some things which are simply me, my way of talking, just as my spoken accent, God help me, is what it is. The king's English was not spoken in Clarksville, Texas, and would sound incongruous in a book set there. I think this would bother your readers less than you think it would. We on our side are quite used to translating for ourselves as we read an English book—or of being pleased by the exoticism. You use an Englishism in your letter to me. You say you are sending Norah an alpha double plus[3] report on my book. Have you any idea how foreign that sounds to an American ear—and how delightful? *I* know what you mean, but by no means every American does (though he can easily enough guess) and I would never use it on this side of the water even to another American who *did* understand it. It would sound affected. It pleased me pink having *you* say it!

Well, let me know your reaction to all this. In the meantime, bless you both again for your kindness to the book. It's especially welcome now when I am in that lull period that comes after sending off a manuscript and before the book is in one's hands. Always a nervous and lonely time, and nothing could have done me more good than having you like the book. I needn't tell you there is no one whom I more wanted to like it. Dorothy joins me in sending you all our love. Write soon.

Yours always,
Bill

1. *Farther Off from Heaven.*

2. WH had encouraged Parsons to publish an English version of selected letters from Jean Lambert and Richard Tedeschi's multivolume edition of *Correspondance André Gide–Dorothy Bussy,* which was to be published in France by Gallimard.

3. A++, the highest grade possible.

TO NICK LYONS

TLS/SMU

[Hudson, New York]
Dec. 29 [1976]

Dear Nick,

Sorry you went and spent your money for E. B. White.[1] There is someone I despise. His is the quintessential "New Yorker" mind and spirit. Shallow, supercilious, arch, snobbish, committed to nothing, upholders of a smug mediocrity which they think is the latest word in smartness. He is the embodiment of the middlebrow, of glossy and fashionable kitsch. Why do you suppose he's so popular? Because he has a mind no better than those of his readers'. You know, right down to what schools they send their kids to, the people to whom he appeals. They delegate E. B. White to confirm them in their opinionated lazy-mindedness. If *he* is superior to Melville,[2] that makes their ignorance of him all right. Really, you don't need to read anything *but* The New Yorker. Our great writers—Sallinger [*sic*],[3] Updike,[4]

Cheever[5]—are regulars, and each tells us how great the others are. Just don't miss a copy and you'll be with it. You'll know how to think and to feel, how to dress, where to go, how to smell. And you will be ever so superior to ever so many other people. I despise anybody so self-important as even to keep copies of his letters—to publish them while he is alive, that's narcissism bordering upon the pornographic. It also means that the author knows there cannot be anything in them if he is willing to share them not just with the persons to whom they were addressed but [with] the world at large. Even as he wrote them he was seeing them in print—not the way to write to a friend. Indeed, it is using a friend for self-promotion. It reminds me of Nixon[6] tape-recording conversations with people without their knowledge. No wonder you were disappointed in them; real letters are addressed in intimacy and written with private passions to their recipients; the E. B. Whites of this world are writing only to themselves. Dead letters. Junk mail.

Glad you like *One Hundred Years of Solitude*.[7] What comic inventiveness, and what a way with words, even in a tongue not his own!

Dorothy has had rather a setback. Fever, nausea, a pain in the region of the left kidney. Terribly weary with being an invalid. Ken Stearns is watching her closely.

Happy new year to you. We did so much enjoy our weekend with you.

Yours,
Bill

1. E. B. White (1899–1985) was a poet and essayist known for his ironic perspective on small things. Starting in 1929 he worked for the *New Yorker* until his retirement. *The Letters of E. B. White*, edited by Dorothy Lobrano Guth (New York: Harper and Row), was published in 1976.

2. Herman Melville (1819–91), regarded by many as America's most distinguished nineteenth-century novelist.

3. The stories of J. D. Salinger (1919–), author of *The Catcher in the Rye* (1951), began to appear frequently in the *New Yorker* in the 1940s.

4. John Updike (1932–), a prolific novelist despised by WH in part because Alfred Knopf praised his productivity at the time WH was making little progress on *The Ordways*. He was a friend of John Cheever's and a frequent contributor to the *New Yorker*.

5. John Cheever (1912–82) began his long association with the *New Yorker* in 1935. He created the genre known as "the *New Yorker* story."

6. President Nixon had a secret recording system in the Oval Office.

7. This novel by Gabriel García Márquez (1928–) was published in 1967. WH is mistaken in saying the novel was written "in a tongue not [the author's] own," for it was originally pub-

lished as *Cien años de soledad.* But perhaps WH means to refer to the experience of reading the novel in a language that was not the author's.

TO BERT ALMON

[Almon, a professor at the University of Alberta in Canada, had written a laudatory review of Farther Off from Heaven, *WH's memoir of his childhood, praising him for shaping each chapter around "a theme or a segment of family history," such as the father's skill as a hunter or his parents' courtship. Almon also notes what WH was most proud of about the memoir's organization, the technique of withholding complete information about some key events: "the full anecdote is always told where it will have the most impact." Finally, Almon says that the book "reveals that very little was ever lost on Humphrey, for what he could not understand as a child, adult reflection and imaginative sympathy would clarify. [. . .] Humphrey has retained the child's sharp perceptiveness, while adding the intelligence and wisdom of a mature artist to this account of life in Clarksville, his flawed heaven" ("William Humphrey's Blue Heaven,"* Southwest Review 63, *no. 1 [Winter 1978]: 85, 86).]*

TLS/PH

Hudson, New York
February 18, 1978

Dear Mr. Almon,

I believe it is not *comme il faut*[1] for a writer to thank a reviewer, but I have never done things *comme il faut* and it seems to me it would be unforgivable not to thank you for your review of Farther Off from Heaven. Believe me, it is not just for the high praise you give the book that I am thankful. No reviewer of any book of mine has ever seen more perceptively what I was trying to do and why I did it in the way I did.

By coincidence you chose to say of me something which I have quoted to three generations of students of creative writing: Henry James' "Strive to become a person on whom nothing is lost." To have it said that I am such a person is the highest compliment I could ever hope to be given.

You say that you read the book in El Paso.[2] Do you live there? If so, do you know my Clarksville childhood friend, Haywood Antone, director of the Texas Western Press at the University? I was in El Paso, for the first time, last May,[3] and saw Haywood for the first time in 40 years.

I am pleased that your review appeared where it did. I went to school at S.M.U. (did not graduate), knew well the editor of The Southwest Review of my time,[4] and was given an honorary degree by the University some years ago.

Again, my deepest thanks to you for your close and careful and sympathetic reading of my book.

Yours,
William Humphrey

1. The French phrase means "as ought to be done."

2. El Paso is Almon's home town.

3. WH gave again one of the lectures originally presented at Washington and Lee University in 1963, "Ah, Wilderness! The Frontier in American Literature," which was promptly published as a pamphlet by Texas Western Press.

4. WH probably refers to Lon Tinkle, who assumed the editorship of the *Southwest Review* in the spring of 1942. Allen Maxwell was the previous editor.

TO HERMAN GOLLOB

[While gathering historical materials for writing No Resting Place, *WH wrote to Gollob of Atheneum Publishers to ask if Marion Starkey's book* The Cherokee Nation *(1946) was still available. Gollob responded that it was out of stock, then added, "There* is *a file copy on the premises, but Ethel Soschin, who masterminds Russell & Russell, (and who, by the way, is a Texan), will not suffer it to leave our offices. She knows how you hombres from Clarksville treat rare books. So why don't you plan to come in here for a day and read it, unmolested, in our conference room; then we might be eligible for a tax deduction as a research center" (Gollob to WH, 2 May 1978).]*

TLS/HR

Hudson, N.Y.
May 6, 1978

Dear Herman,

Now I never meant for you to go wheedling your miss Soschin into lending me her precious book. I can understand her unwillingness to lend it to anybody, especially to a (fellow) Texan. Besides, she has never met me, poor girl, and very likely doesn't even know that in addition to being voted one of The World's One Hundred Best People by *Esquire,* I was once voted one of The World's Fourteen Most Charming Men by *Vogue.*[1] Very likely the news of those events never penetrated darkest Texas, where I envisage her living (on a diet of chittlins and poke salad[2] at the time). Tell her she can keep her old book. Just make her feel mean and rotten with the suggestion that she will always be remembered for having deprived American literature of a masterpiece and me of the Nobel prize. Whether Hudson has got a public library I don't know and am afraid to ask. No native would be able to tell me whether or not there is one, and so far I have been able to pass here by pretending to be illiterate, too. Afraid to come out of the closet now. I know a couple of college profs one of whom may be able to get the book on university inter-library loan and smuggle it in to me in a plain brown wrapper.

Thanks for the wish to be the first reader of the novel I hope to make of all this. We'll talk about it later. As of now, it's just a notion in my head. Nothing may come of it. So far it has fired my indignation more than my imagination. Besides, it has to compete for my attention not only with another novel[3] which I laid aside to write Farther Off from Heaven, but also with another, also vague, notion for yet another novel,[4] and most of all with my deep desire to toss them all out the window and never write another word after what I've been through with my last two books. I'm currently waiting for a response to a suggestion I made to the head editor of a large publishing house not long ago that they subsidize me to the tune of a quarter of a million dollars to be paid in annual installments over the next 10 years and see what they get for it. Ingenious (ingenuous?) notion.

Well, get your cartorosteum segastuating again and come up and see me over this bowl of chili I'm keeping warm for you on the back of the stove. No Pearl. I never promised you Pearl. You'll have to make do with Bud.[5] (Though I swear I do believe I saw Falstaff[6] in the local supermarket the other day. Pearl may be on the way.)

Yours,
Bill

1. Although on occasion in December issues *Esquire* publishes a feature called "The 100 Best People in the World," it does not appear that WH was among those selected in any of these lists. He was, however, featured in "Vogue's Eye View of International Charm," *Vogue,* 15 March 1958, 53.

2. Chittlins (also chitterlings) are the small intestines of hogs, cooked in batter; poke salad (or salit) is the boiled greens of the wild pokeweed. This combination would make a meal for a poor southerner, black or white.

3. "The Horse Latitudes," subsequently called "The Last Refuge," never finished.

4. *Hostages to Fortune.*

5. WH warns that he will not be able to offer Pearl, a Texas beer; Gollob will have to settle for an ordinary Budweiser.

6. A once popular beer that fell into decline in the 1970s.

TO NORAH SMALLWOOD

TLS/UR

[Hudson, New York]
May 21 [1978]

Dear Norah,

Just back from a weekend in Bethlehem, Pennsylvania where we went for the annual Bach Festival—heard the B minor Mass and the St. John Passion—and an overnight stay with Ted and Renee[1] in Princeton. Good to get away from the house and grounds even if only for a short while. Ted groaning deeper than ever even as a flowery and song-bird happy spring was in full bloom. I'm a gloomy gus, but really I am little Goody Two-shoes compared with poor, burdened-with-it-all Ted. Atlas[2] upheld a lighter world than Ted.

Found waiting on my return the page proofs of My Moby Dick from Nick. .[3] [*sic*] I think he has done a very handsome job. Have you seen them yet? I believe you will like them. A nice type, roomy on the page without looking too leaded out to make space. Now he tells me he is going to make also a leather bound limited edition of around 200 copies to sell for $100 per copy. He feels confident he can sell that many.

Found a letter from Mr. Ginna[4] of Little, Brown, saying, among other things that he would like to print a collection of my "stories"—though without any intent to go poaching on Knopf's preserve. I've said I don't have any stories to print, by anybody, and that I have lost all contact with Knopf.

Hope all goes well with you. Both the Weisses and Andy Wanning say they are going to be seeing you soon. Wish we were.

Love,
Bill

1. The Weisses.

2. After the earth was discovered to be spherical, Atlas, the "bearer" or "endurer," who in Greek myth held up the heavens, was in works of art represented as carrying the terrestrial globe.

3. Nick Lyons arranged for the publication of *My Moby Dick* (1978) through Doubleday.

4. Robert Emmett Ginna (1930–), an editor at Little, Brown Publishing Company, was also an instructor in writing at Harvard University and author of essays on Ireland.

TO NORAH SMALLWOOD

TLS/UR

Hudson, N.Y.
June 29, 1978

Dear Norah,

I spent the past two days in New York City lunching and afternooning with Viking,[1] Simon and Schuster, Harper & Row and Doubleday. My proposal: that a publisher give me $300,000 to be paid @ 30,000 annually for the next decade, and see what I produce. None has yet agreed to do it but on the other hand none has yet laughed in my face. Next week I lunch with Farrar Straus in New York, with Little-Brown in Boston. I have engaged Toby Eady[2] and he is working hard to demonstrate that I did not make a mistake in doing so. He's very much on trial with me, and he knows that. Knopf now appears to be halving my sales figures in order to damage my chances with any other publisher. That is a very serious charge to make, but I believe it to be justified. I am puzzled why they should want to hurt me, unless it be as La Rouchefoucauld[3] [*sic*] says, we cannot forgive others for the wrongs we have done them. The sales figures for The Spawning Run and Farther Off from Heaven are about half what they reported to me on their royalty statements. At least, that is my memory of it. Toby told Angus Cameron of Knopf a month ago that I was dissatisfied and considering leaving them; I have still not heard a word from them, this after 24 years of association with the firm.

Ted can't help himself—groaning aloud comes as naturally to him as breathing. He's done it ever since I first met him nearly 30 years ago. Actually, he's no gloomier than I am about the way the world is going, the difference between him and me is that he enjoys hearing himself say it and I don't. On the other hand, I don't mind hearing him say it, for he can be so entertaining! He it was who once, in my kitchen, as we were all moaning over getting older, said, "Yes, the trouble with old age is (long pause, deep sigh) it doesn't last." He's also the man who once said (you really need to have known his absolutely unredeemably unattractive mother to appreciate this) "Oedipus complex? Not me. I just took a second look." That mother, by the way, who deserved nothing whatever from life (and that's about the amount she got, poor soul) on the day when [the] newspaper headline was about the coronation of Elizabeth II, read it and said bitterly, "Some people have all the luck!" She really thought that by the merest accident it was not herself who was queen of England—accident and cruel injustice. But, as I need not tell you, Ted Weiss is one of the very finest people I have ever known, and probably the brightest ever. A staunch friend, and despite what appears outwardly to be a nature sedentary to the point of sloth, a real fighter and always for the right cause.

I am sure you don't expect me to rejoice at the thought of a royalty of only 5%.[4] However, I am sure you would not propose it unless you felt you had no alternative. I agree that 3 pounds is the maximum retail price you can ask for a book of that size. I am sure you would never be ungenerous towards me. So, with reluctance which you will understand, I accept. But please do not be prevailed upon by your associates to hold the book until next Christmas. Life is altogether too uncertain for plans that long-laid. They gang aft agley.[5]

I can't tell you how bewildered, angry and deeply hurt I am by Knopf's treatment of me. It's had me constantly depressed for months now and I can't shake it. The worst of it is, it's made me suspicious and belligerent towards these totally innocent other publishers whom I've been seeing. That's downright stupid, but I can't help myself.

I've written to the reviewer in Canberra, thanking him for his praise and his perceptiveness.[6] Thank you for sending me a copy of his review. I've always thought of Australia as Ultima Thule.[7] One more piece of arrogance to be knocked out of me.

Love,
Bill

1. WH continued to negotiate with Viking in spite of Norah Smallwood's warning. On 14 March 1998, she had written to WH: "I know a lot about Viking. We have done much business with them over the years, but I have to tell you and this again is in the strictest confidence, that since Penguin Books bought Viking things have not been quite the same."

2. Eady, a longtime English fishing companion of WH's, had recently opened his American office on Vanderbilt Avenue in New York City and soon after became WH's literary agent. Eady maintained his association with Hughes Massey Limited in London.

3. François VI, duc de La Rochefoucauld (1613–80), was a moralist and distinguished writer of maxims.

4. For *My Moby Dick.*

5. From Robert Burns's "To a Mouse": "The best laid schemes o' Mice an' Men / Gang aft agley."

6. The reviewer WH is probably referring to is actually a woman, Diane Willman, who reviewed *Farther Off from Heaven* in *Australian,* 28 January 1978.

7. The farthest possible place, sometimes suggesting an ideal.

TO SEYMOUR LAWRENCE

TLS/UM

Hudson, New York
August 21, 1978

Dear Sam,

[. . .][1]

What a hideous time extreme old age can be, usually is! Katherine Anne[2] sounds desperate and I am sorry. She once showed me a 45 caliber automatic pistol in her possession, said she was keeping it to kill herself with should she ever become senile and helpless, and asked me to promise to tell her when that time had come if she herself was unable to detect it. She thought it was unfriendly of me when I refused to accept the responsibility for determining that and telling her to blow her brains out.

Yours,
Bill

1. This letter begins with a short paragraph, here omitted, in which WH explains why it will be impossible for Lawrence and him to meet on 15 September.

2. Memory failure, paranoia, and hostility became increasing problems for Katherine Anne Porter following a stroke in 1977.

TO NORAH SMALLWOOD

[Although WH had written to Smallwood on 22 August 1978 to say that he did not "care for illustrated dust jackets," she had sent him a picture of a trout, which she proposed for the cover of My Moby Dick, *saying, "I think it not only is apt, but I believe if one wants to get the fisherman and not only the readers of fine writing, it is better for the book not to look on the outside as though it might be belles-lettres."]*

TLS/UR

[Hudson, New York]
August 26 [1978]

Dear Norah,

I am returning this to you within minutes of receiving it because we are threatened with a nationwide strike of postal workers here.

You have found a fine picture of a trout,[1] but—and this is a *big* but . . [.] I am reminded of the most famous gaffe in American book illustrating: Rockwell Kent's famous edition of *Moby Dick*. In the very last illustration Ahab is shown in the longboat grappling hand to hand with the great whale's jaws. *And he has got two sound legs.*[2] In this photo of a trout we are shown his *right* side. And he has got a good right eye.[3] Now, I think it would be wonderful to have your artist to give him a bad right eye. It will be wondered at by those who have not yet read the book, but it will intrigue them. . . .

Much love.
Bill

1. Chatto & Windus obtained the photograph from Gens Plough Hansen and Jan Warrer Olesen of Angling Development International in Denmark.

2. Kent's illustration of Ahab is laughable because it ignores the text: "Clap eye on Captain Ahab, young man, and thou wilt find that he has only one leg" (ch. 16 of *Moby Dick* [1851] by Herman Melville).

3. The proposed illustration ignores WH's text: "His eye on that side, his right, was blind. It was opaque, white, pupilless; it looked like the eye of a baked fish" (ch. 4 of *My Moby Dick*).

TO NORAH SMALLWOOD

TLS/UR

[Hudson, New York]
October 10, 1978

Dear Norah,

I've still not settled with any American publisher, but there's no hurry. Harpers is, indeed, a good house, and they are keen to have me come to them. Holt is more than keen and for the very good reason that their list is fairly poverty-stricken, so with them I'd be their fair-haired boy. Little, Brown is still in this poker game, too. We'll see.

Now this is strictly between you and me: Michel Mohrt is a rotter and is anything but an admirer of mine. He advised Gallimard to reject *Farther Off from Heaven,* saying that I was finished and would never write anything more. He also advised them to reject *A Time and a Place.* I have this on good authority.[1]

Oh, dear! If Pritchett[2] thinks American book-reviewing is better than yours then yours must be pretty bad. I've been reading the first ones of *My Moby Dick,* and few of them can even get the facts straight. I believe most of them read no further than the dust-jacket copy. All of them laudatory but nothing is more irksome than imperceptive praise.

Appalled to hear of Trekkie's accident. She is so prone to such freakish and painful mishaps. I have written her today.

I, too, am still waiting to be told the publication date of the French version of Farther Off from Heaven.[3] I'll know better then when to ask Jean Lambert for his Paris flat, and then will know what to say to Rab Raphael, or to any other possible houseowner if the Parsons hear of one in need of a house-sitter. Thank you for speaking further to Raphael. We have rather sentimental feelings about funny old Hove[4] and it would be pleasant to have a stay there.

One last anecdote about Mohrt. I met him first in 1959, for a short chat in his office. He said he would be calling me in a few days to go to dinner with him. Over the years, whenever we found ourselves in Paris, there would be a note from him saying he would be calling in a few days to ask us to dinner. It became a household word in our ménage: whenever the phone would ring we'd say, "That must be Michel Mohrt inviting us to dinner." At last he did, and when we met at his restaurant, he said, "Oh, Humphrey, it's ever so long (he talks very English English, being a faux-Anglais).[5] It must be, what? all of five years?" I said, "No, it's seventeen." I was wearing a hat from Locks[6] and shoes from Church[7] and a jacket from Saville Row.[8] This raised his eyebrows. I am expected to wear feathers in my hair and a ring in my nose. It came out that I knew Ian Parsons. "What!" Mohrt exclaimed. "How is that possible? Why, Ian Parsons knows more about wine than any man I know."

Love,
Bill

1. Internal documents at Éditions Gallimard reveal that WH was premature in his judgment of this editor at the publishing firm. In 1984 Mohrt praised the "authenticité parfaite" (perfect authenticity) of *Hostages to Fortune* and said this "remarkable" novel would without a doubt attract "le plus grand number de lecteurs" (the greatest number of readers) of any of his other books. Later, of *No Resting Place,* he wrote, "C'est une epopee tragique, racontée avec une qualité de style qui font de Humphrey l'un des bons écrivains américains d'aujourd'hui" (It is a tragic epic, told with the quality of style that makes Humphrey one of the greatest American writers today).

2. V. S. Prichett (1900–1997), novelist, critic for the *New Statesman,* and London man of letters.

3. *Plus loin du ciel* was published in 1979.

4. Rab Raphael, an acquaintance of Smallwood and the Parsons, had a house in Hove, a town on the south coast of England between Brighton and Porslade-by-Sea, that the Humphreys could use during the coming year.

5. Imitation Englishman.

6. James Lock in the West End of London, where the most elegant men's clothing stores are located.

7. Church's Shoes, a classic shoe shop in the Burlington Arcade, the West End.

8. In the West End, where the top London tailors are located.

TO NICK LYONS

[WH mocks his own fly fisherman's feelings of superiority toward worm fishermen by implying a parallel to the white bigot's view of black people.]

TLS/SMU

[Hudson, New York]
April 7 [1979]

Dear Nick,

Well, you missed some good grub at Al Clements' Opening Day Breakfast,[1] but you'd have been uncomfortable with the company, as I was. Al had confessed to me a few days before that this year he had invited two (I wish there was a smaller font of type on this machine so I could say this sotto voce)[2] worm fishermen. I couldn't have been more stunned if he'd said he was coming out of the closet. I know that prejudices are not in fashion (even Jimmy Carter[3] now knows it) but I remain unreconstructed. "Al," I said, "that's how neighborhoods get ruined. You let one in . . ." He said these two were really nice guys. I said, "Sure. If they were all like Ralph Bunche . . ."[4] But my clincher was, "Al, would you like your daughter to marry one?" Al winced as though he had a nubile daughter. I don't think they'll be invited again next year. I never learned which two they were (unfortunately, they don't all look alike); to be on the safe side, I ate my breakfast standing up.

Nobody went fishing. To have stepped outside the door would have been to risk death by drowning. Whatever you were doing instead of going fishing this opening day it was time well spent.

Got real excited by a letter received the other day. Some Hollywood agent with a client who wants to buy TV rights to The Ordways for a "2–6 part" serial. Visions of retirement, private jet, 34 miles of personal salmon water, etc. Alas, I sold those rights along with moom-pitcher rts 11 years ago[5] and have long since frittered away in high living all the money I'll ever see.

Having trouble getting back to work. English friend[6] of mine, a painter, was away from hers for a good while once and described the getting back as being like struggling into a wet swimsuit.

How's the Sony of your ownly?[7]

Love to Mari.[8]

Yours,
Bill

1. WH's friend and authority on flyfishing Alford Clements sponsored an annual breakfast on the first day of trout season at his house in Spencertown, New York.

2. In an undertone.

3. Jimmy Carter was president of the United States from 1977 to 1981.

4. Ralph Bunche (1904–71) was a black American diplomat, United Nations undersecretary, and winner of the Nobel Peace Prize in 1950.

5. WH sold the motion-picture rights to the novel to Columbia Pictures fifteen years earlier.

6. Trekkie Parsons.

7. Nick Lyons's only son Anthony.

8. Lyons's wife.

TO NICK LYONS

TLS/SMU [Hudson, New York]
12/12[/79]

Dear Nick,

Did you read those two letters you forwarded to me? One is from Cyril Clemens, great-grand-something-or-other of Mark Twain, editor of "The Mark Twain Journal" out of Kirkwood, Missouri. He wrote me several years ago that for my contribution to American Literature with *Proud Flesh* I had been "elected" (I suspect he is a jury of one) an Honorary Lifetime Member of The Mark Twain Society. I answered saying I thought this was appropriate, as I had been stealing from Mark Twain ever since I grew up and turned writer. Now he writes that for my contribution to American Literature with *My Moby Dick* I have been made a Knight of the Order of Mark Twain. There will be no laying of the sword, I gather. This honor is one, he tells me, that I share with Robert Frost.[1] It appears that he has it also in his power to confer The Mark Twain Gold medal. Maybe if I last long enough I'll share that with Franklin D. Roosevelt,[2] a recipient.

The other letter is from an admirer in Detroit who says he found "great substance" in *My Moby Dick,* then asks me please to answer the question, will civilization as we know it survive the century. It seems to me an impertinent question, because civilization as we know it hasn't survived this far. Could he be resurrected to answer the question, Mark Twain would, I'm sure, agree.

Yrs,
Bill

1. Robert Frost (1874–1963), American poet.

2. Franklin D. Roosevelt (1882–1945), president of the United States, 1933–45.

[LAST YEARS]

1980–93

TO NICK LYONS

TLS/SMU

Hudson [New York]
Dec. 12 [1980]

Dear Nick,

When I've got troubles I let you help me carry them, you should do the same with me. That's what friends are for. Help helps.[1]

I've been blue over the news of Ian Parson's [*sic*] death. He meant a great deal to me. He was 74 and had had a good life and had an easy death but none of those things makes it easier for the people left.

Cold here. Toby Eady is coming up today and I suspect we'll have to stay indoors on account of the weather.

Got the deer on the third day of the season. It had snowed the night before 11 inches. I was over in the northwest corner of the property with Bob Fisher.[2] It was ten minutes past seven in the morning when I heard Bob shoot about 200 yards north of me. I figured he'd killed a deer but readied myself nonetheless. Sure enough in about two minutes I saw the deer through the trees headed my way, and I was downwind of it. I slipped off the safety of the Mannlicher,[3] chose the spot at which I'd take the deer if he came on. He did. I pulled the set trigger, aimed right between his eyes, missed my aim by exactly one inch, and took his right antler clean off at the base and killed him with a shot in the brain. He was dead instantly. About 135 pounds on the hoof. We've been eating him. Good.

Don't be alone with the blues. Let me hear.

Yours,
Bill

1. See editor's note for letter of 28 September 1950 to Porter.

2. WH's friend, a postman, who lived a quarter of a mile down Gahbauer Road toward Hudson.

3. Mannlicher Schoenauer is the maker of the finest European hunting rifles.

TO SEYMOUR LAWRENCE

[In January 1979 WH had signed a contract with Seymour Lawrence, whom he valued as a friend even as he recognized the value of the Seymour Lawrence imprint, which appeared with Delacorte for the publication of Hostages to Fortune, Collected Stories of William Humphrey, Open Season, *and* No Resting Place. *On 23 January 1981 Lawrence responded to preliminary sections of* Hostages to Fortune *and* The Cherokees *(later titled No Resting Place), which WH had sent to him from Paris, France, on 29 December 1980. Lawrence preferred what he had seen of the latter novel: "There's a world in this book and I urge you with all my heart to recreate it. I am sure that* Hostages to Fortune *will be a good book, and a very thoughtful one. But* The Cherokees *has magnificence and a forceful appeal."]*

ALS/UM [Paris, France]
Jan. 28 [1981]

Dear Sam,

I broke the 3rd finger of my right hand yesterday so my script is even worse than usual. My apologies. I'll be brief. Your response to the MSS. is immensely gratifying and I am glowing from yr. praise. It will mean much encouragement to me as I go on. I didn't choose to work 1st on Hostages—it just happened that way. But now I'm well into it and it absorbs my thoughts and it's going well (I'm working here—hard) and it would seem a mistake to drop it at such a time. You may be right that the Indian book is the better one but I've got this one in me and I must be grateful for it and attentive to its dictates. Don't you agree? I'm not sure I could divert my mind from what I'm doing right now if I tried.

We leave here on Feb. 9 for a week or 10 days with Trekkie Parsons, whose letters are very despondent. Then a week in London with Norah[1] before returning home. Meanwhile. Here, I'm basking in being much lionized by the Gallimard people. You'll be pleased to learn that a story from my 1st book[2] is to appear in French trans. in issue #1 of what seems to be a prestigious international revue here edited by Alain Bosquet.[3]

I can't do as you'd like and switch horses now but don't be disappointed. Everything will come of its own will and in its own time.

Again thanks for yr. letter. Best of everything to you and Merloyd.[4]

Yrs.
Bill

1. Norah Smallwood.

2. "The Last Husband," from *The Last Husband and Other Stories* (1953).

3. *Nota Bene*, founded in 1980. Alain Bosquet (1919–98), a French writer of Russian origin, was a poet noted for surrealism.

4. Merloyd Ludington, also an editor-publisher and under the imprint Merloyd Lawrence, who specialized in books on child development, health, natural history, and the environment.

TO NICK LYONS

[When John Kennedy Toole (1937–69) sent the manuscript of his A Confederacy of Dunces *to Simon and Schuster in 1964, it went to Robert A. Gottlieb, who for two years suggested change after change. Frustrated, Toole eventually asked for the manuscript back; he let it lie dormant for three years and then committed suicide. The author's mother, Thelma Toole, worked for fifteen years to get the novel published. In 1980 Louisiana State University Press published the book with few changes. Gottlieb moved to Knopf in 1968 and became WH's editor.]*

TLS/SMU

[Hudson, New York]
April 17 [1981]

Dear Nick,

Did you see the enclosed?[1] What a story! Poor devil down there in New Orleans "on tenterhooks" trying to satisfy Gottlieb's editorial suggestions, and now Gottlieb "does not remember the man, the manuscript or the book." If he really doesn't then he should be shot for his callousness, if he is lying in order to excuse his editorial obtuseness to a book that has just won the Pulitzer prize then he ought to be shot for that. I've read the book and while it does not deserve the praise lavished upon it, it certainly deserved publication. A sordid affair.

Yours,
Bill

1. A cutting of "Pulitzer Novel's Publication Is Tale in Itself," *New York Times*, 15 April 1981, p. 14, sec. A.

TO NICK LYONS

TLS/SMU

[Hudson, New York]
December 29 [1981]

Dear Nick,

I missed that article in the Times[1] so thanks for sending it. It is instructive, [though] not as it intended to be. I had been sent a copy of McMurtry's article (lecture originally) that appeared in The Texas Observer,[2] a publication known as gadfly and mischief-making.

Although McMurtry has made a second career of being Peck's bad boy he was here reacting to Texas chauvinism and bumptiousness which extends from chili con carne to belles-lettres and I agree with most of what he has to say. Of his own books I have read just one and on the basis of it I would say he is quite right in dismissing himself from serious consideration. He is even right in asserting that in her time Katherine Anne Porter was overpraised[3] and should be reexamined, but though slender her gifts were real and lasting and to them he is obtuse. His tone in the piece is contentious and impudent and I like that. But when you set out to make mischief you do well to have all your information at hand. He lets me off far better than he does any other prose writer (something which goes unremarked by the Times' man) but he charges me with laziness.[4] I rather resent that from a fellow who says he has been waiting 17 years for me to produce a third novel. Where was he when Proud Flesh appeared? He also does not seem to know about my second book of stories.[5] And his ignorance of, or his silence about, William Owens' fine childhood memoir This Stubborn Soil[6] is inexcusable.

As for the journalistic accuracy of the Times' reporter: "But no Texas writer, he (mcMurtry [*sic*]) says, has so far equaled even Philip Roth, Norman Mailer or John Updike." Nowhere in McMurtry's piece is mention made of either Updike or Roth, and the one reference to Mailer is slighting.[7] No wonder fish come home from the market stinking: they are wrapped in yesterday's newspaper.

Ummh, I had a bit of my own back out of Ms Oates before quitting Princeton.[8] Not as much of her skin as I hungered for but a bit.

Let us hope that this coming one will be a better year for us all. Keep in touch. Call on me if you need me. Our best to everybody.

Yours,
Bill

1. William K. Stevens, "Texas Writers Assailed by Colleague / Grudgingly Admit He Might Be Right," *New York Times,* 28 December 1981, p. 15, sec. B.

2. "Ever a Bridegroom: Reflections on the Failure of Texas Literature," *Texas Observer,* 23 October 1981, 1, 8–19.

3. McMurtry wrote that most of her fiction is "the work of a half-talent," that it is like Oakland, California" ("There was no there there"), and that her "plumage is beautiful, but plumage, after all, is only feathers" (9).

4. McMurtry suggests that WH too often went fishing when he should have been writing and therefore is among those Texas writers who have been unproductive (13, 15).

5. *A Time and a Place.*

6. William A. Owens (1905–90), born in Pin Hook, Texas, is the author of *This Stubborn Soil: A Frontier Boyhood* (1966) and *Walking on Borrowed Land,* a novel published in 1954. Owens was a consultant on Ken Harrison's 1982 film based on WH's "The Last of the Caddoes," a circumstance which brought the two writers back in touch after not having seen each other for twenty years. They did not know that they were living within sixty miles of each other, Owens in Nyack, New York.

7. McMurtry remarked that as Larry King's career advanced, "he began to make himself a character in his own reportage, sometimes too self-consciously, in the manner of Mailer" (15).

8. Joyce Carol Oates (1938–), novelist, poet, and critic, was a writer-in-residence at Princeton University from 1979 to 1981 and afterward distinguished professor there. WH was a visiting writer at Princeton during the fall semester in 1981.

TO THEODORE AND RENÉE WEISS

TLS/PU

Hudson, New York
February 27, 1982

Dear Ted and Renee,

We were planning a trip to my home town this spring and now we *have* to go. My dear Aunt Rebecca[1] has been found to have inoperative cancer, spread already through her lungs, liver. Chemotherapy will keep her going for a while but not for very long. She's 63. A delightful person.

I had to be rushed by ambulance to the hospital late one night last week, food poisoning from a bad oyster. Second time this happened, the first one in London years ago. I guess I must give them up. This time it was pretty alarming. I was horribly sick, of course, but for the first time my pulse and blood pressure just about disappeared. They put me to bed and fed me dextrose intravenously for half a day and then sent me home. I've been weak as a newborn since but am on the mend now. Said the bookkeeping lady to me as I was on my way out, "You're unemployed?" "Yes." How long? Well, twenty-five years more or less. Have you applied for public assistance? No, I haven't gotten around to that. Your wife is unemployed too? Yes. How long has she been out of work? All her life. Have you tried to find work? No, I've avoided it. Then she revealed that her maiden name had been Dorothy Humphrey. I think she was rather ashamed of having any possible connection to a ne'er-do-well like me.

I wrote that little college in Arkansas saying I might come,[2] it would depend on their fee, as I would be taken from home and work the better part of a week—no further word out of them. I must have scared them off, which is just as well.

The enclosed letter is from the boy who gave me such trouble.[3]

Hope all is well with you. When does the new book[4] come out?

Love from us both.

Yours,
Bill

1. Rebecca Varley, wife of Bernard.
2. Hendrix College, Conway, Arkansas, which WH did visit from 9 to 13 November 1982.
3. Perhaps the letter from Pat Black (see p. 186).
4. *The Man from Porlock: Engagements, 1944–1981* (1982).

TO NICK LYONS

TLS/SMU

[Hudson, New York]
St. Patrick's Day [1982]

Dear Nick,
Critics are human, too, and Wilson, like all of them, was wrong at least as often as he was right. He differs from most of them in being wrong more often in his enthusiasms than in his condemnations. Unlike most critics, he wanted to like; he was by nature generous. Re Hemingway, his worst crime was in having said anything good about Islands in the Stream,[1] which, unlike say Treasure Island[,][2] is unintentionally juvenile. And while he knew a lot about prosody he knew almost nothing about poetry. (Not that I know anything about poetry). His glorification of E. St. V. Millay is laughable,[3] or would be if it weren't so cry-able. I find even more dunderheaded this pronouncement: "Doctor Zhivago will come to stand as one of the great events in man's moral and literary history."[4] But when he's right he's right, just as when your colleague says that Pierre[5] is anything but the worst book ever committed by a great writer he's wrong. And you're right to know he's wrong. Pierre is improbable, pretentious, strained, literary,

atrociously written. There are some absolutes even in the slippery realm of literature. There are, just as there are at the Bureau of Standards the Inch and The Ounce, standards by which to measure and judge and then accept or dismiss. This is counterfeit, this is short of weight, this is lopsided. For example: sentimentality, tendentiousness, factitiousness. No, that a book gets on the bestseller list does not automatically condemn it (though it ought to be made to undergo a lie-detector test) nor was that Wilson's point about Brideshead Revisited;[6] it was that the book would get there for the same reasons as the two books he mentions. It's not that there is nothing good in Brideshead Revisited (and Wilson's disappointment is deepened precisely because of the hopes it raises and the glimmers of the old greatness that occasionally break through—that's what I meant by *adulterated* trash); it's that it's fundamentally bad, and bad in very serious ways. It is a falsification of the past for the sake of nostalgia (born of snobbery), and a falsification of the future for the sake of dogma. And a willful, wishful, wistful distortion of substance can only be accompanied by a degradation of technique.

. . . .

You don't have to accuse yourself of being a redneck when some animal who happens to be black behaves like an animal. That story is a disgrace. I suppose it's true that the college[7] has no way to protect anybody against him but then it's a matter for the police. He should be denounced to them for threats to people and for attacks against them and if necessary those threatened should be given permits to carry a pistol. And the least the school can do is dismiss him. The Dean of Students who advised the girl this ape beat up not to bring charges ought, as we used to say in Texas, [to] be stood on his head in an ant pile and beat in the ass with a dead rabbit. How cowardly of those people to tolerate being intimidated by that character! Kick his ass out.

Snow, sleet, hail, rain, travellers' advisories to stay off the roads, so I haven't mailed off those books to Pennsylvania yet.

As of now I still haven't been told that Chan[d]ler is gone.[8] But it can't be long.

As soon as we can get into Hudson we'll buy plane tickets to Texas. Going around the 25, returning around April 15. I was looking forward to it, now I'm dreading it.

Yours,
Bill

1. Although Wilson calls this posthumously published novel by Ernest Hemingway "preposterous," he admires its "force and dignity" ("An Effort at Self-Revelation," in *The Devils and Canon Barham: Ten Essays on Poets, Novelists and Monsters* [1973], 107, 108).

2. This novel by Robert Louis Stevenson (1850–94) was serialized in *Young Folks,* starting in 1881.

3. Wilson's work *The Shores of Light: A Literary Chronicle of the Twenties and Thirties* (1952) opens and closes with a memorial tribute to Edna St. Vincent Millay (1892–1950), an American poet whose light has now faded. Perhaps WH did not know of Wilson's longstanding sexual relationship with her and that he had proposed marriage to her.

4. See WH's letter of 30 October 1964 to the Weisses.

5. Novel by Herman Melville published in 1852.

6. Novel by Evelyn Waugh (1903–66) published in 1945; see Wilson, *Classics and Commercials* (1950), 298–99.

7. Hunter College of the City University of New York.

8. Chandler Chapman died at the end of March 1982.

TO YANNICK GUILLOU[1]

TLS/EG

[Hudson, New York]
25 April [1983]

Dear Yannick,

We are almost to go off soon on another fishing expedition for *Sports Illustrated* . . . to South America? No. To Alaska? No. After all, it is not just big fish that a fisherman is after—especially *this* fisherman. For as you will have noticed in my essays, I don't ever catch any fish anyway. What I look for when I go fishing is a beautiful river. Scenery. Tradition. A river which inspires such dedication in its fishermen that they don't really care whether they catch any fish. A river is some place where there is something to do with yourself when the fish are not biting. What does this begin to sound like to you? To me it sounds like the Seine in Paris. And so that is where I am being sent "—for a month—" to sit under the Pont Neuf and the Pont Sully to fish for gardons and gougons.[2]

Yours,
Bill

1. An editor at Éditions Gallimard.

2. *Sports Illustrated* paid for WH to sit under the Pont Neuf and Pont Sully, famous bridges in Paris, and fish for a month, but then the magazine refused to publish his article "The Fishermen of the Seine," which was therefore published in *Town and Country,* afterward in *La nouvelle revue française* (1 January 1986) and in *Open Season* (1986). A "gardon" is a kind of fish specific to France and some parts of Spain (in English called a "roach"), and a "gougon" is a small European freshwater fish (in English called a "gudgeon").

TO PIERRE AFFRE[1]

TLS/PH

Hudson [New York]
March 30 [1984]

Dear Pierre,

Your letter came this morning. I am terribly sorry to hear that you have had so many troubles lately: affairs of the heart going wrong, a dismal opening of your new season at the rese[r]voir, the clinic.[2] It seems that winter is always a particularly troublesome time for you. I hope that with the coming of the spring some things at least will begin to look up for you. For me, too. It's been a bleak winter here. Terrible weather. Dark and dreary days. Cold. Right now we are in the second big snow of the last week. And trout season opens only this Sunday. We are going as always to Al's Opening Day breakfast,[3] but of course in these conditions nobody will do any fishing. After the terrible drought of last summer I wonder whether there will be any fishing at all this year. [. . .][4]

I have not been able to settle down to serious work since finishing the novel[5] last October. I have been in a state of constant mental depression. I am always depressed after finishing a book, but seldom has it lasted this long and been so profound. I did write a couple of short stories in the last few months,[6] something I have not done in many years, but have not been able to apply myself to the Indian novel.[7] Again, maybe the coming of spring will help pull me out of my depression. I hope so!

It is very satisfying to see on your envelope: Dr. Pierre Affre, Venerinaire. And I should think that rue Mazat would be a very good address for your clinic. When does your brother join you?

Keep well, be brave, and let's hope everything works out. Dorothy joins me in sending you all our affection.

Yours,
Bill

It was kind of you to say, speaking of my shooting: Your father would have been proud of you.

1. Pierre Affre was "a footloose young bachelor [in Paris, France] who earns his living as a veterinary surgeon but who is usually off somewhere in a far corner of the world fishing" (WH to Norah Smallwood, 19 December 1980).

2. Business was bad at the new veterinary clinic that Affre had recently opened because, according to him, during the bad economic times people were neglecting to care for their animals.

3. See note for letter of 7 April 1979 to Lyons.

4. A short paragraph on Affre's assistance with a Gallimard publication is omitted.

5. *Hostages to Fortune.*

6. "Dolce Far' Niente" and "The Patience of a Saint," both of which were first published in *The Collected Stories of William Humphrey* (New York: Delacorte / Seymour Lawrence, 1985).

7. *No Resting Place.*

TO BARLEY ALISON

[After the relationship between WH and Chatto & Windus ended, WH was adopted by the Alison Press, associated with Secker & Warburg. The first novel published by Alison was Hostages to Fortune; *its dust jacket is the subject of this letter.]*

TLS/RH

Hudson , New York
December 8, 1984

Dear Barley Alison,

I tried to phone you yesterday afternoon but failed to reach you.

I am afraid I must tell you that I think the dust jacket is a disaster. In the first place, the photograph of the author is not by Jerry Bauer,[1] it is by Stan Wayman.[2] In the second place, it is not just the black background of the photograph that I object to, it is (1.) the motif of a fisherman's fly and (2.) the actual fly shown. To me the book now looks like either a book on fishing (salmon fishing, more particularly) or on fly-tying, and this seems inappropriate for such a serious, not to say stark, novel. The fly shown is a double-hooked Scottish salmon fly—a fly for salmon only and in Scotland only. My book is set in America and my protagonist is a trout fisherman. There are no Atlantic salmon to speak of in the U.S. Thus the fly on the cover of the book is totally inappropriate.

I don't see how you can use this jacket, even if this means postponement of publication day.

If I might have my way, I should prefer a jacket composed simply of type, with no illustration of any kind.

Yours,
William Humphrey

1. Jerry Bauer had made the photograph for the American edition of *No Resting Place.*

2. Stan Wayman, a *Life* magazine photographer, had made the photograph of WH for Nick Lyons's edition of *My Moby Dick.*

TO GAVIN WATSON

[John Harrison, a citizen of Bogata, Texas, who had met WH twice, wrote to him, calling him the town's "chiefest cultural hero," on 31 January 1985, and asking him to support efforts to save the Red River County Courthouse from being replaced by a modern structure. Harrison suggested that WH write a letter to the Clarksville Times *that would inform the commissioner's court that its members "would be barbarian rubes to endanger Old Red," the term WH applies to the building in his fiction. The courthouse was renovated in 2000. Gavin Watson was editor of the* Clarksville Times *and a childhood friend of WH.]*

TLS/HR

Hudson, New York
February 6, 1985

Dear Gavin,
Do me the favor, please, old friend, of running the following—prominently—in your next issue:
Dear Gavin,

Will you, should the necessity arise, please run this ad in your paper—full page:

FOR SALE
DUE TO OWNERS' CHANGE IN PLANS
LAST UNOCCUPIED PLOT[1]
in
OLD CLARKSVILLE CEMETERY
CHOICE LOCATION
BENEATH LIMBS OF THE HANGING TREE

and forward all interested inquiries to me? The necessity will arise if and when the County Courthouse is razed and abandoned. It was with the thought in mind of hearing the chimes of its clock in eternity that I bought that plot, and, after it stopped chiming on the midnight, of getting up and ambling over there to gaze at its tower by the light of the moon. Without these satisfactions to look forward to, I might as well be just anywhere, because without its courthouse Clarksville will be just anywhere. Half of this decision was taken by my Brooklyn-born wife, destined to lie alongside me, who loves that unique old pile every bit as much as I do. She adds, and I agree, that we won't want to associate till Judgement Day (when the courthouse will be resurrected along with us) with people so indifferent to their greatest treasure.

Yours,
Bill Humphrey

1. WH had purchased the plot for himself and his wife in 1969. It remains unoccupied, WH's and Dorothy's ashes being buried in the churchyard of St. Paul's Episcopal Church, Tivoli, New York.

TO JEAN LAMBERT

TLS/LC

Hudson [New York]
March 22 [1985]

Dear Jean,

There has been a misunderstanding between me and Gallimard. An editor at Delacorte told me over the phone one day a couple of weeks ago that Gallimard had bought the French rights to the Collected Stories of mine. (Of course, they already own A Time and a Place). I wrote Yannick[1] saying how pleased I was to hear this news. Well, the truth is, not only have they not bought the book, they have not even seen it. Yannick got very alarmed. He phoned here saying he feared that Delacorte had sold the book to some other French house. I assured him that that had not happened. I myself have just received bound proofs of the book, and I am told that a copy has gone to him. Now I must wait to see what his decision is.

Meanwhile he has shown The Fisherman and the Seine to the editors of the NRF[2] and they want to publish an excerpt from it. He tells me that you will do the translation. I hope this is true and that there is not some other misunderstanding.

Within an hour a man is coming here from NYC for the day to look at all my old papers. He is a dealer in autographs and manuscripts and rare books. One of our drawing rooms is heaped high wi[th] an accumulation of 30 years and it has depressed me unbearably to look through them. Letters from dead friends, letters from friends who are friends no longer, projects abandoned, journals detailing my frustrations. I have scribbled my life away. I would really like to burn all this, but I can't because it may be the only income I will have in my old age. The mind of the scholar is a mystery to me. My finished books reflect my effort to do my best; scholars would rather read my rejected versions and the record of my failures. I have said to this man who is coming that I would rather destroy this stuff and that my only reason for not doing so will be a large sum of money.

I hope you are getting around better and are not in such pain. Dorothy wrote you recently, I know, so I have got nothing much to add. Let us hear from you. We both send you, as always, our love.

Yours,
Bill

P.S. I have asked Yannick to ask the NRF to reconsider taking an excerpt from the essay and printing it in its entirety. It seems to me that the excerpt does not stand very well by itself. I have said they may do it if they are determined to, but to reconsider.

1. Yannick Guillou.
2. *La nouvelle revue française.*

TO BARLEY ALISON

TLS/RH

Hudson, New York
March 28, 1985

Dear Barley,
You are very kind to send a copy of the book[1] to my dear friends the Pembers in Rodmell. They are elderly and ailing now. Both are good readers. Tim wrote three novels[2] back in the late 30's and early 40's, and very good novels they are. Then one day he looked out his window (he was living in California then) to see his beautiful little daughter struck and killed by a car. His hair turned white overnight and he never wrote another word. They live like paupers yet he turned down an hereditary lordship and she's a Dupont.[3]

You will be pleased to know that I have just (for the 4th time) won an award for best novel of the year by a Texan (actually one of the 4 times was for a work of non-fiction, the memoir of my childhood). As far as I know, my native state is the only one with such an award. With it comes a nice little check for $1500.[4] There was just a knock on my door, a man from the local florists presented me with a lovely bouquet[5] of lilies and daisies and other pretty plants, a gift from the ladies at Delacourte, all this just minutes ago. Think I'll open a bottle of bubbly this evening.

The news is not always bad—just nine-tenths of the time, and better than that one can hardly ask for.

Take seriously my suggestion that you reconsider publishing me. There can't be much satisfaction in it for you if I get many more such reviews, and god knows it does me no good.

Yours,
Bill

But if you are determined to go ahead with the book of stories,[6] then I think I might have done your cause some good. I phoned Delacorte some time ago, saying, do not ask too much from Secker and Warburg for that book, make it as inexpensive for them as you can do. Yesterday I was told that they had cut in half their price to you for off-sets. I'm not trying to steal credit from your manager's efforts, or Toby's, but I did do my part. I've told them the same thing in regard to my wonderful people at Editions Gallimard.

1. *Hostages to Fortune.*

2. Timothy Pember's three novels are *The Needle's Eye* (1947), *Not Me, Sir* (1948), and *Swanson* (1951).

3. The Dupont family, founders of the Dupont Company, is one of the most prominent families in American history.

4. WH is referring to the Texas Institute of Letters. According to Robert Compton, recording secretary, the institute's records do not show *Hostages to Fortune* as winning the award. However, the novel did win the Texas Literary Festival Award for the outstanding work of fiction published in 1984 by an author who is a native of Texas. This award was given by the Southwest Booksellers Association and the *Dallas Times Herald.*

5. Marking the publication of *The Collected Stories of William Humphrey.*

6. *The Collected Stories* was published by Secker & Warburg in 1986.

TO JEAN LAMBERT

TLS/LC

[Hudson, New York]
January 18, 1986

Dear Jean,
It is a long time since we heard from you. I hope all is well.

I write now to wish you a very happy new year, and to tell you that we were thrilled to receive in yesterday's mail a copy of the January issue of the NRF with its bold red ribbon saying WILLIAM HUMPHREY in big letters. I know of course that it is a most prestigious magazine and I am truly honored. And I am very pleased that the editors were prevailed upon to print the piece[1] in its entirety. Thank you for all your labors on it and for it. What would I do without you.

Along with the magazine, Yannick[2] sent me an invitation to attend a Fete du Livre[3] at Aix-en-Provence[4] in late May, featuring current American literature. I replied that I am really not qualified. That I know next to nothing about the subject. I have looked into the writing of a few of my contemporaries and did not feel encouraged by any of them to pursue their writings any further, and that I don't even know the names of the younger ones. My academic friends, who keep up with such things, tell me I'm not missing much of anything.

Lord knows where you are—off on your travels somewhere, I expect. We have gone nowhere, have seen almost nobody. Our life is routine. I've been hard at work lately after a long session of aridity. Now it is going pretty well and I have about 180 pages of this Cherokee novel.[5] *The Collected Stories,* after a bad start with a destructive review in the daily N.Y. Times,[6] has gone on to do very well. Good, some ecstatic, reviews elsewhere in the country.[7] Meanwhile, *Hostages to Fortune* has just appeared in paperback.[8] How are you coming along on your version of that book? As Yannick says nothing about it, I assume that no publication date has been set.[9]

We were thinking of a trip to Europe in the spring but now we have become victims of the hysteria over here brought about by the hostage-taking and airport shootings.[10] A[s] I said to Dorothy the other day, it would make me mad as hell to get killed by some Arab with this book of mine only half done.

With much love from us both.

Yours,
Bill

1. "Les pecheurs de la Seine (I)" (The Fishermen of the Seine) was published in *La nouvelle revue française,* 1 January 1986, 15–23.

2. Yannick Guillou.

3. Book festival.

4. A city in southeastern France, in the Bouches-du-Rhône department.

5. *No Resting Place.*

6. By Michiko Kakutani, this 22 June 1985 review compared WH's stories to "O. Henry or the worst of John Steinbeck": "There is an unearned sentimentality to many of these stories, a tendency to heap more symbolic weight on ordinary people [. . .] than they can reasonably bear."

7. Reviews pleasing to WH appeared in such places as the *Sunday Peninsula Herald* on 13 October 1985 and the *St. Petersburg (Fla.) Times* on 18 August 1985.

8. A Laurel book.

9. *Ostages du destin* was published by Gallimard before the year's end.

10. Hezbollah's taking of thirty-nine American hostages on a TWA airliner and the Palestinian terrorists' shooting of passengers at the airport check-in counters in Rome and Vienna in 1984.

TO JEAN LAMBERT

TLU/LC

[Hudson, New York]
February 19 [1988]

Dear Jean,

First, your questions about the stories.[1] You are right: in The Last Husband the two men should begin their acquaintance with the formal mode of address "vous" and at some point (you decide when) should adopt the "tu."[2] As for the title, why not call the book simply *Douze Contes*[3] (apologies to Flaubert).[4]

Something has happened to upset and depress us and perhaps to make a revolution in our lives. The apple farm next to ours (on the west) has been sold[5] for a housing development. The surveyors' ribbons are already on the trees just by our mailbox across the road. It has belonged for a generation to a couple now nearing ninety,[6] and none of their 4 daughters wants it. It is 130 acres, which means that by law as many as 65 houses, each on 2 acres, can be put up. For at least a year the noise will be unbearable as the bulldozers rip out the trees. It means also that the value of our property has been greatly lessened. Columbia County (this one) has become the chic place for New Yorkers to come, with the result that land values have soared. This means that if we sell we cannot buy back in the same market. We don't know what to do. I have one friend urging me to move to New Mexico, another to Virginia. We have got to make some move.

Meanwhile, the winter here has been atrocious. I had to hire 3 men to shovel the snow off our roof for fear it would collapse beneath the weight. Now we can hardly see out the windows over the mounds. Temperatures of zero degrees Fahrenheit. Day after day. We go nowhere. Winterbound. Somehow we've got to get out one day next week for me to lecture at Union College in Schenectady.

I now have 250 pages of manuscript done on the Cherokee book. It's got a title. *No Resting Place.* That's taken from the text, a quotation from a prophecy made by the early Cherokees: "The white man will point you to the west, but you will find no resting place there, for he will drive you from one place to another until you reach the western waters."[7] I expect the final manuscript to be no more than another 50 pages, if that much.

This has been a bad winter for me. I have suffered from severe sinus trouble. Have been unable to go outside because of this and the cold. And of course [we are] both deeply depressed over our housing situation. Word today that three more nearby farms, one of over 1100 acres[,] have gone on the market for sale as housing developments. I'll let you know what develops. Meanwhile, love from us both.

Yours,
[no signature]

1. Gallimard published *The Last Husband* in 1988.

2. Formal and informal "you."

3. "Twelve Stories," although there are only ten stories in the volume.

4. The volume by Flaubert alluded to is *Trois Contes* (1877).

5. This real-life event prompted WH to write "The Apple of Discord," a major story in *September Song* (1992).

6. Philip and Harriet Egan.

7. This quotation is from an article titled "Remarkable Fulfillment of Indian Prophecy" in the *Phoenix,* a Cherokee newspaper.

TO SEYMOUR LAWRENCE

TLS/UM [Hudson, New York
early 1988]

Dear Sam,

Thank you for your reading of No Resting Place, and for your offer to publish it should Delacorte refuse. However, I am dismayed at your suggestion that it be presented as non-fiction. The characters in it are caught up in an historical experience but they are not, nor are they based upon, actual people. It is not the story of my family, nor of anybody else's known to me. No real-life boy that I know of listened to the story of his people from his grandfather nor cast a magic spell upon a land-surveyor nor served as a doctor on the Trail of Tears nor saw his father shot to death on Red River. No minister known to me lost his faith through that experience. These are fictional characters and events not drawn from recorded facts but imagined as being expressive of an historical happening. Indeed, as history the book is unreliable, for I have taken liberties with known facts and personages. A common experience that affects the lives of more persons than one is not thereby an impersonal experience. The right to an individual fate is the first right lost in genocide. It was this that I meant to convey. The novel can accom[m]odate such variety. Mine may be a novel with a difference (I hope so) but it is still a novel. From this it will be seen that I would resist appending any sub-title to the book, no matter who should publish it.

The extension of the story into the present generation is a dramatization of Faulkner's dictum: The past is never dead—it isn't even past.[1] I want my story to resonate beyond its local time and place and to affect people long afterward. Were I to follow your suggestion and dispense with the opening section (the section which originally so stirred your enthusiasm) that dimension would be lost. So would the rivalry between Houston and Lamar[2] and The Bowl's [*sic*][3] part therein. So would an understanding of the end of the book.

To say that I am disappointed by your response is to say only a part of what I feel. I am bewildered, especially by your antithetical responses to the opening section.

Yours,
Bill

1. In Faulkner's *Requiem for a Nun* (1951), Gavin Stevens says, "The past is never dead. It's not even past" (1.3).

2. When he was president of the Republic of Texas, Sam Houston worked for unity between the Indians and the white man. When Mirabeau Buonaparte Lamar (1798–1859) succeeded Houston as president, he sought in 1839 to expel the Cherokees from Texas.

3. Chief Bowles led an unsuccessful resistance to the expulsion.

TO BARLEY ALISON

TLS/RH

Hudson, New York
March 9, 1988

Dear Barley,

Toby Eady has sent on to me your note to him regarding *No Resting Place*. I am flattered by your saying you can see no need for improvement in it. I did. I have, I think, finished my revisions. That is to say, I think I've done the best I can with it. I have made deletions, additions and rearrangements of material. As it is too late now for Delacorte to schedule it for publication this fall, it might as well incubate here with me for a while yet. I have read it so many times I need now to get away from it before going over it yet again. What I cannot imagine is why you should want to publish it. The British don't buy my books. They don't even review them. They ignore them. Personally I can see no point in my publishing there. This book seems to me even less likely than the others to find a British audience. However, I suppose I owe it to Delacorte to allow them to recoup through the sale of foreign rights whatever they can to defray their advance to me. And if, despite our discouraging record, you are proud to publish me, then that makes me proud. I had vowed to retire after finishing *No Resting Place;* however, it looks as if I'm off on something new.[1] A bad habit is hard to break. I have worked despite breaking a foot last fall, breaking two fingers two months ago, then one month ago a piece of wood I was chopping for the fire struck my knee, I pitched face-forward, landing on my elbow and on the broken fingers and striking my abdomen a severe blow on a wheelbarrow. I ache all over.

Best wishes to you.

Yours,
Bill

1. Probably "The Apple of Discord," eventually published in *September Song.*

TO WILLIAM A. OWENS

TLS/PH

[Hudson, New York
May 1988]

Dear Bill,
I feel I owe it to you, since you came to my defense against Joan Givner, to tell you that I have read with mouth agape some of the things she says about me.[1]

She says that I have been more influenced by KAP than I would now perhaps be willing to admit. How does she know what I would be willing to admit? Has she asked me? I have never, when asked, early or late, denied or been stinting in my declaration of indebtedness to KAP. (If asked now I would say that I no longer feel the sense of guidance that I felt as a young man in his twenties, but I would say that in addition to finding in her the first voice writing about my own place I admired her stories in their own right, and considered them models). Her remark is snide, gratuitous, and unfounded. Then she speaks of Porter, Goyen[2] and Humphrey discussing certain matters among themselves. I have never discussed anything with William Goyen. I only laid eyes on him twice in my life, once just long enough to sit down, the other with only time to stay on our feet, and neither of us was able to say much of anything to each other on either occasion. I met him the night I met Katherine Anne.[3] It was at her apartment in NYC. Dorothy and I were invited to dinner, he to drinks before dinner. He came bringing a friend, a writer from the Hartford Courant. Now, anybody who knew Katherine Anne will tell you that when she was present nobody else ever got to say anything. It really was a disease with her. (Not that she wasn't worth listening to). I learned years later from Glenway Wescott[4] that one finally had to say, "Katherine Anne, will you please be quiet long enough for me to say a little something?" That night I sensed some sort of not quite out in the open squabble between Goyen and her. As long as he was there I don't believe I got to say two words and after he left probably not one. That night Katherine Anne was so voluble that Dorothy, though she tried again and again, to tell her that the supper was burning, was unable to and it was burned beyond eating, though we were served it nonetheless. I never saw William Goyen again until 22 years later at a party in Princeton. It was a very noisy big party and I didn't catch the name of the man to whom I was presented, and even had I once known him well I wouldn't have known him then because he was plainly dying before your eyes. Finally, seeing that I didn't know who he was, Dorothy whispered his name in my ear. I don't remember a word of the few words that passed between us—they can't have mattered much. That is the extent of my acquaintance with him. Never a word in writing ever passed between the two of us. He is not someone to whom I would have said I hated southerners. A few years after our first meeting he reviewed a book of mine for the Times[5]—a review that so incensed Alfred Knopf he wrote a letter of protest to the editors. Finally this woman suggests that I was drawn to KAP's writing because she was a woman and I, like Goyen, didn't know what sex I was. That is libel.[6] I am astounded that it is considered permissible for a biographer to quote indirectly from the letters of one person without having access to the letters going the other way. In this instance, had she seen the letters of KAP to me she would know that KAP apologized[7] to me for having so completely misundersto[o]d my story about the artists' colony. She later confessed to me that she had misread it owing to her own deficient sense of literary humor. And finally I am flabbergasted to think that the people in charge of that gathering in Austin had the insensi[tivity], the obtuseness to invite me down there to sit and listen to these things being said to my face.

I can't prove this, and wouldn't bother to if I could, but I suspect two things motivated this. In 1965, in Rome, I received a letter from Katherine Anne asking me to be, along with Glenway Wescott (he soon backed out, leaving me alone)[,] her literary executor. I replied that I'd be hers if she'd be mine. And so, by legal document, I was made her executor—much against my wishes because I had then been shown the enormous collection of papers in her Washington, D.C. basement. I didn't want to be the custodian of all that stuff (she hadn't disposed of it to the U. of Maryland[8] then, and suggested I put it in my attic!) [and] responsible for overseeing access to it or quotations from it. But how could I get out of it? Years later, in Dallas, Lon Tinkle told me that Joan Givner had become her executor[9] (I was never told by anybody that I had been relieved of the post). I was glad to hear it—Givner may have thought she had done me out of a job I coveted. We can't forgive those to whom we have done dirt. Second she wrote me while KAP was still alive asking if she could come and spend a week here quizzing me about KAP.[10] I said no, I didn't have a week nor did my wife either to entertain a stranger in our house and lay aside our own work. But I said to console her that I didn't have anything of value to tell her about Katherine Anne anyway. That I had once considered her a good friend without ever feeling I really understood her, and that it was then well over five years since I had heard a word from her. I think Givner cannot forgive me for this, perhaps thinks I am lying about it, maybe even thinks I have juicy things to tell about Katherine Anne that I am saving to write myself.

This has been long and not at all interesting but I thought I owed it to you.

Yours,
Bill

P.S. If you're done with that book about Chief Bowles, I'm nearing the point where I could use it.[11] Yrs.

1. The author of *Katherine Anne Porter: A Life* (1982), Joan Givner was among the participants in a conference on the Texas Literary Tradition held in Austin in 1982. See Don Graham, James W. Lee, and William T. Pilkington, eds., *The Texas Literary Tradition* (Austin: University of Texas, 1983), 58–68. Owens's remarks must have been made after Givner's talk or preceding his own prepared lecture that followed Givner's. WH was in attendance.

2. William Goyen (1915–83), Texas fiction writer, author of *The House of Breath* (1950), *In a Farther Country* (1955), and other works.

3. The night of 13 October 1950.

4. Glenway Wescott (1901–87) was a midwestern writer who drew attention with *The Grandmothers* in 1927 and *Pilgrim Hawk* in 1940, but then his career fizzled.

5. "Tragedy Awaited," *New York Times Book Review,* 12 January 1958.

6. Givner said, "I would like to suggest that the important element in the gravitation of Goyen and Humphrey to Porter was tied with gender considerations. [. . .] I think they were inclined to imitate her style, not in spite of the fact that she was a woman writing as a woman, but *because* of this fact" (Graham, Lee, and Pilkington, *Texas Literary Tradition,* 64).

7. On 21 October 1950, Porter wrote, "I have been thinking about my curious misunderstanding of your entire aim and point of view in *The Fauve*. . [*sic*] Please believe I am not always so near-sighted. [. . .] I got all my clues wrong."

8. Porter's papers are housed in the Hornbake Library at the University of Maryland at College Park.

9. In fact, Isabel Bayley ultimately became Porter's literary executor.

10. Givner's request to interview WH was dated 4 October 1977.

11. *Chief Bowles and the Texas Cherokees* by Mary Whatley Clarke (1971), one of WH's main sources for his historical novel *No Resting Place*. The postscript was added by hand.

TO JEAN LAMBERT

TLS/LC

[Hudson, New York]
March 4, 1989

Dear Jean,

I have been told that my hearing aid is ready and waiting for me in Northampton but have not yet been able to go and get it. I have also been told that I shall really require two. So I am now saying that I shall soon have AIDS. My teeth, the upper ones, are troubling me, I'm getting new glasses today: I feel like an old car going down a bumpy road and shedding parts. My new motto is "Life is killing me."

Many people find it impossible to adjust to a hearing aid. I don't expect to like it. But it will be an improvement over my present condition. And maybe Dorothy won't have to repeat everything she says to me.

I laid aside my apple farmer story[1] to work on something else. A situation between friends of ours, people whom you have met. You possibly remember the Wannings. Not long ago their telephone rang. The caller was a lover of hers from whom she had not heard since their breaking up (his wife found a letter of hers to him) 25 years ago. His wife had died, could he see her? They met, he proposed that she leave her husband of 50 years and marry him. She agreed. She is 78 years old! Her husband consented to the divorce. At the last minute she relented.[2] I know about all this because a friend of theirs who is a friend also of mine[3] has been sending me copies of her letters. My story is finished, but—I can't publish it.[4] Not that I fear a lawsuit, but I have been unable to depart from the facts of the case, and I don't want to hurt them. It must wait either for their deaths or for mine.

Life here goes on in its quiet uneventful way, so I have little news. A strange winter. It has yet to snow! Cold but dry. Publication of *No Resting Place* is scheduled for May, but I have yet to see finished copies of the book, which troubles me. If it *is* to appear in May then copies should be going out now to reviewers and to bookstores. Do not work on your translation from the copy of the manuscript that you have. Further changes have been made in the text. I *have* received page proofs, but even they are not the final version.

I recently got word that the book has been bought by the Dutch. It will be distributed there by the publisher's book club, Holland's largest. [T]hey paid very well for the rights, but I will see none of the money—it goes to Delacorte to defray my advance.[5]

Dorothy joins me in sending love.

Yours,
Bill

1. "The Apple of Discord."

2. Pat Wanning actually left her husband; WH seems to be confusing his story with real life.

3. Sally Thomas, the second wife of Ted Thomas, a longtime fishing companion of WH.

4. The story actually became the title story of *September Song.*

5. WH inserted this sentence by hand.

TO THEODORE AND RENÉE WEISS

TLS/PU [Hudson, New York]
February 14 [1990]

Dear Ted and Renee,
Would you please remember to send me the information about Bellagio?[1] And, to refresh my memory of those parts, that essay of mine on Lenno.[2]

No news from here. Hibernation time. We try not to notice these dark and dreary days by sticking to work. I find that as I sink into silence and avoid company because I don't want to reveal my impairment[3] I write as a mode of talking to the world—if anybody's listening.

I called Esquire and forbade them to run the story of mine[4] they've bought in the same issue with the results of the sexual survey of writers.[5]

They said my wishes would be respected. They seemed bewildered that I had not found it funny. That magazine of course has always had its sensational side but this is a new low. On hearing about the affair, my old friend Paxton Davis, who writes an occasional column on a subject of his choice (and he is a very good journalist) for the Roanoke, Virginia Times asked me to send him the questionnaire. He was as outraged by it as I was. He called yesterday to say that he has written a column about it.[6] I'll send you a copy of it when I receive it.

With much love to you both from both of us.

Yours,
Bill

1. WH had applied for a place in the Rockefeller Foundation Center in this northern Italian town at the fork of Lake Como; his application was denied on 13 August 1990.

2. "The Mountain of Miracles," *New Yorker*, 29 October 1960.

3. Deafness.

4. On 20 July 1989 Will Blythe of *Esquire* sent WH a contract for publishing "Labor of Love"; he was to be paid twenty-five hundred dollars, but the story never appeared in the magazine.

5. A xeroxed questionnaire was sent to between a hundred and two hundred of "America's finest writers"; they were asked questions such as "How many times do you have orgasm in a week?" ("Scandalous! Scurrilous! Sophomoric! . . . That Notorious Survey of Writers' Sex Lives!" *Esquire*, July 1990, 110–11).

6. Paxton Davis, a member of the faculty at Washington and Lee, was a freelance journalist and novelist. His column titled "For Mass Media, Sexual Freedom Becomes Duty" appeared in the *Roanoke Times and World-News* on 16 February 1990, p. 7, sec. A.

[Although WH lived for another six years, his letter writing subsided, in part because of the deaths of longtime correspondents (Leonard Woolf, Ian Parsons, and Norah Smallwood). For those friends remaining, it appears that he merely changed the mode of communication from letter writing to talking on the telephone. There seem to be several possible reasons for this shift. First is the reduction in long-distance rates that began with the breakup of the Bell system in 1984; rates continued to move lower through the 1990s in a fierce competitive market. WH could not resist the bargain rates. I do not believe WH and Shelby Foote ever exchanged letters, but in the 1990s they regularly talked extensively on the telephone. WH and I had long talks on the telephone during the 1990s; he would write to me only if he happened to be sending a book or article through the mail, and even so most of the time just a few lines (I include the most significant letter I received from him during the 1990s). A second reason for WH's

preference for the telephone in the 1990s was that his deafness did not prevent him from using the phone because he could hear on it better than he could hear with his hearing aid. There was a third factor: WH began all-day drinking in 1993, a habit that probably made writing more difficult.]

TO ASHBY BLAND CROWDER

TLS/PH

[Hudson, New York]
February 27, 1991

Dear Bland,

Your review of RP Warren is excellent.[1] You distinguish his virtues as a critic, and I always thought he was best at that. I never cared much for his fiction. Too operatic. Too wordy. It is years since I read the essay on Coleridge[2] but I still remember my reservation: he made a better poem of it than it is.[3]

I doubt that Twayne, or any other publisher, will be interested in a book on my writing. But take warning: if you do write about it don't expect much help from me. When I finish a book or a story I put it out of my mind. By then it will have cost me so much work and worry I want no more of it. I want to get on to the next one, and I don't want to echo myself. Those books are my babies but I put them out for adoption.[4] I just hope they found good homes.

Not only does the Gulf war[5] distress me, its popularity disgusts me. Nothing like a nice clean little war a long way from home to buck up the populace. We're making up for Vietnam.[6] Got something to cheer for this time around.

My best to you both.

Yours,
Bill[7]

1. "Robert Penn Warren: The Once and Future Critic," *Mississippi Quarterly* 33, no. 2 (Spring 1990): 241–7.

2. Warren's "A Poem of Pure Imagination: An Experiment in Reading," an essay on S. T. Coleridge's "The Rime of the Ancient Mariner," was first published in a 1946 edition of the poem and is reprinted in his *New and Selected Essays* (New York: Random House, 1989), 335–423.

3. WH then inserted by hand: "I saw him a few times. He was an amiable man."

4. WH then inserted by hand: "As you've observed, they don't even look as though they had the same father."

5. The First Persian Gulf War (1990–91), between the United Nations–led coalition

and Iraq, was the first major conflict involving the United States since the Vietnam War.

6. The Vietnam War, lasting from 1959 to 1975, was the most drawn-out military conflict in the history of the United States. This war between the communist government of North Vietnam (together with the National Liberation Front) and South Vietnam (supported by the United States) ended with the reunification of Vietnam under a communist government.

7. After signing the letter, WH wrote below by hand: "The film rights to *No Resting Place* have been bought by Home Box Office." Although the scriptwriting was completed, HBO never made the movie.

TO JEAN LAMBERT

[Because cheap telephone rates did not apply to calls to France, Lambert, living in France, would still occasionally receive a letter from WH, especially if they had some business to transact. Lambert was translating WH's final book, September Song, *and had a few questions about the text. This is WH's penultimate letter to his friend.]*

TLS/LC

[Rt. 1,
Hudson, New York]
September 29 [1993]

Dear Jean,

Forgive the long silence. We have had one trouble after another. (I will spare you the details.) Having nothing good to say, I said nothing.

It is pleasant news that you have published the Lewis and Clark. The association with the Louisiana Purachase and with this year's Napoleon observations should guarantee French readers' interest.[1]

It is pleasant news also that you have finished translating the stories and given the mss. to Yannick.[2] It would be pleasant to see one of them in the NRF. I suggest "The Farmer's Daughter" or "September Song."[3] Has there been a decision about a title for the book? I recommended "Chason d'Automne."[4]

Yannick said no. I still like it. I like it very much.

Now, before getting to your queries, one last piece of information: I have sold all my papers—seventeen cartons—the accumulation of forty years—to the library of the University of Texas, for quite a nice sum of money.[5]

. . . .

p. 27: avoiding contractions. Probably untranslateable. French has no (or very few) contractions. In English "I do not," for instance, is more emphatic than "I don't."

p. 150. pull the wool over my eyes. This expression, a very common one, is important to the story; however, I don't know a French equivalent. *m'auvueugler.?* [*sic*] The irony being that she *is* blind.[6]
going for broke. A gambling expression. To stake everything on a turn of the wheel, a throw of the dice, the outcome of which will mean either to win big, or go broke.
Garbo[7] off the lot. The lot is the film-making location. When she was off the lot Garbo made herself drab and unattractive.
carriage trade. Though it refers to an earlier time, the phrase is still in use. A shop's rich customers are those who arrive in their carriages.

. . . .

Our association goes back a long time. To the preface of "[L]'Adieu du Chasseur" and your first words, ["]Je ne connais pas William Humphrey."[8]

Well, we got to know each other pretty well, didn't we[?] I am grateful for your labors, your perception of the nuances of my thought, your own expression and for your friendship.

Yours,
Bill

1. Lambert's *Journal de la première traversée du continent nord-américain 1804–1806,* volume 1, *La piste de l'Ouest,* a translation of Michel Breaking's edition of Meriwether Lewis and William Clark's journal of their expedition to explore the Louisiana Purchase, was published in anticipation of the two-hundredth anniversary of Jefferson's purchase of that territory from Napoleon Bonaparte. Also in 1993 there were continuing observances of major events in the life of Napoleon; it was the two-hundredth anniversary of his role in the expulsion of the British from Toulon, for which at age twenty-four he was promoted to brigadier general.

2. Yannick Guillou.

3. *La nouvelle revue française* selected instead "A Portrait of the Artist as an Old Man" ("Portrait de l'auteur en vieil homme").

4. This is the title under which Gallimard published the collection.

5. A State of Texas Purchase Voucher, dated 20 September 1994 and found in WH's home in Hudson, indicates that he had received the second of three payments, the second being for ten thousand dollars.

6. The French term means "to blind one's self." WH is referring to the character Irene in "An Eye for an Eye" in *September Song.*

7. Greta Garbo (1905–90) was a movie star of the 1920s, 1930s, and early 1940s. WH inserted the following comment by hand: "I must tell you someday about my encounter with her in the little garden of l'Eglise St. Germain."

8. Lambert's preface to his translation of *Home from the Hill* begins with this statement: "I do not know William Humphrey."

Index

WH in the index refers to William Humphrey. Titles of works by Humphrey are listed by title. References to titles of works by other authors are under the names of the authors.